Yale French Studies

NUMB[ER]

Another Look,
Another Woman:
Retranslations of
French Feminism

LYNNE HUFFER   1   Editor's Preface

I. *Approaching The Other*

LUCE IRIGARAY   7   The Question of the Other
LYNNE HUFFER   20   Luce *et veritas:* Toward an Ethics
of Performance
SERENE JONES   42   Divining Women: Irigaray and Feminist
Theologies
PEGGY KAMUF   68   To Give Place: Semi-Approaches
to Hélène Cixous
MARY LYDON   90   Re-Translating no Re-Reading
no, rather: Rejoicing (with)
Hélène Cixous

II. *Other Realities, Other Fictions*

NICOLE BROSSARD   105   The Textured Angle of Desire
LYNNE HUFFER   115   Interview with Nicole Brossard
MARYSE CONDÉ   122   No Woman No Cry
ASSIA DJEBAR   138   The White of Algeria
CLARISSE ZIMRA   149   Disorienting the Subject in Djebar's
L'Amour, la fantasia

III. *Rethinking (French) Feminism*

SARAH KOFMAN   173   The Psychologist of the Eternal
Feminine
CHRISTINE DELPHY   190   The Invention of French Feminism:
An Essential Move

Yale French Studies

Lynne Huffer, *Special editor for this issue*
Alyson Waters, *Managing editor*
Editorial board: Denis Hollier (Chair), Ora Avni, Peter
    Brooks, Benjamin Elwood, Shoshona Felman,
    Françoise Jaouën, Daryl Lee, Christopher Miller,
    Charles Porter, Benjamin Semple, Allison Tait
Staff: Noah Guynn
Editorial office: 82-90 Wall Street, Room 308.
Mailing address: P.O. Box 208251, New Haven,
    Connecticut 06520-8251.
Sales and subscription office:
Yale University Press, P.O. Box 209040
New Haven, Connecticut 06520–9040
Published twice annually by Yale University Press

Designed by James J. Johnson and set in Trump
    Medieval Roman by The Composing Room of
    Michigan, Inc.
Printed in the United States of America by the Vail
    Ballou Press, Binghamton, N.Y.

ISSN 044–0078
ISBN for this issue 0–300–06394–6

In Memoriam

Sarah Kofman

1934–1994

LYNNE HUFFER

Editor's Preface

In putting together this special issue of *Yale French Studies*, an initial question—why talk about French feminism now?—pushed me to think about the historical specificity of the contents of the volume. However, over the course of my work as editor, that incipient question was gradually shadowed by the more general one I often hear from students: what *is* French feminism anyway? So I began by asking, in 1991: What is the interest of yet *another* collection on a question that feminists and academics have been thinking about, digesting, appropriating, and debating for over a decade? And I end, here in this preface, in an attempt to tie up the first question with something of an answer, only to be left with the dangling thread of another confusion. Indeed, from the start, confusion has been the symptom of a basic problem concerning the very constitution of the category "French feminism." In response to that more general uncertainty—what *is* it, anyway?—I offer some brief reflections of my own and, more important, the thoughts of the others included in these pages. Which is to say, as I say to my students when they ask what it is: I still don't really know.

In asking the first, particular question (why now?), I took as my point of departure the 1981 issue of *Yale French Studies*, "Feminist Readings: French Texts/American Contexts."[1] I now read that issue—following on the heels of *New French Feminisms* (1980),[2] the first anthology to introduce the term "French feminism" to an English-

1. "Feminist Readings: French Texts/American Contexts," ed. Colette Gaudin, Mary Jean Green, Lynn Anthony Higgins, Marianne Hirsch, Vivian Kogan, Claudia Reeder, and Nancy Vickers. *Yale French Studies* 62 (1981).
2. *New French Feminisms: An Anthology*, ed. Elaine Marks and Isabelle de Courtivron (New York: Schocken Books, 1980).

YFS 87, *Another Look, Another Woman*, ed. Huffer, © 1995 by Yale University.

speaking audience—as the beginning of a sustained, increasingly academic, feminist interest in the writings of various French intellectuals on the questions of woman, the feminine, and the other. In 1981, the ideas introduced there—my favorite, alas, was *jouissance*—seemed sexy and new. Today, many of us have lost the fervor, or at least the spark, we felt at that initial encounter.

So what happens when the spark goes, when a new encounter becomes old? While it is tempting to discard the old for the ever new, this special issue on "French feminism" was conceived around a different idea: not only can the old be reassessed and critiqued, but in the self-reflexive process of a critical turn toward the old, new thoughts can be sparked and new encounters generated.

In that spirit, I have entitled this issue "Another Look, Another Woman: Retranslations of French Feminism." Because the precise definition of "French feminism" remains suspended, at least for the moment, this volume locates itself in the dynamic space of repetition and movement captured by the concept of "retranslation." The retranslations included here both bring previously untranslated French texts to an English-speaking audience (those by Irigaray, Brossard, Condé Djebar, and Kofman) and, at the same time, critically assess some of the already translated writings of Irigaray, Cixous, Brossard, Djebar, and others (in articles by Huffer, Jones, Kamuf, Lydon, Zimra, and Delphy). What can come out of that layered process of retranslation? What happens when retranslation means asking about sexuality, race, and national identities in addition to the problem of gender? The essays here suggest that in this vexed space of repetition and movement we take responsibility for feminism's limits and failures and also, at the same time, look toward other feminisms for another way of thinking.

This other way of thinking—another look, another theory, another vision—opens up possibilities for the differently structured identities that would constitute another woman, both in an empirical and symbolic sense. Consequently, the volume's focus and organization reflect that commitment to finding other ways: new thoughts and new encounters. The first section, "Approaching the Other," explores the philosophical concept of the other in relation to the question of woman. And while the articles in this section approach the problem of the other from a variety of disciplinary and methodological perspectives, they cohere around a common insistence on the urgency of asking about limits, justice, and the ethical dimensions of feminist thought. Part Two, "Other Realities, Other Fictions," both complicates and gives specificity to the problems introduced in Part One. The pieces in this section implicitly interrogate the homologizing tendencies of a French feminist discourse limited to a conversation between American academics and their Parisian poststructuralist counterparts. Writing across the cultural and geographical terrain of Québec, Guadeloupe, and Algeria, the contributors here also push open the boundaries dividing fiction from essay, utopian imaginings from oppressive realities. Finally, the third section returns to the suspended term of this volume's title, "French feminism," in order to critically evaluate both the construction of the "women" who would be the subjects of "feminism" in general (Kofman) and "French feminism's" specific meaning (Delphy).

"OK, but what *is* it?" I keep hearing. Let me retranslate, and resuspend: I still don't really know what French feminism is. The French feminist garment is cut from a weave that is complex and varied, but its seams are splitting and its hems are frayed . . . that is, if the thing was ever really there. Time for another outfit, I suppose, or a different metaphor altogether. Not because thought is merely a question of fashion, but because in all that attention to intricacies of style we may not have noticed that the whole thing is showing some wear and tear. In attending so diligently to those elegant details, what have we failed to see? And how do we cut and repiece the cloth, together with other fabrics, into other forms that, with luck, will wear well for a politics of liberation?

Whatever "French feminism" is or was, or whatever it becomes, the pieces collected here attest to the importance of a continuing encounter, somehow, somewhere, among the scraps, frayed edges, and bits of thread that keep the conversation going. And what will come of that conversation? As I keep saying to my students: you never know. But you have to keep going. Just don't obliterate all that lies in your way in the process of approaching another: another woman, another thought, another (French) feminism. "Another Look, Another Woman" offers an opening for future encounters of fabric and seam, future rewritings of thought and its limits. Those other encounters and other rewritings promise an ongoing practice of retranslation: "an as yet unwritten world" (Brossard).

I. Approaching The Other

LUCE IRIGARAY

The Question of the Other

Western philosophy, perhaps all philosophy, has been constructed around a singular subject. For centuries, no one imagined that different subjects might exist, or that man and woman in particular might be different subjects.

Of course, since the end of the nineteenth century, more attention has been paid to the question of *the other*. The philosophical subject, henceforth more a sociological subject, became a bit less imperialist, acknowledging that identities different from his own indeed existed: children, the mad, "savages," workers, for example.

These empirical differences had to be respected; not everyone was the same, and it was important to pay a bit more attention to others and to their diversity. Yet the fundamental model of the human being remained unchanged: one, singular, solitary, historically masculine, the paradigmatic Western adult male, rational, capable. The observed diversity was thus thought of and experienced in a hierarchical manner, the *many* always subjugated by the *one*. Others were only copies of the idea of man, a potentially perfect idea, which all the more or less imperfect copies had to struggle to equal. These imperfect copies were, moreover, not defined in and of themselves, in other words, as a different subjectivity, but rather were defined in terms of an ideal subjectivity and as a function of their inadequacies with respect to that ideal: age, reason, race, culture, and so on. The model of the subject thus remained singular and the "others" represented less ideal examples, hierarchized with respect to the singular subject. This philosophical model corresponds, furthermore, to the political model of the leader considered to be the best, indeed the only one capable of governing

YFS 87, *Another Look, Another Woman,* ed. Huffer, © 1995 by Yale University.

citizens more or less worthy of their identity as human beings, more or less civil.

This position relative to the notion of otherness no doubt explains Simone de Beauvoir's refusal to identify woman with the other. Not wanting to be "second" with respect to the masculine subject, she asks, as a principle of subjectivity, to be man's equal, to be the same as, or similar to, him.

From the point of view of philosophy, that position entails a return to the singular, historically masculine, subject, and the invalidation of the possibility of a subjectivity other than man's. If de Beauvoir's critical work on the devalorization of woman as "secondary" in culture is valid on one level, her refusal to consider the question of woman as "other" represents, philosophically and even politically, a significant regression. In fact, her thinking is historically less advanced than that of certain philosophers who ponder the notion of possible relationships between two or more subjects: existential, personalist, or political philosophers. In the same way, she is not at the forefront of women's struggles to be recognized as having their own identity.

Simone de Beauvoir's positive assertions represent, in my view, a theoretical and practical error, since they imply the negation of an/other (woman) [*d'un[e] autre*[1]] equal in value to that of the subject.

The principal focus of my work on feminine subjectivity is, in a way, the inverse of de Beauvoir's as far as the question of the other is concerned. Instead of saying, "I do not want to be the other of the masculine subject and, in order to avoid being that other, I claim to be his equal," I say, "The question of the other has been poorly formulated in the Western tradition, for the other is always seen as the other of the same, the other of the subject itself, rather than an/other subject [*un autre sujet*[2]], irreducible to the masculine subject and sharing equivalent dignity. It all comes down to the same thing: in our tradition there has never really been an other of the philosophical subject, or, more generally, of the cultural and political subject.

> The other (*Of the Other Woman*, the secondary title of *Speculum*) must be understood as a noun. In French, but also in other languages, such as Italian and English, this noun is supposed to designate man and

1. Irigaray's original suggests several possible readings: "of an other," "of a feminine other," "of another subject," and "of another woman." [Translator's Note]
2. Irigaray's original suggests either "another subject" or "a subject which is other." [Translator's Note]

woman. With this secondary title, I wished to show that the other is, in fact, not neutral, neither gramatically, nor semantically, that it is not, or that it is no longer, possible to designate indifferently both the masculine and the feminine using the same word. This practice is current in philosophy, religion, and politics: we speak of the existence of the other, of love for the other, of anxiety about the other, etc. But we do not ask the question of who or what this other represents. This lack of precision in the notion of the other's alterity has paralyzed thought—including the dialectical method—in an idealistic dream appropriated by a single (masculine) subject, in the illusion of a singular absolute, and has left religion and politics to an empiricism which fundamentally lacks ethics insofar as respect for others is concerned. In fact, if the other is not defined according to its actual reality, it is no more than another self, not a true other; it can thus be either *more* or *less* than I, and it can have either *more* or *less* than I. It can thus represent (my) absolute greatness or (my) absolute perfection, the Other: God, the Ruler, logos; it can designate the smallest or the most impoverished: children, the sick, the poor, strangers; it can name the one whom I believe to be my equal. Truly there is no other in all this, only more of the same: smaller, larger, equal to me.[3]

Instead of refusing to be the other gender [*l'autre genre*[4]], the other sex, what I ask is to be considered as actually an/other woman [*une autre*], irreducible to the masculine subject. From this point of view, the secondary title of *Speculum* might have seemed offensive to Simone de Beauvoir: *Of the Other Woman.* At the time of its publication, I sent her my book in all good faith, hoping for her support in the difficulties I encountered. I never received a response, and it is only recently that I came to understand the reason for her silence. No doubt I must have offended her without wishing to. I had read the "Introduction" to *The Second Sex* well before I wrote *Speculum*, and could no longer recall what was at stake in the problematic of the *other* in de Beauvoir's work. Perhaps, for her part, she didn't understand that for

3. Irigaray, *J'aime à toi. Esquisse d'une félicité dans l'histoire* (Paris: Editions Grasset, 1992), 103–04.

4. The word *"genre"* corresponds to the English word "gender" only in the sense of grammatical gender (an element of the French language which cannot be translated into English), and there is no other obvious translation for Irigaray's use of the word. The words "kind," "type," "category," or "sort" do not necessarily imply gendered alterity (whether grammatical or otherwise), and the word "gender" is, strictly speaking, a mistranslation of *"genre"* as it is used here. I have therefore translated it in various ways according to context and have noted parenthetically wherever the word appears in the original text. [Translator's Note]

me my sex or my gender [*genre*] were in no way "second," but that sexes or genders are *two*, without being first or second.

In my own way, and in total ignorance of their work, I pursued a problematic close to that of the American promoters of Neofeminism, a feminism that valorizes difference, one more closely related to the cultural revolution of May 1968 than to de Beauvoir's egalitarian feminism. Let's recall, briefly, what is at stake in this problematic: the exploitation of woman takes place in the difference between the genders [*genres*] and therefore must be resolved within difference rather than by abolishing it. In *Speculum,* I interpret and critique how the philosophical subject, historically masculine, has reduced all otherness to a relationship with himself—as complement, projection, flip side, instrument, nature—inside his world, his horizons. As much through Freudian texts as through the major philosophical methods of our tradition, I show how the other is always the other of the same and not an actual other.

Thus my critiques of Freud all come down to a single interpretation: you (Freud) only see the sexuality, and more generally the identity, of the little girl, the adolescent girl, or woman in terms of the sexuality and identity of the little boy, the adolescent boy, or man. For example, in your view, the little girl's auto-eroticism lasts only as long as she continues to confuse her clitoris with a small penis; in other words, she imagines that she has the same sexual organ as a boy. When she discovers, through her mother, that woman doesn't have the same sexual organ as man, the little girl renounces the value of her feminine identity in order to turn toward the father, toward man, and seeks to obtain a penis by procuration. All her efforts are directed toward the conquest of the male sexual organ. Even the conceiving and engendering of a child has only a single goal: the appropriation of the penis or of the phallus; and this being the case, a male child is preferable to a female child. Thus, a marriage cannot succeed, a woman cannot become a good wife, until she gives her husband a male child.

These days such a description would make many women, and even many men, laugh. But just a few years ago, barely twenty years back, a woman who directed our attention to our culture's staggering machismo was laughed at and was not allowed to teach at the university. Yet today things have not become as clear as it might seem. True, a bit of light has been shed on this subject, but, if Freudian theory is macho, it merely reproduces an existing sociocultural order: Freud, in this sense, did not invent machismo; he merely noted it. Where he goes wrong is in his cures: like de Beauvoir, he does not recognize the other as other; and, albeit in different ways, they both propose that man remain the singular model of the subject, which woman must try to equal. Man and woman, through quite different strategies, must therefore become alike. This ideal conforms to that of traditional philosophy, which seeks a singular model of subjectivity, one which is historically masculine.

At best, this singular model would allow for a balancing act between the one and the many, but the one remains the model which, more or less openly, controls the hierarchy of multiplicity: the singular is unique and/but ideal, Man. Concrete singularity is only a copy of the ideal, an image. The Platonic view of the world, its notion of truth, is, in a certain sense, the inverse of day-to-day empirical reality: you believe that you are a reality, a singular truth, but you are only a relatively good copy of a perfect idea of yourself situated outside of yourself.

Here too, we can't laugh too soon, for we must first ponder the still current pertinence of such a conception of the world: we are children of the flesh but also of the word, nature but also culture. Now, children of culture signifies children of the idea, incarnations that conform, more or less, to the ideal model. Often, in order to live up to this model, we mimic, imitate like children, that which we perceive to be ideal. These are all Platonic ways of being and doing, and all conform to a masculine notion of truth. Even in the reversal constituted by the privilege of the many over the one, a very current reversal often called democracy, even in the privilege of the other over the subject, of the *you* over the *I* (I am thinking, for example, of certain works by Buber and a certain part of Lévinas's work in which these privileges are perhaps more moral and theological than philosophical), we just end up with a stand-in for the model of the one and the many, of the one and the same, in which a singular subject inflects one meaning rather than another. In the same way, privileging concrete singularity over ideal singularity does not allow us to challenge the privilege of a universal category valid for all men and all women. In fact, each concrete singularity cannot decree an ideal valid for all men and all women, and, to ensure cohabitation between subjects, notably within the republic, only a minimum of universality is required.

To get out from under this all-powerful model of the one and the many, we must move on to the model of the two, a two which is not a replication of the same, nor one large and the other small, but made up of two which are truly different. The paradigm of the two lies in sexual difference. Why there? Because it is there that two subjects exist who should not be placed in a hierarchical relationship, and because these two subjects share the common goal of preserving the human species and developing its culture, while granting respect to their differences.

My first theoretical gesture was thus to extricate the two from the one, the two from the many, the other from the same, and to do so horizontally, suspending the authority of the One: of man, the father, the leader, the one god, the singular truth, etc. It involved making the other stand out from the same, refusing to be reduced to the other of the same, to the other (man or woman) of the one, not by becoming him or becoming like him, but by inventing myself as an autonomous and different subject.

Clearly this gesture calls into question our entire theoretical and practical tradition, particularly Platonism, but without such a gesture we cannot speak of women's liberation, nor of an ethical behavior with respect to the other, nor of democracy. Without such a gesture, philosophy itself risks its own demise, vanquished along with other things by the use of techniques that, in the construction of the logos, undermine man's subjectivity, an easier and quicker victory if woman no longer maintains the pole of nature standing opposite to masculine *techne*. The existence of two subjects is probably the only thing that can bring the masculine subject back to his being, and this thanks to woman's access to her own being.

To accomplish this goal, the feminine subject had to be freed from the world of man to make way for a philosophical scandal: the subject is not *one*, nor is it singular.

Next and at the same time, this feminine subject, just barely defined, lacking outlines and edges, without norms or mediations, needed to be mapped out, in order to nourish her and ensure her becoming [*son devenir*]. After this critical phase in my work that was addressed to a monosubjective, monosexualized, patriarchal, and phallocratic philosophy and culture, I thus attempted to define some characteristics of the feminine subject, characteristics which were necessary to affirm it as such, for fear that it might succumb once again to a lack of differentiation, that it might once again be subjugated by the singular subject. One important dimension of assisting the becoming of the feminine subject, and thus my own becoming, was to escape from a single figure of genealogical power, to maintain that "I was born of man *and* of woman, and that genealogical authority belongs both to man *and* to woman." It was thus important to retrieve feminine genealogies from oblivion, not to repress the existence of the father pure and simple, in a kind of reversal cherished by previous philosophical methods, but to return to the reality of the two. But it's true that it takes time to locate and restore this two, and it cannot be the work of one woman only.

Aside from the return to and reconcilation with genealogy, with feminine genealogies—which are still a long way off—woman, women, needed a language, images, and representations which suited them— on a cultural level, even on a religious level, god being the philosophical subject's great accomplice. I began to work on this in *Speculum* and *Ce sexe qui n'en est pas un* and continued the project notably in *Sexes et parentés, Le temps de la différence,* and *Je, tu, nous*.[5] In those works, I discuss the particularities of the feminine world—a world different from that of man—with respect to language, with respect to the body (to age, to health, to beauty, and, of course, to maternity), with respect to work, with respect to nature and the world of culture. Two examples: I attempt to show that life's unfolding is different for woman than it is for man, since it consists for women of much more pronounced physical stages (puberty, loss of virginity, maternity, menopause) and requires a subjective becoming which is far more complex than man's. As far as work is concerned, I show that socioeconomic justice does not consist of merely putting a rule into practice—"equal work for equal pay"—but consists also of respecting and valorizing women in terms of choice in the ends and means of production, professional qualifications, relationships in the workplace, social recognition of work, and so on.

In these works, I also began to speak of the necessity of rights specific to women. As I have written elsewhere, it is my opinion that women's liberation cannot progress without taking this step, as much on the level of social recognition as on the level of individual growth and communal relationships, between women and between women and men. These juridical proposals were viewed with marked interest and a certain mistrust: interest on the part of nonspecialist, nonfeminist women who understood the importance of what was at stake,

5. Several of these books exist in English language editions: *Speculum of the Other Woman,* trans. Gillian C. Gill (Ithaca: Cornell University Press, 1985); *This Sex Which Is Not One,* trans. Catherine Porter (Ithaca: Cornell University Press, 1985); *Sexes and Genealogies,* trans. Gillian C. Gill (New York: Columbia University Press, 1993); and *Je, Tu, Nous: Toward a Culture of Difference,* trans. Alison Martin (New York: Routledge, 1993). *Le temps de la différence. Pour une révolution pacifique* (Paris: Librairie Générale Française, 1989) does not exist in English. [Translator's Note]

interest also on the part of feminists in certain countries who have long been concerned with the necessary mediation of the law in the liberation of humankind, and particularly in women's liberation.

Resistance came from women of two different persuasions. Women in favor of egalitarianism do not understand the necessity of special rights for women; they agree that equal rights with men must be obtained; they are ready to struggle against discrimination; but they do not pay attention to the fact that women are forced to make specific choices in their relationships with men, and that the choices cannot remain individual or private but must be guaranteed by law: the freedom of choice in reproduction, work patterns, sexuality, the raising of minors in cases of divorce or separation, keeping in mind the context of multicultural marriages, where traditional spousal rights differ between cultures. In my view, the lack of special rights for women does not allow them to move from a state of nature to a civilized state: the majority remain nature-bodies, subservient to the State, to the Church, to father and husband, without access to the status of civilians, responsible for themselves and the community.

Women who are more sensitive to a culture or politics of difference also contest the necessity of civil rights specific to women, for they fear the law as requiring servitude to the State. Yet civil rights for individual persons represent, on the contrary, a guarantee that citizens can oppose the power of the State as such; they maintain a tension between individuals and the State, and can even ensure the evolution of a state-controlled society into a civil society, whose democratic character would be supported by people's individual rights.

I can only hope that women understand and promote what is at stake in individual rights, both because these rights are essential to protect them and to affirm their identity, and because as feminine subjects, they are more ready to take an interest in rights having to do with the individual and with relationships between individuals, rather than in rights determined by assets—possessions, property, belongings—rights which make up the majority of masculine civil codes. Existing civil codes and constitutions would have to be completed by including rights for women and rights defined according to women's spirit [*génie*], in other words, beyond sexual specificity, for citizens (both men and women) as people.

The unique character of feminine spirit [*génie*] also leads me back to the question of the other in this final section of my essay.

Having become an autonomous subject, it is now woman's turn to situate herself with respect to the other, and the specificity of her identity allows her to pay much more attention to the dimension of alterity in the process of subjective becoming [le devenir subjectif]. Tradition dictates that woman is the guardian of love and has imposed on her the duty of loving, and of loving despite the misfortunes of love, without explaining why she must perform such a task.

I certainly will not become an accomplice to this kind of imperative on the subject of love, nor to the corresponding imperative of hate which seems to me to be its complementary principle.

Rather, I will pass on to you results obtained from research into the way in which little girls, adolescent girls, and women speak, and will propose an interpretation of the characteristics of feminine language.[6]

The language the most aware of the other is that of the little girl. She addresses herself to the other—in my research sample, to the mother—asking for her agreement concerning an activity they will do together: "Mommy, will you play with me?"; "Mommy, can I comb your hair?" In such statements, the little girl always respects the existence of two subjects, each having the right to speak. Moreover, what she suggests is an activity which involves the participation of both subjects. In this respect, the little girl might serve as a model for all men and women, including the mother, who addresses her daughter using words like these: "You'll have to put your things away if you want to watch TV"; "Pick up some milk on your way home from school." The mother gives orders to the daughter without respecting the right of both subjects to speak, and she proposes nothing that they might do together, as two [à deux]. Interestingly, the mother speaks differently with a boy; she is more respectful of his identity: "Do you want me to come to your room and kiss you goodnight?" As for the little boy, he already speaks like a little leader: "I want to play with the ball"; "I want a toy car." In a way, the mother gives the little boy the you which the little girl has given her.

Why does the little girl like dialogue so much? Doubtless because as a woman, born of woman, with the qualities and characteristics of a woman, including the ability to give birth, the little girl finds herself, as soon as she is born, in the position of having relationships with two subjects. This would also explain her taste for dolls onto which she

6. On this topic, see my J'aime à toi.

projects a nostalgia for dialogue which was not always satisfied by the mother.

Yet the little girl will lose this, her first, feminine partner in dialogue, in the learning of a culture in which the subject is always still masculine—*he, He, they* [*il, Il, ils*⁷]—whether it is a linguistic category [*genre linguistique*] in the strict sense or various metaphors which supposedly represent human identity and its becoming [*son devenir*].

For all that, neither the young girl nor the adolescent girl renounces her relationship with the other: they almost always prefer a relationship with the other over a relationship with the object. Thus, when asked to give a sentence using the preposition "with" or the adverb "together," female adolescents and students, and many adult women, will respond with statements such as: "I'll go out with him tonight"; or "We'll always live together." Male subjects instead respond: "I came with my motorcycle"; "I wrote this sentence with my pencil"; or "Me and my guitar are good together."

This difference between the statements of female and male subjects is expressed in one way or another throughout the majority of responses to a series of questions which seek to define the sexualized characteristics of language. (The research was conducted in a variety of languages and cultures, mostly Romance and Anglo-Saxon.)

Besides the alternation between a masculine choice of subject-object relations and a feminine choice of subject-subject relations, there are other important characteristics of difference: women prefer the present and future tenses, contiguity, a concrete environment, relations based on difference; they prefer being with, being two [*l'être (à) deux*⁸]; men, on the other hand, prefer the past tense, metaphor, abstract transposition, relationships between likes [*semblables*], but only through a relationship with the object, relationships between the one and the many.

Men and women thus occupy different subjective configurations and different worlds. And it's not just a question of sociohistorical determination or a certain alienation of the feminine which could be done away with by making it equal to the masculine. True, women's

7. In the French language, the plural pronominal form is always masculine—even if the pronoun designates as few as one male or one masculine substantive within a group, however large, of females or feminine substantives—unless the pronoun designates an exclusively feminine category. [Translator's Note]

8. The original phrase suggests the notion of "being together with another person" and that the nature of "being" itself (existence) involves duality. [Translator's Note]

language does point to various kinds of alienation and passivity, but it also demonstrates an inherent richness which leaves nothing to be desired from men's language, in particular, a taste for intersubjectivity, which it would be a shame to abandon in favor of men's more inaccessible subject-object relations.

How then can the feminine subject—starting with me—be brought to cultivate a shared experience with the other without alienation? The gesture that must be made is the same gesture I made in *Speculum:* we must be careful to treat the other as other. To be sure, I as woman, we as women, have a nostalgia for dialogue and for relationships, but have we come to the point that we recognize the other as other and that we address him or her accordingly? Not really, not yet. In fact, while the words of adolescent girls and women show a definite leaning toward relationships with others, at the same time there is a desire for an *I-you* relationship that doesn't always recognize just who the *you* is and what *his* or *her* own desires might be.

The feminine subject thus favors a relationship with the other gender [*l'autre genre*], which is something that the masculine subject does not do. This preference for a masculine subject as partner-in-dialogue demonstrates on the one hand cultural alienation, but it also points to various other aspects of the feminine subject. Woman knows the other gender [*l'autre genre*] better than man does: she begets him within her; she mothers him from birth; she feeds him from her own body; she experiences him inside of her in the act of love. Her relationship to the transcendence of the other is, consequently, different from that experienced by man; she always remains exterior to him, is always inscribed with the mystery and ambivalence of the origin, whether maternal or paternal. Woman's relationship to man is linked more closely to shared flesh, to a sensual experience, to an immanent lived experience [*un vécu immanent*], including reproduction. No doubt she experiences the alterity of the other through his strange behavior, his resistance to her dreams, to her wishes. But she must construct this transcendence within horizontality itself, in a sharing of lives which respects the other as other absolutely, extending beyond all intuitions, sensations, experiences, or knowledge which she may have of him. Her taste for dialogue could end up making the other as other into a reductive gesture if she does not construct the transcendence of the other as such, as irreducibility with respect to her: through fusion, contiguity, empathy, mime.

I have tried to show how to move toward a construction of the transcendence of the other in *J'aime à toi* and *Essere due* (the Italian language edition[9]). I pointed out that the operation of the negative, which typically, in order to move on to a higher level in the process of the becoming of the self [*devenir soi-même*] must engage self and self in a dialectical operation, should instead engage two subjects, in order not to reduce the two to the one, the other to the same. Of course the negative is applied yet again to me, in my subjective becoming, but in this case it serves to mark the irreducibility of the other to me and not my subsuming of that exteriority into myself. Through this gesture, the subject gives up being one and singular. It respects the other, the two, in an intersubjective relation.

This gesture must first of all be applied to the relationship between the genders [*les genres*], since gender alterity is real and enables us to rearticulate nature in relation to culture in a truer and more ethical way, thus rising above the essential flaw in our spiritual becoming that Hegel denounces when he speaks of the exile and death of Antigone in *The Phenomenology of Spirit*.

This historic movement from the one, singular subject to the existence of two subjects of equal worth and equal dignity seems to me to be rightly the task of women, on both a philosophical and a political level. Women, as I have already pointed out, are, more than man, destined to a relationship of two [*la relation à deux*], and in particular to a relationship with the other. As a result of this aspect of their subjectivity, they can expand the horizons of the one, the similar, and even of the many, and in so doing affirm that they are an other subject [*sujet autre*], and impose a two which is not a second. By struggling for their liberation, they imply, moreover, that they recognize the other as other, for otherwise they will only close the circle that surrounds the singular subject. Recognizing that man is other clearly constitutes an appropriate ethical task for women, but it is also a necessary step toward affirming their autonomy. Moreover, the deployment of the negative which is required to complete this task allows them to move from a natural identity to a cultural and civil one, without giving up (their) nature, since they belong to a gender [*genre*]. From now on, the negative will intervene in all relationships with the other: in language of course (hence "j'aime à toi"),[10] but also in perception through eyes

9. *Essere due* (Turin: Bollati Boringhieri, 1994).
10. Irigaray's modification here of *je t'aime* (I love you) transforms the "you" from a direct object into an indirect object. [Translator's Note]

and ears, and even through touch. In *Essere due*, I try to define a new way to approach the other, including through the caress.

To succeed in this revolutionary move from affirmation of self as other to the recognition of man as other is a gesture that also allows us to promote the recognition of all forms of others without hierarchy, privilege, or authority over them: whether it be differences in race, age, culture, or religion.

Replacing the one by the two in sexual difference thus constitutes a decisive philosophical and political gesture, one which gives up a singular or plural being [*l'être* un *ou pluriel*] in order to become a dual being [*l'être* deux]. This is the necessary foundation for a new ontology, a new ethics, and a new politics, in which the other is recognized as other and not as the same: bigger or smaller than I, or at best my equal.

—Translated by Noah Guynn

LYNNE HUFFER

Luce *et veritas*: Toward an Ethics of Performance[1]

How can I say it? . . . Our all will come.

—Luce Irigaray[2]

How can we talk about the way things are? How can we know what to do? Though dauntingly broad and hardly original, these basic philosophical questions define the parameters of what I offer here: a challenge to contemporary articulations of the relationship between language and politics. More specifically, this essay critiques recent thinking about speech act theory and queer performativity by asserting the necessity of an ethical call for justice. How do we define the terms of our politics, when we're not even sure who "we" are? What does it mean to call oneself a political agent? a feminist? queer? What is identity anyway, if it's always already the jargonized, spectacularized, institutionalized construction of an infinitely mobile subject position? What happens to politics if everything is a performance?[3]

1. For help on this essay, I would especially like to thank Karl Britto, Cathy Cohen, Beth Huffer, Serene Jones, and Carla Kaplan. The move in this essay toward ethical questions represents a major shift in my thinking about the construction of identities. For an earlier consideration of performance and lesbian sexuality, see Lynne Huffer, "Gendered Figures of Sexual Performance: *The Pure and the Impure*," in *Another Colette: The Question of Gendered Writing* (Ann Arbor: University of Michigan Press, 1992), 71–102.

2. "Le toute va venir." Luce Irigaray, "Quand nos lèvres se parlent," *Ce sexe qui n'en est pas un* (Paris: Minuit, 1977), 212; and, in English, "When Our Lips Speak Together," *This Sex Which Is Not One*, trans. Catherine Porter (Ithaca: Cornell University Press, 1985), 212.

3. My analysis here is drawn primarily from the work of Judith Butler and, to a lesser degree, Eve Kosofsky Sedgwick. Butler has undeniably led the way in popularizing the notion of performativity. See especially *Gender Trouble: Feminism and the Subversion of Identity* (New York: Routledge, 1990); "Gender Trouble, Feminist Theory, and Psychoanalytic Discourse," in *Feminism/Postmodernism*, ed. Linda J. Nicholson (New York: Routledge, 1990), 324–40; "Imitation and Gender Insubordination," in *In-*

YFS 87, *Another Look, Another Woman*, ed. Huffer, © 1995 by Yale University.

The question of performance marks a starting point for this inquiry into broader questions about language, politics, and identity. This essay examines the work of Judith Butler, J. L. Austin, and Luce Irigaray in order to assess performative theory in relation to feminist and queer strategies of resistance. Those performative strategies involve a contestation of identity categories with an aim to bring about political change. And while the intended liberatory aims of feminist and queer performativity are laudable, performative theory tends to be flawed by its disregard for ethical questions, a problem that is particularly striking in Butler's work.[4] Specifically, performativity elides the possibility of an ethical relation that would speak the truth and, in so doing, question identity itself.

Unlike Butler, Irigaray places ethical concerns at the center of her consideration of the epistemological problems of identity and truth. That philosophical stance is made particularly clear in her *Ethics of Sexual Difference*;[5] however, most readers of Irigaray have not recog-

---

side/Out: Lesbian Theories, Gay Theories, ed. Diana Fuss (New York: Routledge, 1991), 13–31; "Contingent Foundations: Feminism and the Question of 'Postmodernism,'" in *Feminists Theorize the Political*, ed. Judith Butler and Joan W. Scott (New York: Routledge, 1992), 3–21; *Bodies That Matter: On the Discursive Limits of "Sex"* (New York: Routledge, 1993); and "Endangered/Endangering: Schematic Racism and White Paranoia," in *Reading Rodney King/Reading Urban Uprising*, ed. Robert Gooding-Williams (New York: Routledge, 1993), 15–22. For Sedgwick, see especially *Epistemology of the Closet* (Berkeley: University of California Press, 1990) and *Tendencies* (Durham: Duke University Press, 1993). Also see Peggy Phelan, *Unmarked: The Politics of Performance* (New York: Routledge, 1993). For work in the social sciences, see James C. Scott, *Domination and the Arts of Resistance: Hidden Transcripts* (New Haven: Yale University Press, 1990); Melvin Patrick Ely, *The Adventures of Amos 'N' Andy: A Social History of an American Phenomenon* (New York: The Free Press, 1990); and I.M. Lewis, *Ecstatic Religion: A Study of Shamanism and Spirit Possession* (New York: Routledge, 1989). My thanks to Cathy Cohen for bringing this work in the social sciences to my attention. Finally, my understanding of performativity is most crucially and significantly indebted to the work of Luce Irigaray, especially in *Speculum of the Other Woman*, trans. Gillian Gill (Ithaca: Cornell University Press, 1985) and *This Sex Which Is Not One*, trans. Catherine Porter (Ithaca: Cornell.University Press, 1985).

4. What constitutes an ethical question? As Claire Nouvet points out, "we can no longer use the word 'ethics' or engage in an ethical discourse without taking note of a certain reticence. . . . The reticence to engage in an ethical discourse thus invokes another kind of ethicity, another and more imperative duty; the duty of a relentless questioning from which not even an 'ethical' discourse should be exempted . . . " (103). "An Impossible Response: The Disaster of Narcissus," *Literature and the Ethical Question*, ed. Claire Nouvet, *Yale French Studies* 79 (1991), 103–34. My ethical critique of performativity follows Nouvet, for whom it is "the question of the other which becomes the ethical question par excellence" (103).

5. Irigaray, *Ethique de la différence sexuelle* (Paris: Minuit, 1984), translated as *Ethics of Sexual Difference*, trans. Carolyn Burke (Ithaca, New York: Cornell University

nized the extent to which she already engages with ethics in *Speculum of the Other Woman* and *This Sex Which Is Not One*. More specifically, in the closing essay of *This Sex Which Is Not One*, "When Our Lips Speak Together," Irigaray inscribes an ethical model of speech that would contest Butler's performative act, despite the apparent affinities between performativity and Irigaray's concept of mimesis.[6] In the lips essay, Irigaray both theorizes and performs a relational model of subjectivity that would allow for the irreducible difference of the other. As theory and performance, Irigaray's lips speak the instability of either a pure truth-telling or an absolute performative concept of language.[7] In so doing, they perform an ethical model of social and discursive relation in which the specular performative subject is put into question by the other's narrative truth.[8]

Press, 1993). On Irigaray and ethics, see especially Margaret Whitford, *Luce Irigaray: Philosophy in the Feminine* (London: Routledge, 1991): "For Irigaray, epistemology without ethics is deadly" (Whitford, 149). Also see Elizabeth Grosz, *Sexual Subversions: Three French Feminists* (Sydney: Allen and Unwin, 1989), especially chapter five, "Luce Irigaray and the Ethics of Alterity"; Drucilla Cornell, *Beyond Accommodation: Ethical Feminism, Deconstruction, and the Law* (New York: Routledge, 1991); Gayatri Chakravorty Spivak, "French Feminism Revisited: Ethics and Politics," in *Feminists Theorize the Political*, ed. Judith Butler and Joan W. Scott (New York: Routledge, 1992), 54–85; and Tina Chanter, *The Ethics of Eros: Irigaray's Re-writing of the Philosophers* (New York: Routledge, 1994).

6. In both *Gender Trouble* and *Bodies That Matter*, Butler draws on Irigarayan mimesis or mimicry to develop her theory of performativity. See especially *Bodies That Matter*, 36–55.

7. Paul de Man describes the "aporia between performative and constative language" as "a version of the aporia between trope and persuasion" that historically defines rhetoric as both oratorical eloquence (persuasion) and an epistemology of figures (trope). De Man suggests that those oppositions themselves are potentially dangerous, because an act of persuasive force cannot be separated from the figuration of truth, regardless of the speaker's intentions. We may be reassured "that it is legitimate to do just about anything with words, as long as we know that a rigorous mind, fully aware of the misleading power of tropes, pulls the strings. But if it turns out that this same mind does not even know whether it is doing or not doing something, then there are considerable grounds for suspicion that it does not know *what* it is doing." See de Man, "Rhetoric of Persuasion (Nietzsche)," in *Allegories of Reading: Figural Language in Rousseau, Nietzsche, Rilke, and Proust* (New Haven: Yale University Press, 1979), 131.

8. Following J. L. Austin and Emile Benvéniste, Shoshana Felman points out that the performative is necessarily self-referential. Further, the self-referentiality of the performative links it to a structure of seduction: "Just as seductive discourse exploits the capacity of language to reflect itself, by means of the self-referentiality of performative verbs, it also exploits in parallel fashion the self-referentiality of the interlocutor's narcissistic desire, and his (or her) capacity to produce in turn a reflexive, specular illusion" (31). See Shoshana Felman, *The Literary Speech Act: Don Juan with J. L. Austin, or Seduction in Two Languages*, trans. Catherine Porter (Ithaca: Cornell University Press, 1983).

Why do we need ethics? Because without it the play of representation is unleashed into a field of power that can harness, abuse, and distort it for the accomplishment of its own ends. Without ethics, "freeplay"[9] can be murderous and illusion can be literalized into the real oppression of persons perceived to be threats. Without ethics as a *foundation*,[10] the force of a performance can become anything at all, commanded by the desire of anyone at all: a democratic president, a fascist dictator, or a progressive academic superstar.[11] As Shoshana Felman has shown, the performative subject plays the role of Don Juan; the political effect of any performance is determined by its success as a seduction.[12] If our performance fails to ask the ethical question, the seduction goes unchecked in its own potential for violence, despite the avowed intention of its agent to contest that very violence.

9. Much has been made of this term in contemporary debates about poststructuralism and postmodernism. In his early formulation of the concept of "play" (*le jeu*), Jacques Derrida makes no claim to its ever being "free," but rather, takes pains to demonstrate the relationship between "play" and the structure that constrains it. See especially "Structure, Sign, and Play," in *Writing and Difference* (Chicago: University of Chicago Press, 1978), and Derrida's response to Gerald Graff in *Limited Inc* (Evanston: Northwestern University Press, 1988), esp. 115–16.

10. My use of the term *foundation* is quite deliberate here. Butler argues against an essentializing foundationalism in "Contingent Foundations" because of the ontological claims upheld by any foundationalist argument. I follow Levinas here in asserting the necessity of ethics, and *not* ontology, as a "first philosophy." As such, ethics accounts for an always prior sociality that subtends ontology, thereby constituting a legitimate, nonessentializing foundation for discourse and politics. We should not annihilate the other, for it is precisely the question of the other that puts "us" into question. That postulation is a foundationalist claim which bases itself on the necessity of being put into question. See especially "Ethics as First Philosophy," in *The Levinas Reader*, ed. Seàn Hand (Oxford: Blackwell, 1989), 75–87, as well as the first section of *Totality and Infinity: An Essay on Exteriority*, trans. Alphonso Lingis (Pittsburgh: Duquesne University Press, 1969).

11. As Butler herself admits: "That the identity-sign I use now has its purposes seems right, but there is no way to predict or control the political uses to which that sign will be put in the future" ("Imitation," 19). Similarly, Butler asserts that "the effects of an action always supersede the stated intention or purpose of the act" ("Contingent," 10). However, she nonetheless makes liberatory claims for a performativity that would suit *her* purposes ("a very different performative purpose" ["Imitation," 24]), that is, the parodic subversion of heterosexual identity. What keeps Butler's purposeful redeployment from being, yet again, redeployed, with perhaps drastically different purposes? Nothing, we all admit, since iterability as repetition is precisely the point. Which is precisely why performativity alone is inadequate as political theory.

12. What is the political effect of a seduction? Because seduction implies a relationship of dependency between the performer and the audience, it seems important here to draw on other political models that would work toward engaging and mobilizing groups to act independently of a performative subject.

So where do we find ethics, this thing that is missing? Not a simple question, since in the moment of finding we face the recognition that there is still, and always, something missing. Armed with a belief in transcendent reason which rests on the universalizing claims of an epistemological *a priori*, but faced with the destabilizing crises of the "postmodern" condition, we still look to theory in order to know what is missing. So doing, we have learned to reject as illusory the totalizing truth of the knowledge to be found there. We have learned that the "true" is contingent, formed and articulated according to particular histories and specific regimes of power. We have learned, ad nauseum, that there is no truth. But who is this "we"? What have we been saying, and to whom? And in dismissing Truth, whose truths have we not been hearing?[13]

ACT I: JUDY

In terms of feminist thought, particularly in the humanities, the loss of Truth and of a "we" who would speak it has led to the theorization of gender as performance. According to Butler, gender identity, like any identity, is founded and regulated through the repetition of signifying practices that appear to naturalize those identities. Consequently, "the feminist 'we' is always and only a phantasmatic construction" (*Gender Trouble*, 142), and " 'identity' as a point of departure can never hold as the solidifying ground of a feminist political movement" ("Contingent," 15). It follows, then, according to performative theory, that a similar process of repetition might subvert those very identities. Butler writes: "It is only *within* the practices of repetitive signifying that a subversion of identity becomes possible" (*Gender Trouble*, 145). Gender is exposed as an "act" (*Gender Trouble*, 146) through practices of parody such as drag; the bodies performing that act "become the site of a dissonant and denaturalized performance that reveals the perfor- mative status of the natural itself" (*Gender Trouble*, 146). Hence, per-

---

13. Patricia Hill Collins's work toward developing a black feminist epistemology can be seen as a model here. In *Black Feminist Thought: Knowledge, Consciousness and the Politics of Empowerment* (New York: Routledge, 1990), Collins examines two con- trasting epistemologies, a traditional "epistemology of separation" and "an epistemol- ogy of connection in which truth emerges through care" (217). While Collins's absolute division between separation and connection is problematic, her call for an ethic of caring questions the very process by which knowledge claims are legitimated. This ethical stance does not deny the possibility of truth, but rather offers a challenge to "what has been taken to be true" (219) by opening a dialogue with those who have been silenced.

formance reveals the naturalized "truth" of gender "as an inevitable fabrication," and exposes "every claim to the origin, the inner, the *true*, and the real as *nothing other* than the effects of *drag*" ("Imitation," 29; emphasis added). The exposure of the instability of that truth has the effect of "proliferating gender configurations, destabilizing substantive identity, and depriving the naturalizing narratives of compulsory heterosexuality of their central protagonists: 'man' and 'woman,'" (*Gender Trouble*, 146).

The loss of "man" and "woman" does not mean, according to Butler, that we've lost the possibility of feminist politics, but rather, it puts the very terms of that politics into question. For Butler, one of those questionable terms is the concept of narrative. Butler replaces narrative, the possibility of telling stories within discursively coherent frames, with a more disruptive performance.[14] This move from narrative to performance corresponds to what many have identified as the epistemological shift of postmodernism, in which the "hegemonical claims of any group or organization to 'represent' the forces of history"[15] are subverted by the locally contextualized speech acts of situated subject positions within specific structures of power. More specifically, American feminists in the early 1970s named women's oppression and, so doing, produced a "quasi-metanarrative"[16] of their own to counter the grand narratives of History and man.[17] However, that feminist narrative about Woman tended to elide the ethnic, racial, economic, sexual, and national differences between particular women. In that context, performance "brings into question the foundationalist frame in which feminism as an identity politics has been articulated" (*Gender Trouble*, 148), exposing as a ruse the "transhistorical commonality" of a feminist "we" constructed through "standards of narrative coherence" ("Gender," 339).

Butler asserts, then, that "performance may preempt narrative as

14. My thanks to Valerie Smith, whose lecture at Yale (Fall 1993) on the two versions of the film "Imitation of Life" pushed me to rethink the terms of that opposition between performance and narrative.

15. Seyla Benhabib, *Situating the Self: Gender, Community and Postmodernism in Contemporary Ethics* (New York: Routledge, 1992), 219.

16. Nancy Fraser and Linda J. Nicholson, "Social Criticism without Philosophy," *Feminism/Postmodernism*, ed. Linda J. Nicholson (New York: Routledge, 1990), 33.

17. See Jean-François Lyotard, *The Postmodern Condition: A Report on Knowledge*, trans. Geoff Bennington and Brian Massumi (Minneapolis: University of Minnesota Press, 1984). For a critique of Lyotard's "ethnological" view of a "prereflexive" or "primitive" narrative of the other, see Benhabib, especially 233n19.

the scene of gender production" ("Gender," 339). Further, not only does she use performance to explain the construction of gendered identities; she also affirms its capacity to subvert the status quo by repeating the very fictions through which those gendered identities were constructed in the first place. Butler implies that the telling "of a unique life-story, of a meaningful tale" (Benhabib, 217–18) is not a viable model for resisting or contesting gender oppression. Rather, we lose narrative along with Man, Woman, History, and Truth, by putting them all in quotations. Having done away with narrative and its purportedly oppressive corollaries, Butler then claims performance as a model for a different form of political practice that would avoid the totalizing tendencies of narrative truth-telling. Indeed, according to Butler, the quotation marks expose the truth as illusory. By mocking that truth, the performative "we" begins to build a "new" politics. "Cultural configurations of sex and gender might then proliferate," and "a new configuration of politics would surely emerge from the ruins of the old" (*Gender Trouble*, 149).

Not surprisingly, Butler's exposure of the trouble with gender has revealed other troubled waters as well. The performative disruption of gender identity seems to work equally well with other categories of difference, be they racial, ethnic, national, sexual, or other. Performativity has been most broadly deployed in recent theories about the multiple identities marked by the term "queer." A term that in itself, according to Eve Sedgwick, is "recurrent, eddying, *troublant*" (*Tendencies*, xii), "queer" dramatically celebrates the explosion of identity, the proliferation of excess and loss set into play by the performative subversion of gender. Thus "queer" can mean "the open mesh of possibilities, gaps, overlaps, dissonances and resonances, lapses and excesses of meaning when the constituent elements of anyone's gender, of anyone's sexuality aren't made (or *can't* be made) to signify monolithically" (*Tendencies*, 8). Indeed, "queer" isn't limited to thinking about gender and sexuality alone; for example, Sedgwick argues that "[i]ntellectuals and artists of color whose sexual self-definition includes 'queer' . . . are using the leverage of 'queer' to do a new kind of justice to the fractal intracacies of language, skin, migration, state" (*Tendencies*, 9). In fact, "[a] word so fraught as 'queer' is . . . never can only denote; nor even can it only connote" (9). Rather, "part of [the] experimental force [of queer] as a speech act is the way in which it dramatizes locutionary position itself" (9). Paradoxically, while both Butler and Sedgwick use "queer" to disrupt the foundations of coher-

ent identity, that disruption does not seem to include the authority—
theirs perhaps?—of the performative "I." "Queer," Sedgwick suggests,
"can signify only *when attached to the first person*" (9).

My argument with "queer" is *not* that Sedgwick or Butler's recurrent, troubling, and eddying first person "queer" doesn't matter, particularly when that person has been marginalized by a society bent on
her or his annihilation. Rather, I think the effect of theorizing a "queer
I" as "a person's undertaking particular, performative acts of experimental self-perception and filiation" (*Tendencies*, 9) has elided the
key ethical questions that must be asked about any communicative
act. First, queer performativity denies the possibility of conversation
between two people with different stories to tell; and second, it fails to
account for the potentially negative, even violent effects of performative experimentation. In regard to the first point, the following questions can be asked: To whom does a performance speak? Can the performer hear the response of the other to whom she would speak? Does
the concept of response, and thus responsibility, even matter in theories of performativity? Another set of issues is raised by the second
point, namely: How might a performance be read? What might cause
the performance to fail, to make it work in ways that veer dangerously
off course, away from the liberatory intentions of its agents?

More pointedly, ethical discourse would have us ask: how does the
first person queer speak to the other? How does the first person account
for and think the second person who would hear her, draw her up short,
put her into question? How does the experimental force of a queer
speech act *do more* than simply "dramatize locutionary position itself"? How does it speak its relation to a "thou," its ethical relation to
an other?

Why do these questions matter? Most urgently, they matter because people continue to suffer, and they suffer as constructed identities. No performance can parodically resignify the harm that is inflicted on a "woman" who is abused, a "fag" who is killed, a "dyke" who
commits suicide, a "black" who is beaten by the "white" police.[18] The

18. Butler herself reads the violent effects of white police brutality on the black body
of Rodney King in "Endangered/Endangering: Schematic Racism and White Paranoia."
She illustrates the twisted logic through which the jury read the videotaped scene of
aggression; in her reading, white racism provides a context for the jury's interpretation of
the video "performance," one that claimed to "see" Rodney King as the source of violence. Butler reads that reversal as a projection of white racist violence onto Rodney
King, who in the jury's view becomes the "black" aggressor, his body the site for the
displacement of "white" aggression. The self-legitimating reversal of that reading of a

quotation marks don't perform away the pain, despite the claim that placing terms like "violence" and "sex" in quotation marks reveals them to be "under contest, up for grabs" (Butler, "Contingent," 19). What might inadvertently be performed away by parodic quotation is the possibility of a narrative which would speak the truth of that pain. Precisely because of the empirical fact that our identities still get us abused, beaten, and killed, we *still* need to elaborate a discourse and a politics about rights and justice,[19] about the relation between "I" and "you." We need to imagine an ethical politics in which, as Levinas puts it, murder becomes impossible.[20] What happens to blacks, women, fags, and dykes? We still need to tell our stories, to narrate the harms that befall us. We still need to speak the truth, a truth that *is more* than "the effects of *drag*" (Butler, "Imitation," 29). Tell the truth. Truth matters.

ACT II: JOHN

Philosophy traditionally claims to separate truth from error, statements of fact from the nonserious play of fiction. At least since Plato, that division between fact and fiction has allowed philosophy to exclude itself from the representational realm of illusion, thereby focusing on the more serious project of finding the truth.[21] J. L. Austin's speech act theory marks an intervention into the exclusion of truth

particular "performance" demonstrates precisely what Butler's theory of performativity lacks: the need for an ethical frame within which to ask about questions of reading.

19. See, especially, Patricia J. Williams, "Alchemical Notes: Reconstructing Ideals from Deconstructed Rights," *Harvard Civil Rights-Civil Liberties Law Review* 22 (1987): 401–33. Williams criticizes the Critical Legal Studies movement's rejection of rights-based theory, arguing that "for the historically disempowered, the conferring of rights is symbolic of all the denied aspects of humanity" (416). "The concept of rights," Williams concludes, "is the marker of our citizenship, our participatoriness, *our relation to others*" (431; emphasis added). For a similar rights-based argument, see Mari Matsuda, "Looking to the Bottom: Critical Legal Studies and Reparations," *Harvard Civil Rights-Civil Liberties Law Review* 22 (1987): 323–99. Also see Elizabeth M. Schneider, "The Dialectic of Rights and Politics: Perspectives from the Women's Movement," *New York University Law Review* 61 (October 1986): 589–652. Many thanks to Carla Kaplan for bringing this work to my attention.

20. Levinas: "The effort of this book is directed toward apperceiving in discourse a nonallergic reaction with alterity, toward apperceiving Desire—where power, by essence murderous of the other, becomes, faced with the other and 'against all good sense,' the impossibility of murder, the consideration of the other, or justice" (*Totality and Infinity*, 47).

21. See Plato's *Republic*, Book X, for the exclusion of imitation from philosophy: "Then the imitator, I said, is a long way off the truth, and can do all things because he lightly touches on a small part of them, and that part an image." Plato, *The Republic: The Complete and Unabridged Jowett Translation* (New York: Vintage, 1991), 365.

from representation by asking about the link between the way things are said and what those things that are said can do. In the first lecture of *How to Do Things With Words*, Austin posits his famous distinction between performative and constative utterances, only to problematize the binarism of his own opposition over the course of the subsequent eleven lectures.[22] A performative utterance is a statement in which to say something "is to do it"; "the issuing of the utterance is the performing of an action" (Austin, 6). Austin opposes performative to constative utterances, the kinds of statements that have traditionally occupied philosophers. "It was far too long the assumption of philosophers," Austin complains, "that the business of a 'statement' can only be to 'describe' some state of affairs, or to 'state some fact,' which it must do *either truly or falsely*" (Austin, 1; emphasis added). The emphasis on performatives makes Austin something of a rebel in the philosophical tradition. By shifting the focus away from philosophy's traditional concern with statements about truth, *How To Do Things With Words* opens the way to contemporary theories of representation in which speaking is acknowledged to be a constructed, context-bound signifying event, an act of force that, rather than providing a means for reaching truth, constitutes the very terms through which that truth is simultaneously affirmed and subverted.

Austin's speech act theory undoubtedly provides a key philosophical base for contemporary articulations of performativity. Significantly, the logic of example through which Austin lays out that theory has had important implications for queer theory as well. As Butler and others have noted, Austin's favorite example of the "performative utterance" is the statement "I do" in the context of the marriage ceremony. To say "I do" is to make the marriage real: to say it is to do it. Austin's reliance on the marriage ceremony to theorize performativity suggests, as Butler points out, "that the heterosexualization of the social bond is the paradigmatic form for those speech acts which bring about what they name" (*Bodies*, 224). Indeed, in repeating the exemplary words "I do" throughout *How To Do Things With Words*, Austin himself is making "it" so, the "it" being theory qua heterosexuality. Performativity therefore is inscribed within a model of heterosexuality as norm that serves to legitimate the power of the performative utterance. Performatives not only perform an action but also "confer a

22. The twelve lectures collected under the title *How To Do Things With Words* were delivered by Austin at Harvard University in 1955. The printed text was constituted from Austin's notes for these lectures. See J. L. Austin, *How To Do Things With Words*, ed. J. O. Urmson and Marina Sbisà (Cambridge: Harvard University Press, 1962).

binding power on the action performed" (Butler, *Bodies,* 225); it follows, then, according to Butler, that "the performative is one domain where discourse acts *as* power" (*Bodies,* 225).

It is Butler who also introduces the term "queer" as a destabilizing intervention into the Austinian construct of a heterosexualized performativity. She asks: "To what extent . . . has the performative 'queer' operated alongside, as a deformation of, the 'I pronounce you . . . ' of the marriage ceremony?" (*Bodies,* 226). Butler thus uses the term "queer" to mark a performative practice that would both destabilize and contest heterosexuality as norm. In this way, "the subject who is 'queered' into public discourse through homophobic interpellations of various kinds *takes up* or *cites* that very term as the discursive basis for an opposition. This kind of citation will emerge as *theatrical* to the extent that it *mimes and renders hyperbolic* the discursive convention that it also *reverses*" (*Bodies,* 232).

How can we know the difference between Austin's heterosexual theatre and the spectacular performances to which Butler refers? The die-ins by ACT UP, the kiss-ins by Queer Nation, and the other varieties of "theatrical rage" (*Bodies,* 233) cited by Butler as examples of a queer-positive opposition to the status quo, are undoubtedly intended to contest the "heterosexualization of the social bond" so shamelessly inscribed in Austin's theory of performativity and played out in the oppressive practices of contemporary society.[23] Further, those contestatory political acts occur within a particular context in which AIDS discrimination, homophobia, racism, and other forms of oppression are being targeted.[24] Austin himself asserts that in order to interpret the force or meaning of an utterance like "I'm queer," the "occasion" or "context" of that utterance "matters seriously" (Austin, 100). Without context, neither the interpretation nor the reception of the utterance can be theorized.

However, a difficulty arises with the following paraodx: context sets limits on the possible meanings of an utterance; at the same time,

23. Sedgwick lists other examples of "queer" identity: "(among other possibilities) pushy femmes, radical faeries, fantasists, drags, clones, leatherfolk, ladies in tuxedoes, feminist women or feminist men, masturbators, bulldaggers, divas, Snap! queens, butch bottoms, storytellers, transsexuals, aunties, wannabes, lesbian-identified men or lesbians who sleep with men, or . . . people able to relish, learn from, or *identify* with such" (*Tendencies,* 8; emphasis added).

24. One difficulty in assessing the political effect of performative practice is the lack of clarity about precisely which institutions are being contested by this "theatrical rage."

context itself is without limits. The particular context of an utterance must be empirically evaluated and understood in any reading of the historical force of that utterance; but, in theory, the possible contexts of that utterance are potentially boundless, because utterances are repeatable. Indeed, as Derrida points out, an utterance has meaning *because* it is repeatable; its force, therefore, cannot be controlled or fixed in place and time.[25] As a result, its contexts are both particular and generalizable, both the irreducible event of a particular performance, and the infinite future of all possible repetitions of that performance. Both that particularity and that generality constitute the "occasions" of the utterance. Further, it is the act of moving from the particular scene of an utterance to the conceptual generality which attempts to think about its other possible occasions that constitutes the act of theorization. Particular scenes of performance by, say, ACT UP, are subsumed by a discourse that attempts to talk about "queer" performance in an evaluative and universalizing way. That theory, in turn, is taken up as a formula for preparing, enacting, and understanding particular scenes of performative practice.

Most crucially, contemporary theories of queer performativity fail to account for the possibility, or even the inevitability, of their own failure. Indeed, the possibility of failure is built into Austin's definition of a performative, since a performative has force only in a context, and contexts are necessarily ever-changing. To use, once again, Austin's favorite example, marriage is paradigmatic as a cornerstone of his theory and yet, as his "doctrine of *Infelicities*" suggests, in marrying there will always be a case in which "something *goes wrong*" (Austin, 14). The performative will fail "if we, say, utter the formula incorrectly, or if, say, we are not in a position to do the act because we are, say, married already" (Austin, 15–16). Another example might be a case in which the person performing the ceremony lacks the authority to "make it so," thus turning the performance into "a mockery, like a marriage with a monkey" (Austin, 24).[26] Failure, therefore, "is not for Austin an *accident* of the performative" (Felman, 66); rather, its possi-

25. Derrida writes: "There is an indefinite opening of every context, an essential nontotalization" (*Limited*, 137). And further: "there is always something political 'in the very project of attempting to fix the contexts of utterances'" (*Limited, 136*).

26. The legitimacy of a marriage is not solely determined by its heterosexualization, although, as in gay marriages, failure to be heterosexual certainly has the effect of delegitimizing the marriage in the eyes of the state. However, other categories of social exclusion have also functioned to delegitimize marriage, as in the case of minors, or African Americans during slavery.

bility is "inherent in it, essential to it. In other words, like Don Juan, Austin conceives of failure not as external but as internal to the prom-ise, as what actually constitutes it" (Felman, 66).

So what if a queer performance goes astray, wanders off its intended path, produces *error* rather than contesting it? That possibility of error and errancy is linked to the question of identity and the violence of totalization. Butler admits, of course, that a "queer" identity, like any identity, can never be total or "fully owned" (*Bodies*, 228); as a word that "carries the pain of social injury," "queer" can never be a term created "from nothing" that would come to "represent our 'freedom'" (*Bodies*, 229). Rather, she argues, "queer" marks both "the *limits* of agency and its most *enabling conditions*" (*Bodies*, 228). In that sense, we can certainly imagine the utterance "I'm queer," to function like "I do," in situations where "something goes wrong" (Austin, 14). It is precisely because those words cannot be pinned down that they can be harnessed and repeated with vastly differing intentions and effects.

The question becomes: who is doing the naming? As Sedgwick points out, there is a difference between the shaming utterance "You queer," and the "I'm queer" that expresses pride. But can we control an effect of shame or pride when, as Sartre famously put it, history de-prives us of our intentions? Butler implies that we *do* have that control when she asserts the necessity of a fixed, self-identical notion of "queer," however provisional that fixing may be: "The temporary to-talization performed by identity categories is a necessary error" (*Bodies*, 230). Although we can never be fully constituted as subjects, "queer" or otherwise—"the subject as self-identical is no more" (*Bodies*, 230)—we must, according to Butler, pretend that as queers we can speak and, like Austin's man and wife, make our identities real. To perform is to act, to "make it so" (Austin, 6); to say "I'm queer" is "to do it."

The problem, of course, is that we can never be sure what the "it" might be, precisely because "it" will be repeated. However, that uncer-tainty should not be a reason for giving up on contestatory politics altogether. Rather, it forces us to think about the *potential* for violence in our own failure to fully know what we think we're doing.[27] And that

---

27. As Felman puts it: "The scandal [of the performative seduction] consists in the fact that the act cannot *know what it is doing*" (96; emphasis in original). Felman calls this scandal Austin's "radical negativity," thus aligning him with thinkers such as Nietzsche and Lacan: "Thus Austin, like Lacan, like Nietzsche, like others still, instiga-tors of the historical scandal, Don Juans of History, are in reality *bequeathing* us what

possibility of violence is linked, however obliquely, to the "necessary error" of identity on which queer performativity depends. Paradoxically, Butler's theory goes too far by allowing a performative act to be anything at all and, at the same time, doesn't go far enough in its reliance on an epistemological structure of analogy that refuses difference. A theory that relies on the "necessary error" of self-identity has the potential for violence because, philosophically, it repeats the mimetic logic that reduces difference to a repetition of the same.[28] Because performativity fails to theorize the other, the identity it stages is totalized, however provisionally, as an ontological force that would subsume the other into its self-identity. And there is nothing to keep that self-identity, produced through error, from erring yet again, from being led astray, from becoming its own failure as violence. In other words, the self-knowing logic of that identity is potentially murderous, as Levinas has shown, because it lacks an ethical *foundation* that would demand a response to an irreducible other.[29]

Without ethics, a performance can be anything it wants to be. Its agents become "identities that are alternately instituted and relinquished according to the purposes at hand" (*Gender Trouble*, 16). The politics of a performance are therefore, by definition, radically "contingent" (*Gender Trouble*, 16), and its value of *force*—as opposed to the *truth* value of a constative utterance—gives it a power of seduction that remains unchecked by truth.[30] Indeed, as Butler herself points out, "one is, as it were, in power even as one opposes it" (*Bodies*, 241), and the "effects of performatives" are "incalculable" (*Bodies*, 241). The theatrical rage of an ACT UP demonstration, or the spectacular

---

they do not have: their *word*, their authority, their promise. . . . Modern Don Juans, they know that *truth is only an act*" (150). While I agree with Felman that the absolute authority of the word is put into question by the very terms of the utterance itself, it seems important to make distinctions between the relative levels of authority that are accorded to particular discourses within historically constituted structures of power.

28. On the collapsing of difference into the self-identical sameness of philosophical truth, see Luce Irigaray, *Speculum of the Other Woman*.

29. Levinas: "Critique does not reduce the other to the same as does ontology, but calls into question the exercise of the same. A calling into question of the same—which cannot occur within the egoist spontaneity of the same—is brought about by the other. We name this calling into question of my spontaneity by the presence of the Other ethics. The strangeness of the Other, his [sic] irreducibility to the I, to my thoughts and my possessions, is precisely accomplished as a calling into question of my spontaneity, my ethics" (*Totality*, 43).

30. On the opposition between truth value and the value of force in Austin, see Derrida, *Limited Inc*, 13. On the seductive force of the performative see Felman.

desire of a butch-femme lesbian performance, cannot know its effects. All the more reason to ask questions about a saying that is also a doing and that, in the moment of that doing, refuses to contest its own identity. Such self-contestation in saying can only happen in a form that articulates the horizon of an ethical relation, one that cannot tolerate self-identity but, rather, produces an opening toward the other.

INTERMISSION: BEHIND THE CURTAIN

[I]n ancient Persia . . . to consecrate the marriage, the boy makes his agreement heard loudly and clearly; the fiancée, the girl, is put in the next room amid other women, near the door over which a curtain falls. In order to make the necessary yes audible, the women hit the young girl's head against the door, causing her to moan.[31]

As the paradigmatic model of performativity, marriage requires a "necessary yes," an utterance of acquiescence to the bond of matrimony that transforms boy and girl into man and wife. Does Austin's "I do" mask a moan of pain, as in Assia Djebar's account of the curtained "yes" that falls between the Persian girl and the boy she is forced to wed? Is there in marriage a necessary violence that undergirds the "necessary yes"? If so, what might that marital violence suggest about the possible violence of performativity itself?

Not only does Austin's performative rest on an assumption of the unquestioned legitimacy of all heterosexual marriage, its intrinsic possibility for failure is illustrated by marriage ceremonies in which the implicit "rightness" of the marital bond is put at risk by occasions where "something goes wrong." But why is marriage necessarily right and its failure "wrong"? Austin appears never to have asked himself that question, despite his attention to the rights and wrongs of "accuracy and morality" (Austin, 10), or his concern for the "solid moralist" (Austin, 10) who surveys "the invisible depths of ethical space" (Austin, 10). In fact, for an unwilling bride in a forced marriage where a moan of pain is taken as "yes," the failure of that "necessary yes" might be welcome. Similarly, a survivor of domestic abuse might argue that it is precisely in those cases in the ceremony where "something goes wrong" that something "right" has happened, particularly if the failure represents an avenue of escape from a cycle of violence. In

31. Assia Djebar, *Women of Algiers in Their Apartment*, trans. Marjolijn de Jager (Charlottesville: University Press of Virginia, 1992), 145.

focusing on the ceremonial trappings of an utterance, Austin fails to account for the sociopolitical institutions that ground the utterance within oppressive systems of power. In the case of "I do," the institutional context for the utterance is a system of power that perpetuates a gendered structure of domination and subordination. Not only does Austin take the privilege of the "he" ("a solid moralist"?) within that structure for granted, he unwittingly exposes the hidden violence through which the binding power of his "moral" act is imposed and reinforced.

In Austin's "doctrine of 'illocutionary forces'" (Austin, 100), the "act performed," or "illocution" (Austin, 100), acquires its force through a particular "context" (Austin, 100). In taking seriously the notion that "the occasion of an utterance matters seriously" (Austin, 100), Austin shows how mere meaning—a locution—is necessarily contextualized and thus becomes an "illocutionary act" (Austin 101). To illustrate this point he comes up with the following example:

Act (A) or Locution
    He said to me [Austin? the solid moralist?] 'Shoot her!' meaning by 'shoot' shoot and referring by 'her' to *her*. [Austin, 101]

Just who is this italicized feminine pronoun and why is she going to be shot? Might she be the solid moralist's wife or wife-to-be? Austin leaves out that part of the story, but the least we can surmise is that, as in all of Austin's examples, the agent of the speech act is a "he" with a considerable stock of authority. As Austin's tale continues, we read about illocution and perlocution finishing up the job: "He urged (or advised, ordered, &c.) me to shoot her;" "He persuaded me to shoot her;" "He got me to (or made me, &c.) shoot her" (Austin, 102). By the time we get to what might be dubbed a counter-locution ("He said to me, 'You can't do that'" [Austin, 102]), Austin's attempt at resurrection appears somewhat feeble, since by that time *she* is already dead. The performance is over and she is just a statistic like, say, the four American women killed every day in incidents of domestic violence. If a performative is a marriage in which a "he" weds a "she," its broader "occasion" (Austin, 100), to use Austin's term, is a system of violence that perpetuates "his" power, as well as that of the dominant group of which he is a member. Both theory and empirical data suggest that "he" gets away with it: no matter how "it" is performed, "she" ends up getting shot.[32]

32. Austin: "Getting away with things is essential" (30).

How would Butler's performatives avoid the error of Austin's inter-missionary, misogynist violence? I know that Butler does not want women to be shot, any more than she wants them to be married. But her theory, like Austin's, fails to articulate the terms through which that murder would become impossible. In ethical terms, the force of performance cannot be thought without the response of she who would be bound by its terms. We need to hear the story of the one who gets shot, beaten, raped, or abused, and survives to narrate its truth. We need to hear so that she, with another, can perform a different economy of speech, resistance, pleasure, and love. That's what the lips are say-ing. Listen.

ACT III: LUCE

Darkness. A murmur of voices. The curtain rises.

Luce 1 (backstage): So did it work? Did he seduce you?

Luce 2 (in the audience): Who? Don Juan?

Luce 1: Yeah. You know, Don John Austin. Was it a felicitous scene? He has a reputation, you know. So did it work?[33]

Luce 2: Are you kidding? His failure to seduce me may have been infelicitous for him, but I assure you that, for my part, it was a happy bungle. I'd rather not end up being shot to prove a point, thank you very much. Besides, I don't know about you, but I prefer girls.

Luce 1: Yeah, I know. I do too. So what about the girl? Did she seduce you?

Luce 2: Who? Judy? Well, I was tempted. But it didn't quite work. You see, I've heard it all before. Take this stuff we wrote on hysteria, for example. Not so very different from what Judy says. (Reading from *Speculum*): "And anyway why would she not be 'hysterical'? Since hysteria holds in reserve, in suspension/suffering, something in com-mon with the mime that is a sine qua non of sexual pleasure" (60). We've all learned to interpret that language: the hysteric repeats and exaggerates the gendered fictions that construct her as "woman." But you know, I don't think it necessarily gets her anywhere. The phallus always stops her, and his play keeps on going: "The problem is that the ludic mimicry, the fiction, the 'make believe,' the 'let's pretend'—which, as we know, made the hysteric subject to all kinds of disbelief, oppression, and ridicule—are stopped short, impeded, *controlled by a master-signifier*, the Phallus, and by its representative(s)" (*Speculum,*

---

33. Felman: "I had better declare at once that I am *seduced* by Austin" (73); "To seduce is to produce felicitous language" (Felman, 28).

60). Or take the chapter in *Speculum* on Plotinus as another example. Nothing but quotes. Quite audacious, if I do say so myself. But what do we have to show for all that work?

Luce 1: So you no longer believe in mimicry? We put a lot of stock in it for a while, to say nothing of all the others.[34] (Reading from *This Sex*): "To play with mimesis is thus, for a woman, to try to recover the place of her exploitation by discourse, without allowing herself to be simply reduced to it . . . to make 'visible,' by an effect of playful repetition, what was supposed to remain invisible. . . . If women are such good mimics, it is because they are not simply resorbed in this function. *They also remain elsewhere . . .*" (76). That's what we're famous for, you know.

Luce 2: I suppose. But to tell you the truth, I think it's a stop-gap measure, to keep us from disappearing altogether. And as I said before, it's hard work. (Reading from *Speculum*): "And hysterical miming will be the little girl's or the woman's work to save her sexuality from total repression, disappearance" (72, translation modified). You know, our real story never quite gets going—"let us say that *in the beginning her story would end*" (*Speculum*, 43; translation modified).

Luce 1: Which is why I thought: OK, let's stop being stagehands and put ourselves in the spotlight, just like Charcot's hysterics every Tuesday at the Salpêtrière. Quite a show, you know. If we can't have a story, let's perform. (Pause). Luce, you look tired.

Luce 2: I am tired. Or rather, we're tired. The performance is still on his stage, the props and the story are his. (Reading from *This Sex*): "You imitate whatever comes close. You become whatever touches you. . . . Taking one model after another, passing from master to master . . ." (210). As Audre says, the master's tools, the master's house . . . it just seems like there's no way out.[35] And there's no telling how they'll read us. Look what happened to those poor hysterics. So we perform, be-

34. On Irigaray and mimicry or mimesis see especially Toril Moi, *Sexual/Textual Politics: Feminist Literary Theory* (New York: Routledge, 1985); Jane Gallop, *Thinking Through the Body* (New York: Columbia University Press, 1988); Elizabeth Grosz; Naomi Schor, "This Essentialism Which Is Not One: Coming to Grips With Irigaray," *Differences* 1/2 (1989): 38–58; Christine Holmlund, "I Love Luce: The Lesbian, Mimesis and Masquerade in Irigaray, Freud and Mainstream Film," *New Formations* 9 (Winter 1989), 105–23; Maggie Berg, "Luce Irigaray's 'Contradictions': Poststructuralism and Feminism," *Signs: Journal of Women in Culture and Society* 17/1 (1991): 50–70; Rosi Braidotti, *Patterns of Dissonance: A Study of Women in Contemporary Philosophy*, trans. Elizabeth Guild (New York: Routledge, 1991); Margaret Whitford, *Luce Irigaray: Philosophy in the Feminine*; and Drucilla Cornell.

35. Audre Lorde, "The Master's Tools Will Never Dismantle the Master's House," *Sister Outsider: Essays and Speeches* (Freedom, CA: The Crossing Press, 1984).

come the symptom of an aetiology, and then we simply disappear. Either way, the abuse continues.[36]

Pause. Faint light on the audience, then backstage. The stage remains dark.

Luce 2: What about the lips? Are they still hiding among us, here in the audience, backstage?

Luce 1: Ah yes, the lips. They're still here, repeated, like a poem. But they're not just about pleasure, you know.

Luce 2: Sounds pretty pleasurable to me. All those wonderful, funny combinations: mouth to mouth, mouth to labia, labia to mouth, labia to labia, inner labia to outer labia, outer labia to mouth, outer to outer, inner to inner, outer to inner, to mouth, to labia . . . (Reading from *This Sex*): "Doesn't that make you laugh?" (209).[37]

Luce 1: Sure, it makes me laugh, and it's pleasurable too. But there's pain here as well.

Luce 2: Wait. Listen. The lips are speaking. From behind the scenes, moving across the stage, toward the other listening lips: we're here to

36. See Judith Herman, *Trauma and Recovery* (New York: Basic Books, 1992), on the connection between hysteria and sexual abuse. Freud's publication of *The Aetiology of Hysteria* (1896), which describes that connection, was met with disbelief and ridicule by his colleagues. He subsequently abandoned what has now become known as the seduction theory.

37. Humor is a funny thing, as Freud and others have noted. A case in point is Felman's reading of Austin's jokes, which she highlights in order to emphasize the subversive, self-deprecating impulse underlying Austin's speech act theory. However, to what extent does such a reading of subversion depend on a shared cultural code? Indeed, as outsiders to a hegemonic, masculinist code of laughter, feminists are often accused of having no sense of humor. Conversely, those who do not share the marginal or "lesbian" code of Irigaray's labial play may not find her essay funny. In that regard, I would like to thank Galen Sherwin for our illuminating discussions about Irigaray's "inside" jokes. James Scott points to a similar dynamic of shared humor as part of a culture of resistance in *Domination and the Arts of Resistance*. See also Sigmund Freud, "Jokes and their Relation to the Unconscious" (1905), *The Standard Edition of the Complete Psychological Works* 8, trans. James Strachey (London: Hogarth, 1960): "Every joke calls for a public of its own and laughing at the same jokes is evidence of far-reaching psychical conformity" (151). For a feminist critique of Freud's "Jokes" essay as a reinforcement of the homosocial bonding between elite men, see Jane Gallop, "Why Does Freud Giggle When the Women Leave the Room?," in *Thinking Through the Body*, 33–40. The assumption of a shared code between the teller of a joke and its public is demonstrated by Freud himself in his later lecture, "Femininity" ("New Introductory Lectures on Psycho-Analysis" [1933], *Standard Edition* 22, 122–35). Ostensibly addressing both "Ladies and Gentlemen" (112), Freud opens his lecture on "the riddle of the nature of femininity" (113) with a remark about women being the "problem," thus dismissing the "Ladies" as participants in the joke's humor. Also see Irigaray, in "The Blind Spot of an Old Dream of 'Symmetry'" (*Speculum*, 11–127), who mimics Freud's exclusionary humor.

hear them. Hear them, to speak our story, here, hear, to laugh with pleasure. That's what I call making love. Between us, the lips make love.

Luce 1: But in all that speaking and all that loving, the stage is still there. Even in darkness, the actors are set and ready to go, waiting to trap us as we start to move. And it's all there for his satisfaction, his happiness, his felicitous doctrine. His pleasure keeps us quiet, frozen. His blank, the *"semblant,"* white blood.[38]

Luce 2: Yes, I know. (Reading from *This Sex*): *"Env(i)olées* into proper names" (*This Sex*, 205). Violated by his words but, still, with words, taking flight toward something else, moving over and through and under the stage. Oh, how can I say it? Trapped in his "proper skins" (*This Sex*, 205) to keep the meaning up, to keep those "dead skins" (*This Sex*, 212) from drooping. His meaning is our blood, his *sens* is our *sang*, the blood of our lips for his show, his story. Our story? Gagged and raped. Our lips parted, *"écartées."* For him "they would have to stay apart" (*This Sex*, 208). The word is our bond and our bondage: "the gag upon our lips" (*This Sex*, 212).[39]

Luce 1: (*Sigh*). I know. But I still think there's hope. Remember catachresis? Like the "face" of a mountain or a "head" of cabbage. That's what our lips are. Impossible. What those eggheads call "an abuse of trope."[40] No way to say it, except as something it's not. Non-existent on his stage, except in his image, as his "face" or his "head." So how can we say it? And yet we say it, our lips, together . . .

Luce 2: We're doing it now . . .

Luce 1: Well, you can never be certain. But, yeah, something's happening, some sort of murmur. Backstage, and in the audience, speaking together. And look, the stage is still dark. Why should we continue to

38. Irigaray uses the word "semblant," or resemblance, to describe the logic of identity that reduces women to a repetition of the same. The structure of the "semblant" is like its homophone, "sang blanc," or white blood, which freezes difference into a homogenous blank. "And what about your life? You must *pretend* to receive it from them [Tu dois faire *semblant* (*sang blanc*): la recevoir d'eux]" (*This Sex*, 208/*Ce Sexe qui n'en est pas un*, 207, emphasis added).

39. J. L. Austin: "Accuracy and morality alike are on the side of the plain saying that *our word is our bond*" (10).

40. See Pierre Fontanier, *Les Figures du discours* (Paris: Flammarion, 1977), 189, and Andrzej Warminski, *Readings in Interpretation: Hölderlin, Hegel, Heidegger* (Minneapolis: University of Minnesota Press, 1987), liii and lix. Also see Gayatri Spivak who, in "French Feminism Revisited," argues that we must "accept the risk of catachresis" because the *"political* use of words, like the use of words, is irreducibly catachrestic" (72).

keep Man's play going? Avid spectators, devoted stagehands, mesmerized, working, doing anything for him.[41] For what? For his world, his stage, his knowledge, his pleasure? No. Let's get going, move our lips in another direction. No more lighting up his Truth on his stage. A different truth, listen . . .

Luce 2: OK, it sounds great. Let's move our lips. But how can we say it? I know, you're talking about love . . . funny, lesbian, outrageous love. An ethics of lips, making love. (Reading from *Ce sexe*): "Entre nous: toute(s) . . . between us: all" (*Ce sexe,* 217). "How can I say it? . . . Our all will come" (*This Sex,* 212). "Le toute va venir . . . entre nous: toute(s)." How can I say it? (Reading from *This Sex*): "I love you" (206). (*Pause*). But really: "I love you"? Have you ever heard such a trite cliché?[42] Doesn't "I love you" just prop up his play? Give a face to his mountain? Turn a stupid vegetable into a talking head?

Luce 1: I know. It's inescapable. All those cabbage heads. And then some can't even speak, like the corn. No head for you, just an ear. All those body parts, and they still can't hear. . . . But we can still say it: our lips. And hear them, differently, and then try again: how to say it? How to say it, our lips, together? And hear them, our lips, another way? Speaking, making love, with our lips. This is what happens when we get aroused: our lips fill with blood, turn red. (Reading from *This Sex*): "While our lips are growing red again. They're stirring, moving, they want to speak" (212). It's the truth about us, together. That's what happens when we get excited. Lesbians, we're men's blank, but when we speak together, we speak the truth about another pleasure, another love. (Reading from *This Sex*): " 'I love' lies in wait for the other" (206).

41. See Marilyn Frye, "To See and Be Seen," in *The Politics of Reality: Essays in Feminist Theory* (Trumansburg, New York: The Crossing Press, 1983), 152–74. Frye compares phallocratic reality to a play where the actors are men and the stagehands are women; women exist as such by "*loving* the actors and taking actors' interests and commitments unto themselves as their own" (169). For Frye, lesbianism means a shift of attention from the actors to the stagehands: "If the lesbian sees the women, the woman may see the lesbian seeing her. With this, there is a flowering of possibilities" (172).

42. As Jonathan Culler puts it: "I love you is always something of a quotation, as many lovers have attested" (*On Deconstruction: Theory and Criticism after Structuralism* [Ithaca: Cornell University Press, 1982], 120). More radically, Paul de Man describes the figure of the erotic as an illusion of intimacy and connection: "Rather than being a heightened version of sense experience, the erotic is a figure that makes such experience possible. We do not see what we love but we love in the hope of confirming the illusion that we are indeed seeing anything at all" ("Hypogram and Inscription," in *The Resistance to Theory* [Minneapolis: University of Minnesota Press, 1986], 53n23.) However, I would suggest that in performing an ethics of love, Irigaray's lips contest the radical negativity of such critiques of the clichés of humanism.

And when we speak, we break the icy silence that hides our wounds. And their blank, white blood, becomes red. How can I say it, this impossible blank, like a blank of corn or a cabbage blank? Don Juan Austin would call it nonsense, the refusal to be blank, to be seduced by his promise. The refusal to hide the truth of our pain behind the curtain of his happy play.

Luce 2: But still, as they say, all the world's a stage . . . Listen, his play is starting again.

Luce 1: Yes, there they go. (*Loudly*): You may kiss the bride! (*Laughing*): But look, it's just a curtain, drooping and rising, the one that marks *his* stage.[43] *Read my lips:* another opening, another woman, red lips filling with blood, with other stories, with other lips to open. . . .

Luce 2: Kiss me.

Luce 1: I thought you'd never ask. I love you.

Luce 2: (reading from *This Sex*): "Two lips kissing two lips: openness is ours again. Our 'world' " (210).

---

43. Lacan: "The phallus can only play its role as veiled" (Jacques Lacan, "The Meaning of the Phallus," in *Feminine Sexuality: Jacques Lacan and the école freudienne,* ed. Juliet Mitchell and Jacqueline Rose, trans. Jacqueline Rose [New York: Norton, 1982]), 82.

SERENE JONES

Divining Women: Irigaray and Feminist Theologies

> Religion marks the place of the absolute *for us*, its path, the hope of
> its fulfillment. All too often that fulfillment has been postponed or
> transferred to some transcendental time and place. It has not been
> interpreted as the infinite that resides within us and among us, the
> god in us, the Other for us, becoming with and in us—as yet manifest
> only through his creation (the Father), present in his form (the son),
> mediator between the two (spirit). Here the capital letter designates
> the horizon of fulfillment of a gender, not a transcendent entity that
> exists outside of becoming.[1]

The gathered group of over 2,100 women was expectant and restless as
it waited for the opening worship to begin. The women had traveled
from every state in the U.S., arriving in Minneapolis by car, bus, bike,
and train. In addition, some had just flown in from Mexico; others had
taken long night flights from Nairobi, Manila, and Hong Kong, while
still others had simply walked that morning from their jobs to the
downtown convention center. Among their ranks were women clergy,
seminary students, church workers, teachers, and program coordina-
tors representing Christian communities ranging from Lutheran and
Episcopal to Baptist and Roman Catholic. There were also many
women who brought stories of their work outside the church, stories of
struggling with aging, retirement, disabilities; of leading Bible studies
in rural Appalachia and of teaching history in inner-city schools; of
fighting against racist environmental practices in the South and the
exploitative employment practices of corporations which had fled the
unions of the North; of working as counselors, activists, and organizers
dealing with AIDS, domestic violence, substance abuse, and reproductive rights. They had come to hear and converse with women theologians of equally diverse backgrounds and interests—Mujestra
theologians, Asian and Asian-American theologians, womanist theo-

1. Luce Irigaray, "Divine Women," *Sexes and Genealogies*, trans. Gillian C. Gill
(New York: Columbia University Press, 1993), 63.

YFS 87, *Another Look, Another Woman*, ed. Huffer, © 1995 by Yale University.

logians and biblical scholars, Lesbian ethicists, Euro-American feminist liturgists, African liberationists, Latin American liberation theologians and Roman Catholic church historians—all of whom were prepared to bring their critical reflections to bear upon the topic of the conference simply titled, "RE-imagining."[2] And when a silence finally fell over the crowd, this reimagining commenced with a collective voice calling upon the blessing of Sophia, woman-wisdom, "the God within us and among us this day."

In the days that followed, the conference organizers and participants had no idea that the public response to this event would be as quick and as passionately critical as it was. Within a week, articles began appearing in newspapers across the country claiming that feminists in the church were teetering on the edge of heresy, that the God of the Christian tradition and scriptures was being deposed by some strange Goddess called Sophia, and that feminists were threatening to "get rid of Jesus' cross," supplanting its power with some mystical, erotic "nectar" which flows from "within and among" the bodies of women. Echoing the sentiments of conservative protectors of "family values," critics of the conference claimed that now, even in the church, the secularizing impulses of "political correctness" promised to destroy what they believed to be the last bastion of moral integrity in the nation, the tradition of church teachings and the Bible.

For feminist theologians like myself, the force of this backlash was quite disturbing, not because it represented such a stridently negative assessment of feminism in the church—after all, those kinds of responses have been directed at feminists for years—but because so many local presses and many more local pastors were so eager to decry, as if they were a new and dangerous threat, the voices of women and men who are calling for Christianity to continue its long history of reimagining God and Christ in a language that is meaningful to historically particular communities of faith. Insofar as the conference took up this task of reimagining, it did not seem to me, nor to many others like me in church communities across the nation, that it was all that radical, all that outlandish, all that "heretical." In fact, it seemed quite

2. The conference was planned as part of the Ecumenical Decade of the Churches in Solidarity with Women, a ten year emphasis of the World Council of Churches which, in part, seeks to "affirm—through shared leadership and decision-making, theology and spirituality—the decisive contributions of women in churches and communities" (Conference Program Booklet, Minnesota Council of Churches, Minneapolis: 4–7 November 1993).

healthy and full of promise that women should gather and creatively construct new discursive economies for the language of faith, and that this conversation should have at its center the critical challenge of rethinking our God-talk through the multiple axes of race, gender, class, sexuality, and ethnic particularity.

For many years now, this process of "reimagining" the language of church theology has drawn heavily upon the insights of feminist theorists who work in nontheological disciplines but who nonetheless struggle with questions concerning relations of power and the multiple axes of identity-construction raised in events such as the Minneapolis conference. Without their guidance and critique, feminist theology would have long ago become a theoretically static and archaic enterprise, lacking focus and a critical edge sharp enough to elicit even cries of heresy. The purpose of this essay is to continue the conversation between theologians and feminist theorists by exploring the significance of Luce Irigaray's work for feminist studies in religion.[3] Among feminist theorists, Irigaray holds particular promise for theologians because she explicitly takes up theological questions and calls women not to give up on God-talk, but to engage creatively in collective reimaginings, again, not unlike the corporate task of the Minneapolis event. The fact that she so clearly gestures toward the Divine in her work allows theologians to struggle with her theoretical insights into the role of gender in the construction of divine rhetorics without having to overcome the antireligious bias one finds in much current feminist theory. Irigaray's work also has the added advantage of being situated on the extreme margins of Christian discourse, a location

3. In 1984, the first extensive discussion of French feminism and theology was held in a section on "Women and Religion" at the annual meeting of the American Academy of Religion. Prior to this meeting, Irigaray was most frequently read as a companion piece to works of Hélène Cixous and Julia Kristeva, but as the papers at the conference soon made apparent, the facile collapse of the works of these theorists into one school of thought called "French feminism" was to be short-lived. In these initial papers, it became clear that readers of Cixous were quickly moving toward "goddess spirituality," and an essentialized vision of women's religious experience. In the years since, this movement has continued as Cixous has become the star theorist of religionists whose agenda leans towards New Age assessments of piety and personal spirituality. In contrast, theorists who were drawn to the writings of Kristeva expressed interest in the possibilities that feminist psychoanalysis raises for the study of religion. Since that initial meeting, Kristeva's work continues to inspire an aesthetic understanding of faith that focuses on the spirituality of such women as the medieval mystics, and the field of mariology. For an overview of theological uses of French feminism, see *Transfigurations: Theology and the French Feminists*, ed. C.W. Maggie Kim, Susan M. St. Ville, Susan M. Simonaitis (Minneapolis: Fortress, 1993).

which allows her to push questions and issues that theologians who feel the constraints of church commitments might miss.

The insights of current feminist theology hold particular promise for expanding and pushing the perimeters of Irigaray's agenda as well. As an activist and political rhetorician, Irigaray continually positions her work vis-à-vis communities of women who are struggling against the oppressive logic of phallocentrism and its conception of the Divine; and yet her principal audience has been and continues to be academic feminists whose disciplinary interests rarely lead them to construct liturgies and other socially enacted rhetorics designed to test the practical force of Irigaray's theological reflections. Such is not the case, however, with feminist theologians whose peculiar ecclesiastic commitment requires them to locate their reflections in the context of active, worshiping communities. In this regard, it may well be that feminist theologians have the unique advantage of providing Irigaray's writings with the audience she desires but is institutionally unable to reach. And not surprisingly, this audience is one which, like myself, may not only embrace her agenda, but also constructively challenge it at some of its most critical points.

TWO THEOLOGICAL DISCOURSES

In order to trace the multiple ways in which feminist theologians can both constructively deploy and critically challenge Irigaray's reflections on God and religion, one must note from the outset that she has developed, over the course of several decades, two very distinct theological discourses, each of which has different implications for feminist theology. The first discourse, found primarily in her earlier work, *Speculum of the Other Woman*, follows a deconstructive agenda.[4] In these texts, Irigaray explores notions of God that fill the canonical texts of western philosophy, texts in which the God encountered is rendered through a phallocentric logic which either makes woman invisible or relegates her to a discursive space where she can do nothing but reflect back to God/man a morphology of his desire. Accordingly, the critical gestures that Irigaray extends toward these conceptions of the Divine are largely negative: she seeks to expose the instability of such notions by uncovering the repressed role that assumptions of sexual difference play in theological discourses where God is falsely

4. Irigaray, *Speculum of the Other Woman*, trans. Gillian C. Gill (Ithaca: Cornell University Press, 1985).

constructed as an icon of unitary presence and stable, undifferentiated truth. In terms of the larger social function of this first discourse on the Divine, Irigaray makes these critical gestures in order to dethrone this God by "jamming the discursive machinery" which sustains Him.[5]

Having deployed these deconstructive gestures, however, Irigaray is not content simply to leave empty the discursive space that God has traditionally occupied. Instead, she offers her reader a second discourse on the Divine, a discourse whose principal function lies in reenvisioning a conception of God that might prove liberating for women or, to use her language, might "save women." In order to generate a rhetoric that could sustain such a conception of the Divine, Irigaray shifts theoretical gears and moves on to an analytic terrain where a pragmatic assessment of what "women need," and not a philosophically grounded series of deconstructive gestures, serves as the principal evaluative criteria. This second discourse on God finds its clearest articulation in her more recent text, *An Ethics of Sexual Difference*, and in the lectures collected in *Sexes and Genealogies*.[6] In these works, the Divine master trope of western philosophy is replaced by images of a God who mirrors a morphology of female desire, one which profits from an economy of fluid relationality and irreducible difference, as opposed to an economy of phallic transcendence which consumes the other it posits. In this second discourse, Irigaray moves from a project of critique to one of construction, from a conceptual arena where God is revealed as the empty sign of an untenable phallus to an arena where the Divine is figured in the fecund space of "woman"; from a God who condemns and devours woman to a God who has the power to save her. This shift in discourse also marks a move in Irigaray's work from an analysis which focuses on questions moored in the classical world of ontology and metaphysics to one which encourages utopian reimaginings anchored firmly in a practical assessment of the politics of feminist action.

By distinguishing these two discourses (the deconstructive and the utopian), I do not mean to imply that one has nothing to do with the other. It is clear that even in Irigaray's early work, her deconstructive gestures are intimately tied to a constructive vision of an alternative female morphology; and similarly, the more utopian gestures of her

5. Irigaray, "The Power of Discourse," in *This Sex Which Is Not One*, trans. Catherine Porter with Carolyn Burke (Ithaca: Cornell University Press, 1985), 78.
6. Irigaray, *An Ethics of Sexual Difference*, trans. Carolyn Burke and Gillian C. Gill (Ithaca: Cornell University Press, 1993); *Sexes and Geneaologies*.

later work never cease to recapitulate a deconstructive appreciation for the illusions of phallic mimesis.[7] Despite the interdependence of these two discourses, however, one must conceptually mark their distinctive social functions and their subsequent use of different kinds of language and evaluative criteria. If such distinctions are neglected, one risks misconstruing the second discourse as an essentializing project which fails to stand up to the deconstructive criteria of the first; and such readings of Irigaray, I believe, overlook the complexity of her project. Further, if the two discourses are collapsed into a single discourse, one misses the agility of Irigaray's ever-shifting rhetoric and mistakenly maps the play of her theoretical travels along the lines of a single trajectory.

IRIGARAY'S DECONSTRUCTION OF THEOLOGY

Let me begin by focusing on the ways in which feminist theologians have already profited and might continue to profit from a critical dialogue with the first of these two discourses. On the most obvious level, Irigaray's dismantling of the God who governs the order of classical metaphysics and Enlightenment epistemology provides feminist theologians with a map for uncovering and critiquing patriarchal assumptions buried in classical and Enlightenment accounts of Christian doctrines. It is not, however, a map which is useful for analyzing all parts of the Christian tradition, for Irigaray's perspective is limited to the conceptual strictures of Western philosophy, and such strictures, fortunately, do not obtain equally for the whole of Christian scriptures and theology.[8] Once these distinctions are made, however, Irigaray's analysis of the logic of phallocentrism can be applied, with interesting results, to traditional Christian understandings of such notions as God's transcendent otherness, God's self-generative origin, and doctrinal conceptions of divinely stabilized truths and immutable presence. By illustrating that the master trope of Western thought rests on a false

7. See Margaret Whitford, *Luce Irigaray: Philosophy in the Feminine* (London: Routledge, 1991), 70–71.

8. In order to follow Irigaray's map, one must first distinguish between those moments in doctrine which are inextricably bound to western philosophical schemes (in all their variety) and those which find their roots in the Hebraic biblical tradition, for the latter do not conform as easily to the contours of her critique as the former. This requires positioning Irigaray's analysis squarely "in Athens," and not, conversely, "along the road to Jerusalem"—to use a well-worn pair of images often deployed by theologians to mark two distinct trajectories within early Christian thought.

logic which eclipses the productive difference that sustains it,
Irigaray's analysis provides the basis for several constructive criticisms
of the phallic logic that also structures Christian doctrines such as
providence, atonement, and creation *ex nihilo*. Each of these doctrines
similarly eclipses difference while valorizing a static and closed conception of a God whose identity is secured only through a series of
mimetic reductions.

Given that Christian theology has traditionally made a good deal
out of the divine attributes of omnipotence, simplicity, and immutability, the force of such a critique should not be underestimated—for
each Sunday, in churches around the world, Christians sing praises to a
God who closely resembles a classical Roman overlord, deliver sermons in which an epistemically assessable notion of Divine truth
holds sway, and offer prayers to Platonic forms of the true and the good
which remain untouched by the supposedly fallible cries of those who
ask.[9] In each of these instances, the theological rhetoric deployed is
designed to protect God's sovereign otherness by reaffirming the radical difference between the Divine and the creaturely and by reminding
the creature that supplication is owed to the more powerful Other who
reigns eternally. What Irigaray's critique makes clear, however, is that
such a rhetoric is predicated upon the prior positing of a binary opposition (God-creature) in which the privileged term (God) garners its definitional force only by hiding the role that the other (the creature) plays
in the production of its truth. By revealing the play of this logic, Irigaray
shows that this God is not as radically different as the discourse about
Him suggests—insofar as one can define His identity only in relation
to the other which He can supposedly do without. As for His power,
Irigaray illustrates that it too depends on the repression of His relation
to a second term that generates the very difference He alone supposedly controls.[10] While it would be too strong to say that by unveil-
ing the play of such a logic, Irigaray single-handedly deals a death-blow
to all theological notions of Divine otherness, power, and transcendence (in fact, I will later argue that we need to keep them), her critique

9. I do not mean to imply that all Christian liturgy and piety can be categorized
according to these philosophical typologies. I am simply suggesting that echoes of a
variety of classical metaphysics can be found in the church's worship books and sermons
on any given Sunday morning.

10. For a fuller discussion of Irigaray's critique of phallocentric renderings of the
Godhead, see Serene Jones, "This God Which is Not One: Irigaray and Barth on the
Divine," in *Transfigurations*, 109–41; Elizabeth Grosz, "Irigaray and the Divine," in
Transfigurations, 199–214.

does suggest that feminist theologians who want to retain such terms need to reconceive the discursive framework which engenders them, a task that requires much more, as Irigaray points out, than simply renaming God in the feminine.

In addition to providing feminist theologians with a map of the phallocentric impulses that undergird particular aspects of traditional doctrines of God, Irigaray's deconstructive gestures also raise a number of challenges which feminist theologians who are offering alternative doctrines of God need to consider. In recent years, it has been fairly commonplace for feminist theologians to turn to a variety of different contemporary philosophies in search of a conceptual framework that avoids the pitfalls of the old versions of phallic logic and that subsequently offers an economy of Divine-human relating wherein difference is honored and tyrannical conceptions of power are subverted. This tendency is most evident in the work of feminist process theologians who use the ontologies of Alfred North Whitehead[11] and Charles Hartshorne[12] to gain critical leverage against Classical notions of Divine immutability and to generate, in turn, an understanding of the God-world relation in which change, mutual reciprocity, and fluid process prevail.[13] This turn to philosophy is also apparent in the work of feminist theologians who situate their reflections firmly within the field of transcendental phenomenology.[14] Here, the opera-

11. The work of Whitehead that has accumulated the most conceptual capital in the field of process theology has been his *Process and Reality* (corrected edition), ed. David Ray Griffin and Donald W. Sherburne (New York: The Free Press, 1978). For further developments in Whitehead's metaphysics, see *Adventures of Ideas* (New York: The MacMillan Co., 1933); *Modes of Thought* (New York: The Free Press, 1968).

12. For Charles Hartshorne's perceptive analysis of natural theology and its relation to an ontology of process, see Hartshorne and William L. Reese, *Philosophers Speak of God* (Chicago: University of Chicago Press, 1953); see also Hartshorne, *The Logic of Perfection* (La Salle, Ill.: Open Court, 1962) and *Omnipotence and Other Theological Mistakes* (Albany: State University of New York Press, 1984).

13. For representative works in feminist process theology, see Sheila Davaney, ed., *Feminism and Process Thought: The Harvard Divinity School/Claremont Center for Process Studies Symposium Papers* (New York: Edwin Mellon Press, 1981); Rita Nakashima Brock, *Journeys By Heart: A Christology of Erotic Power* (New York: Crossroads, 1988); Marjorie Hewitt Suchocki, *God-Christ-Church: A Practical Guide to Process Theology* (New York: Crossroads, 1984).

14. This orientation is most pronounced in the philosophical commitments of students of Karl Rahner, a twentieth-century Roman Catholic theologian whose analysis of Christian existence is rooted in a revised system of Thomistic metaphysics (see Joseph Maréchal, *Le Point de départ de la métaphysique*, 5 vols. vols. 1, 2, 3, Bruges and Paris: 1922–23; vol. 4, Brussels, 1924; vol. 5, Louvain and Paris: 1926) and the existential philosophy of Martin Heidegger, *Being and Time*, trans. John Macquarrie and Edward

tive terms of discourse are not wedded to metaphysical assumptions about divine process, as they are in process thought; rather, the conceptual arena for reworking the Divine-human relation is grounded in an analysis of the "structure of consciousness," the assumption being that a more immanental and relational view of God emerges once "women's experience," as a species of general experience, is shown to be structurally oriented toward the Divine.[15] A third and even more recent example of this turn to philosophy appears in the work of feminist theologians who hope that Lévinasian ethics[16] will mark the beginnings of a path which, moving beyond phenomenology, introduces the possibility of conceiving God in communal terms.[17]

What might Irigaray, in her first discursive mode, say to these different models of reimagining the Divine? It would be too simplistic to suggest that Irigaray's critique of the totalizing impulses of philosophy would render these attempts at reimagining either unintelligible or irredeemably problematic. After all, Irigaray herself never breaks entirely free from such impulses, a fact she acknowledges when she warns that such a break would require one to step outside of discourse itself; and that, she adds, is conceptually impossible. Short of rejecting

---

Robinson (London: SCM Press, 1962). See Karl Rahner, *Spirit in the World*, trans. William Dych (New York: Herder and Herder, 1968) and its development in *Foundations of the Christian Faith: An Introduction to the Idea of Christianity*, trans. William Dych (New York: Seabury, 1978). In recent years, a materialist mediation of Rahner's thought (for example Johann Baptist Metz, *Faith in History and Society: Toward a Practical Fundamental Theology*, trans. David Smith (New York: Seabury Press, 1980), has appealed to feminist theologians in search of grounds for a more overtly historicist ontology of "women's experience."

15. Two recent works which reflect this phenomenological orientation are Elizabeth A. Johnson, *She Who Is: The Mystery of God in Feminist Theological Discourse* (New York: Crossroads, 1992) and Catherine Mowry LaCugna, *God For Us: The Trinity in Christian Life* (San Francisco: Harper Collins, 1991). An older and perhaps better known example of this play between phenomenology and theology is found in the early work of Mary Daly, whose philosophical bearings are taken not from Rahner but from the existentialism developed by the liberal Protestant theologian, Paul Tillich. See Tillich, *Systematic Theology*, 3 vols. (Chicago: University of Chicago Press, 1967). For Daly's most Tillichian work, see *Beyond God the Father: Towards a Philosophy of Women's Liberation* (Boston: Beacon Press, 1973).

16. Emmanuel Lévinas, *Totality and Infinity: An Essay in Exteriority*, trans. Alphonso Lingis (Pittsburgh: Duquesne University Press, 1969) and *Otherwise than Being or Beyond Essence*, trans. Alphonso Lingis (Boston: M. Nijhoff, 1981).

17. Ellen T. Armour and Amy Hollywood introduced me to this newly emerging trend in feminist theology. See Hollywood, "Beauvoir, Irigaray and the Mystical," *Hypatia* 4 (1994): 158–85 and Armour's forthcoming contribution to *Feminism and Interpretations of Derrida*, ed. Nancy Holland (University Park: Pennsylvania State University Press, 1995).

these models, however, Irigaray's critique of philosophical closure offers a word of caution to feminist theologians who believe it possible to
find a conceptual scheme which resists, in its totality, the phallocentric reductions of traditional doctrines. Such a system is not to
be found, she would argue, because the very drive to systematize
discourse—by drawing the world into tightly coherent frames of reference where universals rule and where meanings are categorically
constrained—will always create discursive contexts in which differences are eclipsed and incommensurable otherness is inconceivable.
Thus, even though a philosophy might valorize processes of being and
becoming over a logic of static presence, or focus on structures of
consciousness that bring the immanent and transcendent infinite together as opposed to pulling them apart, these philosophical systems
will nonetheless create definitional borders which, in turn, generate
margins of difference that must be repressed in the name of conceptual
coherence.

In this regard, Irigaray's critique suggests that feminist process
theologians would do well to consider the margins engendered by a
metaphysics of Divine becoming. Similarly, the practitioners of transcendental phenomenology, on the one hand, and Lévinasian ethics, on
the other, would profit from exploring the repressions instantiated in
phenomenology's account of universal structures of knowing and Lévinas's formulation of a universal ethic. Such considerations, if taken
seriously, again would not require these models of feminist theology to
completely eschew philosophical inquiry; rather, in a more tempered
manner, Irigaray's critique reveals the benefits of practicing a more *ad
hoc* deployment of philosophical gestures which, if they are analytically diverse enough, could counter the restrictive urge to construct
tightly coherent theological schemes which may appear liberating but
which nonetheless harbor potentially oppressive closures. When one
views the projects of current feminist theologians through the lens of
Irigaray's critique of philosophical closure, one may also more fully
appreciate the value of those feminist theologies that already practice
this kind of pragmatic *bricolage*.

Four examples of such a practice are: first, the critical enterprise of
womanist theologians who conceptually root their "reimaginings"
in the literary traditions of African-American texts and culture;[18]

18. Several names associated with womanist theology are Kelly Brown Douglas, *The
Black Christ* (Maryknoll, New York: Orbis, 1994); Emily Townes, ed., *A Troubling in My
Soul: Womanist Perspectives on Evil and Suffering* (Maryknoll, New York: Orbis, 1994);

second, the project of feminist theologians whose "reimaginings" focus on functionalist accounts of doctrinal meaning, drawing upon the traditions of British analytic and linguistic philosophy;[19] third, theologies which use the tools of cultural anthropology to analyze the nature of doctrinal claims;[20] and fourth, the work of a growing number of theologians who are attracted to the methodological rootlessness of the American pragmatist tradition.[21] While I do not mean to suggest that these theologies are immune to further feminist criticism— indeed, they are not—they are methodologically positioned to better accommodate Irigaray's critique of philosophy than are those theologies which embrace notions of philosophical coherence and systematic closure.

In addition to marking the ways in which Irigaray might challenge feminist theological uses of philosophy, it is important to note that her position raises equally serious challenges to many current theologians who assume that by embracing a poststructuralist approach to religious discourse, they thereby avoid the phallic pitfalls of process thought or transcendental phenomenology. If Irigaray were simply a poststructuralist theorist, her work might be used to defend theologies

---

Katie G. Cannon, *Black Womanist Ethics* (Atlanta: Scholars Press, 1988); Delores S. Williams, *Sisters in the Wilderness: The Challenge of Womanist God-Talk* (Maryknoll, New York: Orbis, 1993); Jacquelyn Grant, *White Woman's Christ, Black Woman's Jesus: Feminist Christology and Womanist Responses* (Atlanta: Scholars Press, 1989); and M. Shawn Copeland, "Wading Through Many Sorrows," in *A Troubling in My Soul,* 7– 129. For a definition of womanist theology, see Toinette Eugene, "Womanist Theology," in *The New Handbook of Christian Theology,* ed. Donald Musser and Joseph Price (Nashville: Abingdon Press, 1992).

19. Janet Martin Soskice, *Metaphor and Religious Language* (Oxford: Clarendon Press, 1985). Although it is not a work in analytic theology, Sallie McFague's recent book, *The Body of God: An Ecological Theology* (Minneapolis: Fortress, 1993) represents an interesting model of a feminist theology that is willing to "methodologically travel" along a course that weaves in and out of existential phenomenology, scientific empiricism, and cultural-linguistic theory.

20. Kathryn Tanner, *Theology and the Study of Culture* (Minneapolis: Fortress, 1995); *The Politics of God: Christian Theologies and Social Justice* (Minneapolis: Fortress, 1992); *God and Creation in Christian Theology: Tyranny or Empowerment?* (Oxford: Basil Blackwell, 1988). Also see Amy Plantinga Pauw's review of George Linbeck's cultural linguistic assessment of the nature and function of religious language and doctrine: Pauw, "The Word is Near You: A Feminist Conversation with Lindbeck," *Theology Today* 50 (April 1993): 45–55.

21. Rebecca Chopp, *The Power to Speak: Feminism, Language, God* (New York: Crossroads, 1991). Also see her article on the pragmatic tenor of American feminists' theological encounter with French feminism, "From Patriarchy into Freedom: A Conversation Between American Feminist Theology and French Feminism," in *Transfigurations,* 31–48.

which move in this direction, theologies often referred to as "negative theology."[22] However, her insights into the patriarchal remainders which haunt deconstruction suggest otherwise. Negative theologians are largely academic philosophers of religion who, having become excited by the possibilities that poststructuralism opens up for theology, have undertaken to deconstruct traditional doctrines of God by articulating notions of divinity that cut against illusory valorizations of presence, autonomy, stasis, and immutable sovereignty. They do so by positing a counter discourse that celebrates emptiness, chaos, prophetic critique, radical indeterminacy, and the anarchical dimensions of mystery, where God stands, without foundations, as an infinitely open sign. It is also not uncommon to find negative theologians suggesting that their theology has profoundly positive implications for a feminist agenda, insofar as they believe that this God, the empty sign, has the power to discursively topple the master trope of phallocentric doctrines. However, the claim that feminists should appreciate the force of this negative discourse is not accompanied by a willingness, on the part of negative theologians, to name their project as feminist; in fact, they actively resist such a title, arguing that their critical enterprise has implications which are broader than a feminist agenda would allow—for their audience is "the arrogant Western subject" whose gender marks but one among many of his identities.

What might Irigaray say about this approach to theological discourse? Can this radically indeterminate God, the infinitely emptying sign, save women? If the only thing at stake in Irigaray's critique of phallocentrism were the destabilizing of both traditional ontologies of being and the foundationalist impulses of Enlightenment epistemology, then she might be able to answer the latter question affirmatively.

22. The term "negative theology" has a long and complex history in the field of Christian doctrine, ranging from medieval to modern mystical reflections on the "Via Negativa" to eighteenth-century Congregationalist debates on piety. The most recent conversations on the topic have focused specifically on both poststructuralist accounts of meaning and Heideggerian renderings of ontology. See Mark Taylor, *Altarity* (Chicago: University of Chicago Press, 1987); *Deconstructing Theology* (New York: Crossroads, 1987); *Erring: A Post-Modern Theology* (Chicago: University of Chicago Press, 1984). Also see Charles Winquist, *Epiphanies of Darkness: Deconstruction in Theology* (Philadelphia: Fortress, 1986); *Derrida and Negative Theology*, ed. Harold Coward and Toby Foshay (Albany, New York: State University of New York Press, 1992); Carl Raschke, *The Alchemy of the Word: Language and the End of Theology* (Missoula: Scholars Press, 1979). For an assessment of postmodernism, Derrida, and a Christian theology that seeks to avoid the problems attending an uncritical valorization of fragmentation and chaos, see Walter Lowe, *Theology and Difference: The Wound of Reason* (Bloomington: Indiana University Press, 1993).

But she makes it quite evident that much more is at stake. Even in its most distinctly deconstructive moments, Irigaray's analysis of philosophical phallocentrism is driven not by a general theoretical interest in showing that truth claims and ontological presences are illusory, but by a feminist concern to expose the ways in which such discourses silence women. To the degree that this political agenda guides her reflections, she never lets her focus stray far from the issue of gender and the construction of sexual difference, a fact that keeps her from wielding the tools of poststructuralist analysis as if destabilizing discourse were an end in itself and not a means of exposing discursive constraints which are oppressive to women. Keeping her gaze focused on women and, correlatively, on the role played by gender in the construction of discursive economies thus allows Irigaray to interrogate the gender relations which structure even the most destabilized of deconstructive discourses.

When one directs this gaze at the God of negative theologians, one finds a gendered fault line which runs through this seemingly indeterminate terrain. This fault line appears, in all its oppressively gendered elegance, if one simply asks about the utility of valorizing notions such as emptiness, chaos, and radical indeterminacy in a context where women have long been associated with these attributes. Are not these theologians finally celebrating, as if it were unambiguously liberating, the very space (or non-space) that has served as a prison for women? It would seem so—particularly if we do not allow poststructuralist flights of fancy to occlude the issue of gender. And although it may be true that when the masculine subject occupies such a space, a critical subversion of his gender occurs, in their quest for a general audience, negative theologians never pause to consider that those who deploy discourse (and who are deployed by discourse) are never just general Western subjects whose arrogant but illusory claims to truth and presence need to be tempered; rather, they are always persons who have discrete histories that are marked by different relations to the dominant discourse. For women, it hardly seems emancipatory to step into a theological economy where the prison that has held them is suddenly disguised as an airy, open meadow where they can supposedly move with freedom. Having lived under the weight of a rhetoric that fragments her as the chaotic, and having occupied the position of the open sign which simultaneously recapitulates and disintegrates her relations, the woman of Irigaray's gaze might not welcome this "indeterminate God/man." Rather, she might desire to kill this new philosopher king who, having walked in truth, now chooses to enter her prison as if it too were his home, his open field of play.[23]

IRIGARAY'S ESCHATOLOGICAL THEOLOGY

Moving beyond Irigaray's deconstructive moment, what are the theological implications of her second, more constructive discourse on the Divine, the discourse that she claims may be able to "save women?" As I previously noted, when Irigaray turns to the task of describing this second God, there is a pronounced shift in the discursive machinery of her reflections. Instead of deploying analytic gestures aimed at jamming the conceptual apparatus that drives phallocentric renderings of God, she generates a rhetoric designed to help women "construct a space for ourselves in the *air* for the rest of our time on earth—air in which we can breath and sing freely, in which we can perform and move at will" ("Divine Women," 66). As the images evoked by this statement suggest, the second discourse is driven by strongly utopian impulses and consequently is crafted in a language that seeks to inspire hope, to open up space for new imaginings and namings, and to encourage bold gestures of creative envisioning in a theological context where constraint, confusion, and silence have traditionally reigned. Such a rhetoric is, in short, Irigaray's pragmatically feminist answer to the negative theologians' empty discourse.

Interestingly, it is this second discourse, and not the first, which comes closest in its form and function to mirroring the constructive agenda that guides much of the feminist theology written for use in church contexts. Such theological literature is designed to serve as a kind of communal discipline or a form of collective spiritual direction where both the crafting of character and the shaping of disposition are of primary importance. For feminist theologians, this crafting and shaping often utilizes the rhetorical logic of Christian eschatology, a logic wherein the social transformation of the subject unfolds through the discursive power released by a vision of the future. This future, the Christian eschaton, is for feminist theologians one in which God's promise of a coming reign of justice and peace abounds with concrete images of what this might mean for women as well as for others who presently live in the time and space of injustice and oppression. The eschatological agenda of feminist theology thus seeks to measure and

23. See the conclusion of Irigaray's "Plato's *Hysteria*," in *Speculum*, 346–64 and "*La Mystérique*," ibid., 191–202.

reconfigure the present, or the "already," by reference to an admittedly utopian future, the "as yet" of the parousia.[24] Furthermore, the success or failure of such a rhetoric is gauged not by some ethereal, otherworldly logic but by the ethical quality of the character it authors and the social relations it constructs. The force of its truth, then, lies not only in the propositional form or the analytic content of this eschatological vision but, even more importantly, in the ethical integrity of communal identities and relations such a vision instantiates.

Before turning to the ethical commitments which drive Irigaray's discourse on the Divine that can save women, let me first, in broad terms, explore the conceptual framework she sets up for defending the usefulness of engaging in this kind of eschatological reflection on God. In her essay,"Divine Women," Irigaray, following the lead of Ludwig Feuerbach, observes that feminists should not abandon theological discourse because "no human subjectivity, no human society has ever been established without the help of the Divine" ("Divine Women," 62). The Divine builds subjectivity and culture, she further argues, by serving as an infinite goal or horizon which, in turn, as the ultimate telos of our envisioned future, has the power to shape our present.[25] As this telos, the Divine horizon determines the path of our becoming by providing a genre or essence which we subjectively actualize in the time and space of our unfolding futures. According to Irigaray, however, this path of becoming is not authored by a divine, transcendent being who exists quite apart from our will to become. Rather, the God who authors this path is nothing more (nor less) than an imagined screen onto which human beings project genres and essences that originate in and thereby mark their own material finitude.

Irigaray argues that, as this screen, the God who has for centuries reigned in Western culture is, not surprisingly, male, a God who mirrors back to the arbiters of patriarchal culture a morphological reflection of their own masculine desire. To this observation, Irigaray adds

24. There are a variety of eschatological paradigms that structure Christian reflections on the time and character of its Divine telos. The one I refer to here is found both in the tradition of "liberal Protestant thought" and in contemporary theologies of liberation. In many instances, this focus on the "already/not yet" dialectic is drawn from biblical interpretations of Pauline eschatology.

25. Ludwig Feuerbach, *The Essence of Christianity*, trans. George Eliot (New York: Prometheus Books, 1989). For an interesting theological account of Feuerbach's position on religion, see Karl Barth, *From Rousseau to Ritschl* (New York: Harper, 1959). Barth's critique of Feuerbach and its significance for Irigaray's analysis of philosophical mimesis is explored further in "This God Which Is Not One."

that, given the proclivity for human beings to become images of the very Divine which they create, women need to have a conception of God which will mark a path of their own distinctive becoming rather than one which, as the mirror of man, requires women to seek a future in which they must also become an image of man and a function of his desire. Until this new God is imagined woman will have no "mirror wherewith to become woman"; and "as long as woman lacks a Divine made in her image, she cannot establish her subjectivity or achieve a goal of her own. She lacks an ideal that would be her goal or path in becoming" ("Divine Women," 63).

Given Irigaray's assertion that the God who will accomplish these ends is a human construct, it makes sense that she should turn to an analysis of women's present situation or, to use Feuerbach's terms, the shape of women's material finitude as the principal source for determining the characteristics of this new Divinity. However, in an interesting turn of argument, Irigaray suggests that simply imagining a Goddess with supposedly female attributes or invoking a horizon that is spiritually feminine will not provide women with the divine path they need in order to become, for such Goddesses can easily reproduce an economy of relating which simply reverses the old economy of phallocentric discourse. Instead of constructing a new Goddess out of valorized attributes that remain caught in a reductive fascination with essences and a correlative ontology of being, Irigaray looks to women's material finitude (but not essential being) in search of grounds for a constructive ethics. This move—again, a move away from an ontology of attributes and into the realm of social ethics—finds it parallel in the work of recent feminist theologians who are not as interested in making God female as they are in constructing a theological discourse that disposes the community of faith to act in an ethically just manner.[26]

In *An Ethics of Sexual Difference*, Irigaray presents her account of two ethical constraints which she believes should limit and shape this emergent, emancipatory vision of God. First, she indicates that this new theology must author a discursive space in which the other is not consumed by a desire to establish a totalizing definition of subjectivity. Rather, it must be a space of love where two touch in an embrace that respects difference while also permitting the constitutive power

26. I do not mean to suggest that figuring God in the feminine is unimportant or necessarily dangerous. As many conference participants at "RE-imaginings" would attest, imagining God as woman can function as a decisive component in the process of forming an ethically emancipatory Christian character.

of relation to flourish. In her essay on Descartes's treatment of the first passion, Irigaray describes this kind of relating as a meeting marked by "wonder":

> This first passion is indispensable not only to life but also or still to the creation of an ethics. Notably of and through sexual difference. This other, male or female, should *surprise* us again and again, appear to us as *new, very different* from what we knew or what we thought he or she should be. Which means that we would look at the other, stop to look at him or her, ask ourselves, come close to ourselves through questioning. *Who art thou? I am* and *I become* thanks to this question. Wonder goes beyond that which is or is not suitable for us. The other never suits us simply. We would in some way have reduced the other to ourselves if he or she suited us completely. An *excess* resists: the other's existence and becoming as a place that permits union and/through resistance to assimilation or reduction to sameness.
>
> Before and after appropriation, there is wonder.[27]

In order for this wondrous and nondominating love to exist, Irigaray explains, a second ethical constraint is required. The self (woman) who loves must inhabit a space of subjectivity that cannot be simply reduced to the desire of the other; her relating must move out from a space in which self-love grounds her own desire and subjectivity. Taking on the voice of "woman," Irigaray explains why circumscribing the boundaries of this female identity remains so difficult for women. Under the strictures of the male gaze, "we look at ourselves in the mirror to *please someone*, rarely to interrogate the state of our body or our spirit, rarely for ourselves and in search of our own becoming" ("Divine Women," 65). But, she continues, another kind of gaze is necessary for wonder to flourish, a gaze which is self-referential. "I have yet to unveil, unmask, or veil myself *for me*—to veil myself so as to achieve self-contemplation, for example, to let my gaze travel over myself so as to limit my exposure to the other and repossess my own gestures and garments, thus nestling back into my vision and contemplation of myself" ("Divine Women," 65). Irigaray further suggests that by repossessing her own gestures and garments, woman can create a nest or an envelope which, by containing her subjectivity, makes it possible for her to love, enfold, and contain the other without sacrificing her own becoming:

27. Irigaray, "Wonder: A Reading of Descartes, *The Passions of the Soul*," in *An Ethics of Sexual Difference*, 74. See René Descartes, *The Passions of the Soul* in *The Philosophical Works of Descartes*, vol. 1, trans. E. S. Haldane and G. R. T. Ross (Cambridge: Cambridge University Press, 1931; reprinted, Dover, 1955).

If she is to be able to contain, to envelope, she must have her own
envelope. Not only her clothing and ornaments of seduction, but her
skin. And her skin must contain a receptacle. She must lack
    —neither body,
    —nor extension within,
    —nor extension without,
or she will plummet down and take the other with her.[28]

Within the context of the two-fold ethical constraints of wonder
and self-love, Irigaray turns to the question of God and generates a
vision of the Divine which, she argues, encourages both the construction of a space of subjective integrity for women and a relating to the
other which is not predicated on a logic of consumption. The language
she uses to describe this God comes from her account of a morphology
of women's continual self-touching in the caress of two lips, a morphology in which one "thinks through mucous."[29] It is, however, quite
difficult to get a handle on the character of this God because Irigaray's
own language becomes extremely elliptical when she speaks of an
economy of exchange mediated through the fluid substance of mucous. For the most part, her references to the Divine in this context
emphasize immanence and indwelling. Instead of imagining God as
the immutable, transcendent Other who founds identity through the
eclipse of difference, Irigaray portrays this God as one who moves
through and among women as spirit, "the respiration of lovers,"[30] as
the "sensible transcendental" that "is not alien to the flesh" ("Love of
Same," 110) but "surrounds them and envelopes them in their *jouissance*. Clothing them in that *porousness* and that *mucous* that they
are."[31] In this economy of exchange, God and woman touch and caress
as two lips, rendering a knowledge that is undifferentiated from the
relating which stirs it. Cast in the language of immanence, this God is
both matter and movement (place and interval) within which subjectivity coalesces in time-space—"the infinite that resides within us
and among us, the god in us, the Other for us, becoming with and in us"
("Divine Women," 63).

Despite her obvious preference for immanental language about
God, however, Irigaray is not prepared to abandon entirely images of

28. Irigaray, "Place, Interval: A Reading of Aristotle, *Physics IV*," in *An Ethics of
Sexual Difference*, 35.
29. Irigaray, "Love of Same, Love of Other," in *An Ethics of Sexual Difference*, 110.
30. Irigaray, "An Ethics of Sexual Difference," in *An Ethics of Sexual Difference*,
129.
31. Irigaray, "Love of Self," in *An Ethics of Sexual Difference*, 69.

God's transcendent otherness. This dimension of Irigaray's Divine appears most clearly in passages where she emphasizes the difference between woman, as finite creature, and God, the infinite Other, "who keeps track of our limits and our infinite possibilities—as women— who inspires our projects" ("Divine Women," 67). She explains the need to retain this distinction as follows:

> If we are to have a sense of the other that is not projective or selfish, we have to attain an intuition of the infinite:—either the intuition of a god or divine principle aiding in the birth of the other without pressuring it with our own desire,—or the intuition of a subject that, at each point in the present, remains unfinished and open to a becoming of the other that is neither simply passive nor simply active. ["Love of Same," 111–12]

And the intuition of this unfinished subject itself requires the Divine Other which, as infinite horizon, keeps the subject always "half open" ("Love of Same," 111).

In sum, the primary function served by this God lies in securing the normative force of the two ethical constraints that shape Irigaray's broader emancipatory vision: as matter, God secures the space and provides the boundaries which permit self-love; as nonconsuming movement, God is that wondrous moment when the other is encountered in the caress. God thus functions as both the envelope which contains female desire and the powerful impulse which sends that envelope forth and empowers the other to graciously receive it. The ethical constraints of wonder and self-love are thus grounded not only in the matter/movement/God which *is the subject* but the matter/movement/God which *is more than the subject;* this God is inside as well as outside ourselves, both a divinity that *we are* and a divinity that *we relate to* as the beckoning, defining Other.

In recent feminist scholarship devoted to reshaping Christian doctrines of God, one finds similar descriptions of the Divine emerging which try to hold together conceptions of divine transcendence and immanence and which correlatively seek a balance between images of God: those which strengthen an understanding of the subjective wholeness (containment) of the fragmented female subject, and those which suggest that the borders of subjective identity are constituted through relationally fluid encounters (wonder) between the subject and God, neighbor, discourse, and history. Like Irigaray, feminist theologians seek to articulate a vision of God that holds these notions together, because their analysis of women's oppression points to the need for a God who both heals the fractured self-loss experienced by persons whose social identity has been consumed by a debilitating emphasis on "self-giving," and who simultaneously marks the way toward an ethic of relationality that insists on keeping the healed self open to wondrous interactions with others.

Attending to this balance between a God who authors subjective integrity and a God who embraces the opening of the self to the other has led feminist theologians to suggest several interesting reformulations of the narrative of traditional Christian discourse. One observation about this narrative which has become a standard part of feminist theology concerns classical descriptions of sin as pride or narcissistic self-love. Feminist theologians have argued, in short, that if one looks to the material finitude of woman and notes that she has not been permitted to contain herself, to let her gaze travel over herself, then it becomes clear that the sin of pride does not describe her loss or the fallen state of her becoming; rather, her sin is better described as the sin of fragmentation, of subjective dissolution.[32] Once her sin is identified in this manner, it then becomes apparent that her salvation rests not in a vision of the Divine who breaks through the wall of her narcissistic gaze, but of a God who inscribes borders within which she might begin to conceive of herself as a coherent self, capable of relation and yet contained enough not to let the relation dissolve her. As feminist theologians continue to work through the implications of this way of understanding sin and salvation, Irigaray should remain a productive conversation partner, particularly for the challenge of carving out a conception of self-love that does not lead to the reproduction of a rhetoric which inscribes false notions of autonomy. In this regard, the value of Irigaray's eschatological vision lies in its ability to affirm both a postmodernist appreciation for the social construction of the subject who is constituted by her relations, and the more pragmatic observation that this subject is also an agent who pulls these relations into an

---

32. In the field of feminist theology, the structure of women's oppression and its relation to traditional doctrines of "sin" has been explored in works by Judith Plaskow, *Sex, Sin and Grace: Women's Experiences and the Theologies of Reinhold Niebhur and Paul Tillich* (Washington, D.C.: University of America Press, 1980); Susan Thistlethwaite, *Sex, Race and God: Christian Feminism in Black and White* (New York: Crossroads, 1989); Mary Potter Engel, "Evil, Sin, and the Violation of the Vulnerable," in *Lift Every Voice: Constructing Christian Theologies from the Underside*, ed. Susan Thistlethwaite and Mary Potter Engle (New York: Harper Collins, 1990).

order, thus giving her action meaning and allowing her to make ethically responsible decisions.[33]

In addition to reconceiving the character of sin and salvation, feminist theologians have also tried to open up traditional renderings of God's identity in such a way that it, too, honors both self-love and relational wonder. In this regard, traditional construals of the Trinity have proved to be a long-neglected but fertile field of discursive possibility; and Irigaray's description of the God who is interval and place helps to expand the conceptual horizons of Trinitarian thought. According to the logic of Trinitarian conceptions of the Divine, the identity of God is figured not simply as a singular subject but as a community of persons in mutual relation where both substantive difference and fluid exchange constitute a Divine being who is at once self-contained and radically open to relation.[34] Because the divine economy of exchange which marks God's identity is internally both multiple and unitary, this God does not need an external other in order for there to be self-knowledge, for such knowledge is eternally generated through the relations of the Trinity. Such a God can thus relate to that which is truly other than God (humanity) without reducing the other to a function of divine, narcissistic desire, as is the case in phallocentric conceptions of the Divine-human relation. Rather, this Trinitarian God might be self-contained enough to encounter humanity with wonder and to inspire, in turn, a wondrous response which need not consume in order to know. As these brief comments on the Trinity

33. The pragmatic critical theory of Seyla Benhabib, *Situating the Self: Gender, Community and Post-modernism in Contemporary Ethics* (New York: Routledge, 1992), provides a model of how the normative impulses of critical theory and the constructivist drives of poststructuralist thought meet in a theory of subjectivity where ethical responsibility, normative rules, and the relativized subject coexist. Also see Charles Taylor, *Sources of the Self: The Making of Modern Identity* (Cambridge: Harvard University Press, 1989). In the field of feminist theology, similar strategies for negotiating a constructivist/ethically normative vision can be found in the work of Rebecca Chopp, *The Power to Speak*; Katie G. Cannon, *Black Womanist Ethics*; and Sharon Welch, *Communities of Resistance and Solidarity: A Feminist Theology of Liberation* (Maryknoll: Orbis, 1985).

34. This particular formulation of divine relationality was first developed in the writings of the fourth-century Eastern Trinitarian theologians, the Cappadocians, especially Gregory of Nyssa. See Cornelius Plantinga, Jr., "Gregory of Nyssa and the Social Analogy of the Trinity," *The Thomist* 50 (1986): 325–52. For a general introduction to the doctrine of the Trinity and the variety of ways contemporary theologians characterize the types of relation that exist both between each "person" in the Godhead (Father, Son, and Spirit) and between God and humanity, see Ted Peters, *God as Trinity: Relationality and Temporality in Divine Life* (Louisville: Westminster/J. Knox, 1993).

indicate, it may well be that thinking through this unitary/relational character of God will require a shift in the morphological imaginary of theology. Such a shift would reject the reductive desire for symmetry, closure, and binary order which, according to Irigaray, typifies Western thought, and would move toward an imaginary which plays with the morphological economy of exchange described by Irigaray as female desire. Could feminist theologians think this Godhead through a morphology of mucous, an imaginary driven by a mechanics of fluid, an economy modeled on the caress of two lips—always touching yet half open?

ON GOD THE OTHER

As I suggested in my opening comments, the conceptual traffic between Irigaray's Divine and the more explicitly Christian God of feminist theology does not move only in one direction, from Paris to Minneapolis; it also moves from the U.S. back to Paris, and from the church back to the academy. What critical challenges might theologians raise to Irigaray's conception of a "sensible transcendental" God who can save women? Are there limits to the use to which Christian theology can put her theory, limits which might point to weaknesses in her own argument? Similarly, are there moments in her reflections on God which must be expanded and nuanced if her theory is to accomplish its intended eschatological function in practicing communities of faith?

Let me begin by returning to Irigaray's conception of God's otherness and, more specifically, her use of Feuerbach to ground her discussion of the need for God in human society. Feminist theologians who try to avoid using phenomenology in their efforts to reenvision God might ask of Irigaray why she so uncritically imports a nineteenth-century philosophical scheme which clearly deploys the kind of universalizing gestures she rigorously critiques in her earlier work. According to Feuerbach, it is possible to give a coherent account of the process whereby society in general and the universal subject in particular construct the Gods they need in order to become. Insofar as Irigaray appears to applaud Feuerbach's account, she too embraces a totalizing gesture that reduces the thick particularity of diverse religions and views of God into a mirror of the same. If Irigaray intends to reproduce, at a methodological level, her ongoing commitment to honoring incommensurable difference, then she needs to qualify her use of Feuerbach with an acknowledgment that she is using his philosophy for its explanatory power and not as a universal ground for analyzing all religious discourse. For as long as she allows his analysis to serve a foundational function, she risks replicating a totalizing logic in which the rich diversity of the world's religions is reduced to and consumed by a master philosophy which claims to know the "truth" about their varied productions.

In addition to questioning her seemingly uncritical importation of a philosophically reductive scheme, one might challenge Irigaray's use of Feuerbach in particular. Does it really allow her to generate a discourse on God that differs significantly from the phallocentrism she critiques? While it is clear that Irigaray plays her two conceptions of God against one another, contrasting the God of man who is stable, immutable, and singular with the God of woman who is fluid, infinitely open, and capable of holding the endless variety of goals that woman might conceive for herself, these two Gods nonetheless bear a remarkable resemblance to one another. Both Gods are, according to Irigaray's analysis of Feuerbach, the product of a projected desire; they are each the term of gender's becoming and in this regard function to secure the infinite horizon of accomplishment which the finite human will needs to survive and grow. And, even though Irigaray points out that the specific contours of each gender's horizon are different, the God who is this horizon in each case serves the human will by taking on, as mirror, the attributes of the concrete human subject creating the Divine. It thus appears that the God of man and the God of woman, although they may be generated from different morphological economies, share a similar origin: each originates in the productivity of a consciousness that creates God in his or her own image.

Although this similarity does not seem to trouble Irigaray, there are good reasons why it should. As illustrated above, the economy of exchange that produces these Gods is a mirror image of the economy of exchange that Irigaray so rigorously critiques in her readings of phallocentrism. According to that "old dream of symmetry," (*Speculum*, 11–129) the other (woman) has no being or space of becoming of her own because she is continually positioned as an other who mirrors man back to himself, defining the borders of his identity and securing the stability of his presence. In this phallic economy, woman is thus consumed by man's projective desire, reduced to a blank screen toward which he directs his narcissistic gaze. In short, she is the fictive product of his subjectivity, a function of his need to be and become; and as Irigaray states, "[t]o be the term of the other is nothing enviable. It paralyzes us in our becoming" ("Divine Women," 71). Given Irigaray's critique of this discursive economy, it seems strange that she would turn around and offer us a God who, like woman, can be nothing more than a blank horizon or the term who serves the consumptive needs of the subject who requires an imagined God in order to become. To the extent that she does this, she appears not to have thwarted but to have resurrected the logic of classical ontology and Enlightenment episte-mology by simply putting God in the place traditionally held by woman. One might therefore ask Irigaray how far she has really moved the conversation. Although her new God may be clothed in the gar-ments of female desire, this God still occupies the space of an empty sign, a blank screen of transcendence who can finally author nothing but the same. And when woman meets this God, she is really only meeting herself; she thus remains caught in the logic of discourse which as "a tight fabric . . . turns back upon the subject and wraps around and imprisons him [her] in return" ("An Ethics," 120).

One might push this point further by asking Irigaray if this God can secure the ethical constraints she puts forth and if, so doing, this God can subsequently encourage *in practice* both self-love and wondrous relation. With regard to self-love, Irigaray makes it quite evident that the God who will save women will do so by authoring a space of becoming where relations are not conceived through a binary logic of dialectical loss and where fragmentation is not sublated as gain. Rather, in that other conception of God, gain would begin with an affirmation of women's autonomy as well as a celebration of historical particularity and incommensurable otherness. Such a God, she argues, would invite women to a new becoming by affirming the limits of their subjectivities, by giving boundaries to their presently fragmented and dissimulating selves—in short, by containing and enveloping them, as with skin, within a discursive receptacle that relishes the open coher-ence of unique differences. But can Irigaray's God actually teach women to conceive of themselves in this manner? Not, it seems, if the very God who is to author this contained subjectivity is Herself with-out container or envelope, without a limited identity, who as the unen-viable term of another is without skin, boundary, horizon, or historical particularity, who is nothing but infinite expanse, relation, space and interval. More specifically, it seems that Irigaray asks women to imag-ine a God who will teach them self-love and containment; but the God she then goes on to describe is, in fact, incapable of a Divine self-love because this God is nothing but an empty sign—not so unlike the one invoked by negative theologians—that functions only to contain the love of another. At a pragmatic level, she thus ties her rhetoric into a theological knot, constructing an eschatological vision that, on the one hand, requires us to rethink our present in terms of subjective containment. On the other hand, Irigaray asks us to think that present through the future horizon of a God who, as a term of women's self-love, has no envelope, no incommensurable otherness.

The same problem occurs when one explores Irigaray's notion of wonder. Irigaray is not simply content to leave woman subjectively isolated in her own self-loving envelope, but seeks instead to pair this discourse of containment with a discourse about God that would lead the subject to reach out to the other in a wondrous caress. In that caress, difference would be celebrated, mutual respect would abound, and woman would remain forever half-open to the transformative power of relation:

> Attracting me toward, wonder keeps me from taking and assimilating directly to myself. Is wonder the time that is always covered by the present? The bridge, the stasis, the moment of *in-stance?* Where I am no longer in the past and not yet in the future. The point of passage between two closed worlds, two definite universes, two space-times or two others determined by their identities, two epochs, two others. A separation without a wound, awaiting or remembering, without despair or closing in on the self. . . . Wonder must be the advent or the event of the other. The beginning of a new story? ["Wonder," 75]

To inscribe a discourse of divinity in which such wonder is imaginable, Irigaray must be willing to permit wonder to flow between the subject woman and the God who beckons her. In terms of pragmatically modeling this understanding of relationality through theological discourse, one should argue that the God toward whom woman is attracted must be a God that she cannot assimilate directly to herself. For the relation between woman and God to be wondrous, there must be the division of two worlds, two definite universes, two space-times, two others, for it is only in the difference that passage is possible. Furthermore, this difference need not reside in opposition or contradiction, as in the phallic economy of divine exchange. Rather, it exists when one meets the other "always as though for the first time."[35] But if God is a projection of woman's desire, such difference is repressed while assimilation is valorized, and the economy of exchange that

35. Irigaray, "Sexual Difference," in *An Ethics of Sexual Difference,* 12.

ensues proves consumptive and wounding. In this sense, between God and woman there is no advent or event of the other. And what new story has begun? It is her story alone, not "theirs, together." Is this the parousia that Irigaray imagines into the future of woman? Her elaboration of wonder suggests not, but the question remains: can a religion in which there is no wonder between persons and a God (who is incommensurably other) encourage an ethic of wonder between men, between women, and between women and men?

From a Christian perspective, such an ethic of wonder is made possible through the concept of a divine, transcendent (as well as immanent) agent who comes into relation with the world and thereby with women through the promisory act of unmerited love—through grace. In feminist terms, this God can be conceived as the Divine who saves woman from subjective dissolution by containing her in an envelope of grace and by calling her into wondrous relation where an ethic of mutual reciprocity holds normative weight. The God who meets women in this manner is not simply a term of human consciousness but a subject capable of acting, of freely pouring out the grace that enfolds woman, and of pronouncing judgment upon economies of relating that are consumptive and oppressive rather than reciprocal. And in each of these actions, God remains other to woman as one who meets her, who meets us, with a message of hope. God as Other shows us another way into our future, a way which we are only capable of glimpsing within the projective limits of our discourse, yes, but which remains always beyond as the *more* which draws our projected desires up short. For Christians, this God is encountered as the incommensurable Other both in the Law of Moses—which discursively marks the contours of a divine will that is decisive and material and not simply an infinitely expanding horizon—and in the person of Jesus Christ, whose life, work, teachings, death, and resurrection render the complex identity of a person (not an infinite expanse) who is neighbor, friend, and lover, as well as savior and judge. To the extent, then, that feminist theologians remain committed to affirming the otherness of the Divine—in Her multiple manifestation as the Trinity, the Law, and Jesus Christ—their conversations with Irigaray will include a constant reminder that the God of woman's desire is, like the woman She calls, a subject both contained and half-open in the enveloping caress of self-love and wonder.

PEGGY KAMUF

To Give Place: Semi-Approaches to Hélène Cixous

FIRST APPROACH

A matter of some gravity: that which pulls toward the earth, the lowest
level, below ground even, the weight and volume with which heavier
substances displace air or water. We say a matter is grave to remind
ourselves to ponder it, to weigh it carefully, to exercise acute ethical
vigilance: all the moral senses alerted to those imponderables that at
every moment risk being swept aside or, worse, trampled underfoot by
the ponderous march of gravity's law. If the matter is grave, then, by
definition, it should not be taken lightly. Moral seriousness, it seems,
requires that weight be given.

Approached from another angle, however, the scales tip in an apparent paradox: what is wanted is lightness, not weight or gravity. And it is
above all a question of approach, approach to the other, under the
gravest imperative to let the other escape the force of our gravity, the
inertial wave that can level everything in its path, crush whatever does
not have time to get out of the way. The most responsible and most
serious approach advances carefully and slowly, but above all lightly—
which may mean obliquely, or imperceptibly, or even not at all. For
there is perhaps no more careful approach than a stillness that would
let the other come out of her own, his own movement.

How to approach stillness stilly enough, lightly enough, and yet
seriously enough to make some advance into the distance holding me
at such a remove from the other's encounter? The question is placed
here at the brink of this approach to the writing of one who could
imagine the following exchange between two women's voices on the
subject, precisely, of writing:

YFS 87, *Another Look, Another Woman,* ed. Huffer, © 1995 by Yale University.

—Parce que le rêve secret de l'écriture, c'est d'être aussi délicate que le silence.

—Mais est-ce qu'il y a une écriture d'une telle délicatesse?

—Il y en a une, mais je ne l'ai pas. Parce que pour écrire délicatement de la délicatesse, il faudrait pouvoir non-écrire.

—Il faudrait pouvoir écrire l'effacement. Mais est-ce qu'on peut "écrire" l'effacement?[1]

"Because the secret dream of writing is to be as delicate as silence."

"But is there a writing of such delicacy?"

"There is one, but I don't have it. Because in order to write delicately about delicacy, one would have to be able not-to-write."

"One would have to be able to write effacement. But can one 'write' effacement?"

This question arises for the writer who would send a first letter of love, while fearing that her words will ensnare, entrap, and finally crush the beloved beneath their law. A fear presides over this "première lettre" or first approach to the other in writing: "Comment faire pour que soit libre? Souci: Peur que l'aimer lui fasse loi" [How can I do things so is free? Concern: Fear that loving her will impose a law on her] (21). Slowly, lightly, she approaches the "last sentence" and the "Ultimate Book" for which this book will have been a sort of prolegomenon, a writing-toward the "melodical cell of an entire book" (275).

If, then, the task proposed is to "write on" a writing that itself wishes secretly to approach silence and effacement, at every turn the risk, or rather the certainty, is that one will displace that delicate stillness with the volume—both the noise and the weight—of one's own descriptions. Such "writing on," the more serious and pondered and concrete it becomes, the more it flattens the intricate retreats of the other's effaced discretion into recognizable or familiar patterns, general molds, one-size-fits-all patterns of thought. The question is, then, how to write on without ruthlessly crushing beneath the weight of discourse that to which one wants above all to grant the chance of a certain lightness on the page, the chance of flying to meet the other, of touching her or him without touching.

Toward the beginning of the same text, the unnamed "she" who throughout will seek the "Ultimate Book" and the last phrase, recalls her earlier attempts at sentences, all of which had been discarded for making too much noise, for being "too long, too narrow, too cold, not

---

1. Hélène Cixous, *Limonade tout était si infini* (Paris: des femmes, 1982), 252–53; my translation.

carnal enough, much too timid, meager and heavy as lead." She is then portrayed thinking:

> La légèreté aussi pèse. Ce qui j'ai à dire est plus léger que la légèreté ou n'est pas. Le mot 'légèreté' est déjà un poids. Il n'y a pas de mot assez léger pour ne pas alourdir la légèreté de la légèreté.
>
> Et ce que j'ai à dire est du domaine de la légèreté propre. [*Limonade*, 17]

> Lightness also weighs down. What I have to say is lighter than lightness or else it is not. The word 'lightness' is already a weight. There is no word light enough not to weigh down the lightness of lightness.
>
> And what I have to say is of the realm of lightness proper.

The predicament "she" begins to uncover here—that "la légèreté propre" is itself improperly named, too heavy—and the predicament that is ours as we approach the serious lightness of this writing are not, of course, encountered uniquely in the vicinity of texts signed by Hélène Cixous. Indeed, as we will try to make clear, it is the very generality of the dilemma that accounts for its inextricableness and inevitability. This is not to say (but this too will have to be shown) that these texts display any less singularly the marks of this general problem. There is, however, another circumstance dictating an especially circumspect approach to the writings of Hélène Cixous if we would not crush them under too much critical weight.

It is the circumstance of Cixous's reception as "French feminist theorist" in certain Anglo-American circles. Much has now been written about the imprecise, hasty divisions that this label has fostered as commentators struggled to justify its application. This hastiness or heaviness has been especially evident with regard to the writings of Cixous despite the fact, or perhaps, rather, *because* of the fact that, for a long time, and to a certain extent it is still the case, the "theorist" characterization was constructed on the basis of a very few English translations of Cixous's work. For most intents and purposes, it was based on the translation of two essays in the journal *Signs* in 1976 and 1981.[2] It is indeed one of the more remarkable aspects of this reception

2. "The Laugh of the Medusa," trans. Keith Cohen and Paula Cohen, *Signs* 1/4 (Summer 1976): 875–93; and "Castration or Decapitation," trans. A. Kuhn, *Signs* 7/1 (Fall 1981): 41–55. For a bibliography of English translations of texts by Cixous, see Morag Shiach, *Hélène Cixous: A Politics of Writing* (London and New York: Routledge, 1991). In addition to the thesis on Joyce (*The Exile of James Joyce*), translated in 1976, fifteen essays or extracts from essays have been translated in various journals or collections, as have several works for the theater. If Shiach's bibliography is accurate, there have been

that so few translations have appeared and yet Cixous's name is almost always included whenever the "French-feminist-theory" construction is called up.[3] Perhaps this oddity says something about such a construction's potential disregard for what happens in the encounter between languages or idioms, and more generally in the encounter with the other that is given a space in writing. In any case, we will be led to examine more closely below the reluctant relation Cixous's writing maintains to translation, not only in the narrow or "proper" sense, but all forms of transportation or transmutation, beginning with the transmutation into a "theory," French, feminist, or other.

First, however, consider how the construction of Cixous as theorist has not hesitated to dismiss or merely disregard this reluctance. One of the most symptomatic examples of such commentary is Sandra Gilbert's "Foreword" to the American translation of The Newly Born Woman in 1986, which is titled "A Tarantella of Theory."[4] The symptom it exhibits is in fact double, for Gilbert seems undecided whether to try to make the "French feminist theory" label stick or, on the contrary, to dispute its pertinence. The result is a version of the "kettle logic" that Freud immortalized in his famous joke: all of this French stuff is very foreign to us American feminists; besides, our English-speaking women writers already invented it; and what they didn't invent is probably bad for you anyway. On the one hand, Gilbert insists on the strangeness of Cixous's "dazzling tarentella of theory" for the typical American readers whom she supposes for this purpose. Inadvertently, no doubt, her descriptions of this encounter manage to call up comical images: provincial American tourists squirming with disap-

---

only two complete translations (Angst and Dedans) of Cixous's twenty-four or more (depending how you count) "fictional" texts. Doubtless others are forthcoming.

3. In her introduction to Revaluing French Feminism, Nancy Fraser writes that "for many English-speaking readers today 'French feminism' simply is Irigaray, Kristeva, and Cixous," (1). This repetition by rote feeds Fraser's complaint, which seems to be primarily that there has been a misapprehension of "a much larger, more variegated field," (1). This is, of course, quite true. And yet, although her introduction makes a point of mentioning other feminist thinkers in France, the anthology she is introducing (and which she edited with Sandra Lee Bartky) conforms pretty much to what she calls the "curious synecdochic reduction" (1) by concentrating its essays on Irigaray and Kristeva, adding only an essay by Sarah Kofman to the mix. It would thus seem that the principal "revaluation" this anthology proposes is to eliminate altogether Cixous, whose name indeed is never again mentioned by any of the contributors.

4. Hélène Cixous and Catherine Clément, The Newly Born Woman, trans. Betsy Wing (Minneapolis: University of Minnesota Press, 1986). Originally published as La jeune née (Paris: Union Générale d'Edition, 1975).

proval as they watch some Mediterranean peasant festival in which the women, really, get far too carried away with the rhythms of the dance. On the other hand, however, Gilbert also manifestly wants to domesticate and reappropriate "French feminist theory" by comparing (and postdating) its tenets, procedures, or assertions to those of some of the Anglophone world's most respected "madwomen in the attic," Emily Dickinson or Virginia Woolf. This side of the strategy leads Gilbert to try to purify the "Dickinsonian" strain in Cixous by denouncing its admixture with a decidedly less savory association (at least for Sandra Gilbert and her imagined "typical American readers") to Lady Chatterley. "Didn't D.H. Lawrence . . . begin to outline something oddly comparable to Cixous's creed of woman before she did? . . . This often misogynistic English novelist defines an 'orgasm' whose implications, paradoxically enough, appear to anticipate the fusion of the erotic, the mystical, and the political that sometimes seems to characterize Cixous's thought on this subject. . . ." (xvii). Despite the hedging ("appear to," "sometimes seems to"), Gilbert's tactic here is unmistakable: appropriate the "good things" in Cixous by assimilating them to respected English-speaking precursors and, once the technique of comparison is in place, switch the poles to a negative, "often misogynistic" association to repel whatever cannot be assimilated.

Whereas commentary like Gilbert's seems simply not to have noticed the resistance Cixous's texts pose to this kind of appropriation, elsewhere the elaboration of the French-feminist-theory construct has shown greater awareness of the forcing required to make the mold of "theory" fit. Here is how another commentator, Toril Moi, makes her approach to what she calls "Cixous's textual jungle":

> Between 1975 and 1977, [Cixous] produced a whole series of theoretical (or semi-theoreitcal) writings, all of which set out to explore the relations between women, femininity, feminism and the production of texts. . . . The fact that many central ideas and images are constantly repeated, tends to present her work as a continuum that encourages non-linear forms of reading. Her style is often intensely metaphorical, poetic and explicitly antitheoretical, and her central images create a dense web of signifiers that offers no obvious edge to seize hold of for the analytically minded critic. It is not easy to operate cuts into, open vistas in or draw maps of Cixous's textual jungle; moreover, the texts themselves make it abundantly clear that this resistance to analysis is entirely intentional. Cixous believes neither in theory nor analysis.[5]

5. *Sexual/Textual Politics: Feminist Literary Theory* (New York: Methuen, 1986), 102.

One may be intrigued by the slight hesitation betrayed at the outset between "theoretical (or semi-theoretical)" to qualify the so-called "whole series" of writings in question; nevertheless, the potentially interesting notion of the "semi-theoretical" is simply dropped as Moi proceeds to dismiss the "abundantly clear . . . resistance" to the kind of analysis (or semi-analysis) she wants to perform. The principles of that analysis are themselves made clear in this initial paragraph and they derive from the familiar set of distinctions that includes expression vs. thought, style vs. substance, metaphoric vs. literal, and poetic vs. theoretical. All of the first terms in these pairs designate or describe what makes it difficult for this "analytically minded critic" to seize and to cut. Difficult, perhaps, but not impossible as long as one remains confident that, whatever the complications and implications, expression, style, metaphor, and poetry may finally be treated as incidental adjuncts to thought, substance, and so forth. And, most important, they are considered to be without relevance to what interests Moi above all: politics. Given the more or less unquestioning assumption of these conventional analytical categories, the fact that Moi goes on from there to find little good to say about Cixous's "whole theoretical project" (105) cannot come as too much of a surprise.[6] Things would perhaps look different if one pursued the less predictable category or the noncategory of the "semi-theoretical." For her part, however, Moi is intent on nailing down "the *kind* of feminist theory and politics [Cixous] represents" (104).

The pairing of "theory" with "politics," here in Moi's phrase but also in the title of her book, may be read as confirming a widely shared axiom: a literary theory, which is to say, a theory of meaning and value, is necessarily a theory of politics, even or especially if it does not explicitly claim to be so. The axiom is the distilled result of an intense exploration, over several decades (in fact, ever since Nietzsche), of "theory"'s limits. We now call "theory" the practical demonstration of how and why theory is not in fact possible as an act of thinking uncontaminated by contingency, particularity, or experiential differences.[7]

---

6. Moi's general disregard for what she calls here "style" should be surprising if one recalls that the subtitle of *Sexual/Textual Politics* is "Feminist Literary Theory." After a first section on "Anglo-American Feminist Criticism," however, the second part of the book is titled "French Feminist Theory"; hence the announced "literary" component seems to have slipped into the crack between Anglo-American "criticism" and French "theory."

7. At the beginning of his now famous essay "Resistance to Theory," Paul de Man observes that an inherent difficulty for literary theory is that it must "start out from empirical considerations" if it is not to ground itself in "an *a priori* conception of what is

Because it cannot avoid putting these differences materially and practically into play, "theory" is political: it is implicated necessarily in the very process of signification and symbolization it describes, the process by which some differences are made to represent difference in general. In this sense, "theory" is always semi-theory.

It is not easy to reckon with this insight. If "theory" is always semi-theory, then there is no telling absolutely when and where the semi-theoretical and semi-political may shade off into the semi-poetic or semi-fictional or some other semi-recognizable mode since such distinctions are rendered rather dubious by the contaminating non-category of the "semi-." Nevertheless, the "semi-" is not, as some may want to claim, an excuse for renouncing literary theory, which is to say, a thinking about written texts that seeks a certain generality. On the contrary, and this is the difficulty, such thinking opens onto a responsibility to that which is only glimpsed beneath the effacement of the prefix *semi-* on all names and general concepts. A semi-name is not altogether there, it does not name a presence, nothing that *is;* rather, it calls for something to present itself otherwise. If semi-theory responds to, is responsible for, this semi-effacement that carries so little weight in the present, it is because it gives place to that which as yet has no name: a future.

Cixous is one of our age's greatest semi-theoreticians. And as such, she will disappoint whoever supposes that theory's political responsibility begins and ends in a present "reality," by which is meant that which is fully present to itself rather than disseminated by the semi-. Moi's critique, for instance, is inscribed by that supposition:

> It is just this absence of any specific analysis of the material factors preventing women from writing that constitutes a major weakness of Cixous's utopia. Within her poetic mythology, writing is posited as an absolute activity of which all women *qua* women automatically partake. Stirring and seductive though such a vision is, it can say nothing of the actual inequities, deprivations and violations that women, as social beings rather than as mythological archetypes, must constantly suffer. [123]

'literary' by starting out from the premises of the system rather than from the literary thing itself—if such a 'thing' exists" (In *The Resistance to Theory* [Minneapolis: University of Minnesota Press, 1986], 4–5). This opening statement, and its reprise in the essay's conclusion regarding theory's impossibility ("Nothing can overcome the resistance to theory since theory *is* itself this resistance" [19]) may stand here synecdochically for what we are calling "theory's" limits.

The motive and the endpoint of this critique is to be found in the phrase "women, as social beings rather than as mythological archetypes. . . ." The term "mythological archetype" is not Cixous's, of course, but has been chosen here to qualify the "women" of whom Cixous speaks in her semi-theroetical writings. Such so-called archetypes have no social being, which is not to say they are false, or that the evocation of these nonbeings is in error. In this, Moi agrees with Catherine Clément when, in her exchange with Cixous in *The Newly Born Woman*, she said: "Your level of description is one where I don't recognize any of the things I think in political terms. It's not that it's 'false,' of course not. But it's described in terms which seem to me to belong to the level of myth or poetry . . . " (124). The politics invoked by Clément or Moi implies first of all an ontology. Which means that the "women" to whom they would refer are those beings classified (and restricted) as such, that is "social beings." This is, ultimately, but a tautology of reference: "women" means (those beings who are called) women. And "women"'s sociality is understood here as that which is named by the fundamental social convention of a stable referential language.

Cast in its starkest terms, the distinction Moi (or Clément) invokes is between a politics and a poetics of "women." The former, it is supposed, cannot do without a stable reference to the "actual" experience of social beings (in Moi's phrase above, "the actual inequities, deprivations and violations that women, as social beings rather than as mythological archetypes, must constantly suffer"). The latter, on the other hand, dispenses not with reference but with referents; it is a practice of what has been called reference without a referent.[8] But once again as regards such distinctions, are we not obliged to have recourse to the notion of the semi- in order to account for a politics that must also be a poetics? For indeed what kind of politics would be possible given a stable referential system, in which tautology stands in for ontology? If in fact "women" were confined (but on whose order? by what law?) in the tautology of reference, in the actuality of the present, if one could name with that term only an ontologically predetermined being (the "social being" in question for Moi), then could there even be a politics of women, a feminist politics? The term "woman" is a political term because it can be expropriated from any "actual" referent, turned aside

8. See Jacques Derrida, "La double séance," in *Dissémination* (Paris: Editions du Seuil, 1972), 234.

from a given coded function, just like any other term, and still differently. A politics is possible only to the extent that the referential tautology can be expropriated, indeed, has already expropriated itself, which is to say, it is possible only to the extent that, between "women" as "actual, social beings" and as *something else, something other* than this apparent actuality, the distinction is unenforceable because unlocalizable. This possible politics is that of semi-reference, or of reference without referent, which names the impossible "thing which is not."

A practice of semi-reference like Cixous's will, therefore, require one to read this expropriability at work within texts that appear to be making theoretical statements about "women." To illustrate, we may recall any one of a number of frequently cited passages from "Sorties" in *La jeune née*, for example:

> Je dirai: aujourd'hui l'écriture est aux femmes. Ce n'est pas une provocation, cela signifie que: la femme admet qu'il y ait de l'autre. Elle n'a pas effacé, dans son devenir-femme, la bisexualité latente chez la fille comme chez le garçon. Féminité et bisexualité vont ensemble. . . . A l'homme, il est bien plus difficile de se laisser traverser par de l'autre. L'écriture, c'est en moi le passage, entrée, sortie, séjour, de l'autre que je suis et ne suis pas, que je ne sais pas être, mais que je sens passer, qui me fait vivre,—qui me déchire, m'inquiète, m'altère, qui?—une, un, des?, plusieurs, de l'inconnu qui me donne justement l'envie de connaître à partir de laquelle s'élance toute vie. Ce peuplement ne laisse ni repos ni sécurité, trouble toujours le rapport au "réel", produit des effets d'incertitude qui font obstacle à la socialisation du sujet. C'est angoissant, ça use; et pour les hommes, cette perméabilité, cette non-exclusion, c'est la menace, l'intolérable. . . . Que soit "féminine" une certaine réceptivité, c'est vrai. On peut bien sûr exploiter, comme l'Histoire l'a toujours fait, l'accueil féminin en aliénation. . . . Mais je parle ici de la féminité comme conservant en vie l'autre qui se fie à elle, la visite, qu'elle peut aimer en tant qu'autre. . . . Par la même ouverture, qui est son risque, elle sort d'elle-même pour aller à l'autre, voyageuse de l'inexploré, elle ne dénie pas, elle approche, non pour annuler l'écart, mais pour le voir, pour faire l'expérience de ce qu'elle n'est pas, qu'elle est, qu'elle peut être. [158–59]

I will say: today, writing is woman's. That is not a provocation, it means that woman admits there is some other. In her becoming-woman, she has not erased the bisexuality latent in the girl as in the boy. Femininity and bisexuality go together. . . . It is much harder for the man to let himself be traversed by some other. Writing is the passageway, the entrance, the exit, the dwelling-place of the other in me—the other that I am and am not, that I don't know how to be, but that I feel passing, that makes me live—that tears me apart, disturbs me, changes me, who?—a feminine one, a masculine one, some?—several, some unknown, which is indeed what gives me the desire to know and from which all life soars. This peopling leaves neither rest nor security, always disturbs the relationship to the "real," produces an uncertainty that gets in the way of the subject's socialization. It is distressing, it wears you out; and for men this permeability, this nonexclusion is a threat, something intolerable. . . . It is true that a certain receptivity is "feminine." One can, of course, as History has always done, exploit feminine reception as alienation. . . . But I am speaking here of femininity as keeping alive the other that is confided to her, that visits her, that she can love as other. . . . Through the same opening that is her danger, she comes out of herself to go to the other, a traveler in unexplored places; she does not deny, she approaches, not to do away with the space between, but to see it, to experience what she is not, what she is, what she can be. [85–86; trans. modified]

There is a potentially vertiginous effect set off by the series of semi-referential turns negotiated here. It begins with the first assertion, "aujour'hui l'écriture est aux femmes," which advances its sense only on the condition of a reciprocal untying of "écriture" and "femmes" from their ordinary, or "actual," referents. The assertion consists of a coassignment of each term's meaning to the other: hence (and henceforth: "aujourd'hui") I will say "writing" is that which is given over to "women" and, with the same gesture, that a "woman" is whoever is given to "writing." The coassignment in question, however, is less something to be asserted or described than forcefully put in play by the very practice that writes "writing" and "women" as each given over to the other, as the site of the admission "qu'il y ait de l'autre." It is, however, a *coup de force* against near insuperable odds, against the resistant logic of opposing names. For Cixous here would rename "women" with the name of the other even while retaining the same name. The text thus advances through *contradiction*, countering logical diction with force, which precipitates more than one difficulty.

For example: "Femininity and bisexuality go together. . . . It is much harder for the man to let himself be traversed by some other." If "femininity" is the welcome given to the other "that I am and am not" then linking it to or renaming it "bisexuality" appears to accommodate that welcome. Yet, the "bi-" also indicates a duality, one whose other face is recognizable by its symmetrically opposed features: man or masculinity, that which does not easily let itself be traversed by the other. There would thus seem to be a limit posed on the "bisexual" welcome given to the other, and it is the limit setting off "masculine" exclusion from the "feminine" welcome. But this limit determines a "bisexuality" that in effect excludes the "masculine," or, what amounts to the same, a "bisexuality" that is exclusively "feminine." Which is to say, a "bi-" that is precisely not dual or, still less, pluralized, but gathered up within a single and same concept, "la féminité," even as the latter is being rewritten here as the mark of a certain plurality. It would seem that the intractable logic of opposition has played its formidable hand to counter the text's pluralizing movement. In so doing, that logic uncovers a seemingly paradoxical *identity of the plural* constructed over against the identity of the same, "masculine" identity. But that is not all. For if, finally, a logic of identity prevails here over its pluralization, tracing a limit that falls between "feminine" and "masculine" along a division that remains in place despite the nominal introduction of "bisexuality," then there will have been all the same a crossing of the border between the two, a kind of contamination of the feminine by its masculine other. This crossing occurs less as a welcome laid out for the other, however, than as an unadmitted admission, when admission is refused to that which is defined as refusing admission to the other. But what is refused is thereby admitted since "féminité," if it wants to keep its name, must admit that for which the other is named "masculin": the desire, precisely, to keep its name and with that an identity. "Féminité" cannot name only itself precisely because it would name itself to the exclusion of the other name, the name of exclusion. And in that sense, which is the sense in question here, the "feminine" is "masculine." The price of keeping the name is losing it.

At the same time, with the same gesture, drawn here and crossed over is the limit of a possible theory of the "feminine," that is, of a certain concept of "woman" posed, or imposed, by its name. In the construction of "French feminist theory," is it not this limit that has to remain unremarked? Perhaps, however, in the appropriation of Cixous's writings for that construction, the limit has been translated, so to speak, into the limit of translation. That is, perhaps the fact that this appropriation has relied on limited translations can itself be interrogated for its theoretical import.

With its very name, "French feminist theory" presumes that the theory in question is translatable. And indeed what kind of theory could ever presume otherwise? Tied to an idiom, to a particular, singular linguistic site of formulation, theoretical concepts would be prevented from posing their universal, generalizable validity. Which is why, by "theory," we always also understand a certain theory of translation, in fact the necessity of a translation without remainder or resistance. "French feminist theory" is theoretical to the extent it is translatable. This explains in part why the construction could occur, or even had to occur, as a phenomenon in a language other than the original. (And given the presumption of translation, the "French" label, which cannot be the mark of linguistic particularity, ends up thematizing some unspecified cultural difference and provoking the sort of uneasy and defensive recuperations we saw in Sandra Gilbert's commentary.) By remarking the apparent resistance of Cixous's texts to translation in the ordinary sense, we are pointing once again to the notion of the semi-theoretical. Here "semi-" would mark the tie to a language or idiom, at the same time as it works to loosen the referential link, to open meaning's construction to the deconstruction of a future. Translation, in effect, has to reverse this process, at least in part: it reasserts referential value in order to sever the relation to the other language. The point, however, is not to reiterate this limit on translatability, and thus on theory, but to advance always under the necessity of thinking, in terms that are as rigorous as possible, the semi- (semi-theoretical, semi-translatable, semi-referential, semi-fictional), there where a difference crosses with the generality of the concept.

This necessity has been made more apparent than ever by the impasse into which a certain thinking of difference (gender difference, but not only gender difference, of course) seems to have been led in recent years. Naomi Schor is certainly not alone when she insists on "the urgency of rethinking the very terms of a conflict which all parties would agree has ceased to be productive."[9] The "conflict" is understood here as that between essentialism and anti-essentialism, one which Schor and others want to rethink in a way that will preserve an essential unity of the feminine without which feminism, as a theoretical construct and political position, seems incoherent. But whether one adopts the terms essentialism/anti-essentialism or others to qualify the nature of the opposition, the rethinking that is called for must finally rethink, which is to say displace, opposition itself as the struc-

9. "This Essentialism Which Is Not One: Coming To Grips With Irigaray," *Differences* I (Summer 1989): 40.

turing concept of difference. This is the condition of marking a difference, making a difference that does not return, like a debt to be paid, to
the concept of the same.

In a note to the same essay, Schor writes: "The question that arises
is: how to theorize a subjectivity that does not reinscribe the universal,
that does not constitute itself by simultaneously excluding and incorporating others?" (56, n.5) If indeed such a question arises, is it not
given its impetus by the experience of a certain impossibility at the
heart of such a theorization? An experience that is inscribed in the very
terms of the question as posed here? It asks: what would a subject be
that excludes exclusion and yet at the same time avoids incorporation
of what it does not exclude? But this question soon begets others, for
example: How can such a subject exclude exclusion without excluding
itself as nonexclusive? And what would be the difference, finally, between this wished-for subject-in-theory and the classical subject described as "simultaneously excluding and incorporating others"? Each
is consigned to an *essential* impossibility of reserving the subject exclusively for itself and no other. Each is delivered over to the experience
of the impossibility of being its own subject, of presenting itself to
itself without difference, without delay, without others. The wished-
for theorization is, moreover, the very form in which this impossibility
imposes its limit at every moment on my experience of a subjectivity
which is never "mine." For the subject in question is already theorized,
that is, it has the form of a general concept, and this theorization or
generalization is the condition of its impossible appropriation by anyone, any *one*. A call to retheorize the subject, in order more properly to
take account of the differences that remain uninscribed by the universal, must set out from this limit on appropriation, rather than from the
wishful desire to lift it so as finally to overcome the exclusion of exclusion. It is as the site of the experience of the impossible that the "subject" in all its difference from "itself" can be rethought otherwise than
as a new inscription of the exclusive universal; an experience of the
impossible, which is to say, of the other. This task for an active thinking cannot be reduced, however, to a theorization of the limit or the
impossible appropriation: at some point, it will have to encounter that
limit *in itself* as the limit posed, each time differently, to the theorization it would perform. Of necessity, the theory in question, if it is to be
rigorous, must affirm itself as semi-theory. What is needed and what is
called for is not, therefore, a new theory of the "subject," for that
project always lures one with the promise of appropriation, of a finally

appropriate concept of difference in all its difference. Rather, it is to the possibility of the semi- (the possibility, if you will, of an impossible name) that the excluded other of the subject calls.

"The semi-" would be here an impossible name, a semi-name for that which each time must be addressed differently. With its hyphen, or *trait d'union*, it signals the space within the name of a heterogeneity, that for which there is no common measure other than the minimal mark of coappearance—minimal, almost weightless as it waits for the other's approach. A spacing . . . that which gives place to writing.

SECOND APPROACH

Toward the end of *Limonade tout était si infini*, the writer recounts a remarkable event. It is a *grazing* encounter, which nevertheless has the force of a tremendous explosion. A man (F.) was taken by his friend (M.) to meet a third (O.) who was blind. When the two were presented to each other, standing face to face, F., the visitor, silently executed a bow of the head to O. in acknowledgment. This gesture, unseen by the one to whom it was addressed, nevertheless managed to touch him because when the visitor, who was Franz Kafka, lowered his head, his hair *grazed* the blind man's forehead. Neither Kafka nor his friend, Max Brod, knew what had happened, but the third man, the addressee, consigned his experience the next day to a typewritten account, which Cixous transcribes in part as follows:

> Ce fut comme si la foudre m'avait frappé. J'ai éprouvé au contact de ces cheveux une douleur inavouable à mes amis, mais c'était *une joie* qui m'a causé cette douleur: je n'ai pu retenir mes larmes. Elles semblaient jaillir directement de mon coeur. Alors, comme si par la violence du ruissellement, une toile de nuit était arrachée de mes pupilles, j'ai cru voir—je mens—: j'ai vu—avec certitude,—de mes yeux comme si je voyais soudain la lumière. [245–46]

> It was as if lightning had struck me. At the contact of that hair, I felt a pain which I could not confess to my friends, but that pain caused me *a joy;* I could not hold back my tears. They seemed to flow directly from my heart. Then, as if by the violence of the flow, a veil of night was torn from my pupils: I thought I saw—I am lying—I did see, with certainty, with my eyes as if I were suddenly seeing the light.

"For the first time," he wrote, "someone considered my infirmity to be a fact that concerned only myself" (244).

The writer of *Limonade* recounts this extraordinary event with infinite caution so as not to crush its diaphanous miracle with words. "Ce qui rend cette scène si fragile, un mot pourrait la briser, c'est qu'elle n'a pour ainsi dire presque pas de lieu, parce qu'elle s'est passée dans l'invisible. L'indicible délicatesse du geste: c'est de faire signe à voir devant un homme aveugle: et ainsi de ne pas le priver du plus diaphane respect" [What makes this scene so fragile, which could be broken by a word, is the fact that it almost does not take place, so to speak, because it happened in the invisible. The unsayable delicacy of the gesture: to make a sign for sight in front of a blind man, and thus not to deprive him of the most diaphanous respect] (241). "Chaque mot jette plus d'ombre" [Each word casts more shadow] (ibid). "Peut-être que j'ai utilisé des mots trop gros, trop visibles?" [Perhaps I have used words that are too gross, too visible?] (240). Like Kafka, she would bring an extreme discretion to the encounter with the other. Called upon to render a silent gesture and an invisible touch, words are too loud, too visible. And yet, the grazed forehead also touches the dream of an impossible address for the Cixousian writer, "the secret dream of writing," which is to be "as delicate as silence." To write of this scene is to dream of reproducing it, to take it as the model of writing. But it is an ungraspable model, or rather, it is the ungraspable as at once model and without model, at once a generalizable, repeatable mark and an unreproducible singularity. This doubled mark is the mark of a dreamed-of writing. How so?

Kafka bows his head to the other. He executes, that is, a highly conventional gesture signifying respect, assent, greeting, or obedience, but which, precisely because it belongs to the code of polite address, does not address his interlocutor specifically. Instead, it is a general address, and the respect it signifies is a function of this generality. It addresses the other as, in effect, the same as all those to whom one owes respect, regardless of any and all difference. More precisely, it acknowledges the other as other than him- or herself, as more than or greater than a contingent, finite self, and finally, it addresses its respect to no one in particular, but to a concept of the other as that to which respect is owed.[10] This is the condition of iterability of any mark, here the mark of respect. While it is usually buried beneath the very convention it makes possible, this condition of repetition is made to appear in a singular manner in the event recounted by Cixous's writer. It appears,

10. Cf. *The Critique of Practical Reason* where Kant defines duty [*Pflicht*] as the respect owed to the moral law (Part I, Book I, Chap. 3).

so to speak, in its invisibility to the blind man for whom the conventional address seems most inappropriate. But because the mark is inappropriate with regard to his blindness, because it addresses him without respect to this contingency but in the mode of respect for a general concept of the other, it closes a gulf there where a different, though no less general mark (grasping the hand, for example) would have had no such effect.

This is not all, however, for it does not yet account for the effect of the doubling of the mark. Kafka bows his head to the other. He touches his interlocutor, *this one and no other*, with the same gesture that repeats a general address. This other mark is accidental, contingent, inadvertant, and therefore singular, but also indissociable from the conventional, deliberate, and general mark. The stunning effect of the episode derives, finally, from this indissociability, from the fact that the same gesture does and does not address the other in his singularity, does and does not address the other as general concept. The one and the other indissociably, and thus effectively. If the accident had not accompanied the execution of the gesture, then of course the blind man would not have known he had been addressed as he was, which is to say, not as himself but as a general other. But precisely because he did perceive the mark—*he himself and no other*—it was no longer simply the general mark he perceived, but that mark doubled by its singular address. What has occurred, no less by chance than by convention, is an implication of the singular in the general and vice versa, the one made possible by and given to the other: difference literally grazes, crosses its general concept.

In what sense is this event an event of writing? In the sense that its sense is disseminated, and therefore there can be gift, something given without return and without reappropriation. Cixous is here thinking through the paradoxical noneconomy of the gift, more powerfully and consequently than in the semi-theoretical terms advanced in *The Newly Born Woman*. In the earlier essay, what is called gift does not give without taking, without reappropriating what is given in a return to the giver. Nevertheless, a distinction is made there between two kinds of "giving-for," which are in turn aligned with masculine and feminine economies of identity:

Dans le mouvement du désir, de l'échange, [l'homme] est partie *prenante:* la perte, la dépense, est prise dans l'opération commerciale qui fait toujours du don un don-qui-prend. Le don rapporte. La perte se

transforme au bout d'une ligne courbe en son contraire et lui revient
sous forme de gain.

Mais est-ce qu'à cette loi du retour la femme échappe? Est-ce qu'on
peut parler d'une autre dépense? En vérité, il n'y a pas de don "gratuit".
On ne donne jamais pour rien. Mais toute la différence est dans le
pourquoi et le comment du don, dans les valeurs que le geste de donner
affirme, fait circuler; dans le type de bénéfice que tire le donateur du
don, et l'usage qu'il en fait. . . .

Elle aussi donne pour. Elle aussi donnant se donne—plaisir, bon-
heur, valeur augmentée, image rehaussée d'elle-même. Mais ne cher-
che pas "à rentrer dans ses frais". Elle peut ne pas revenir à elle, ne se
posant jamais, se répandant, allant partout à l'autre. [160–61]

In the movement of desire, of exchange, he is the en-grossing party;
loss and expense are stuck in the commercial deal that always turns
the gift into a gift-that-takes. The gift brings in a return. Loss, at the
end of the curve, is turned into its opposite and comes back to him as
profit.

But does woman escape this law of return? Can one speak of another spending? Really, there is no "free" gift. You never give something
for nothing. But all the difference lies in the why and how of the gift, in
the values that the gesture of giving affirms, causes to circulate; in the
type of profit the giver draws from the gift and the use to which he or
she puts it. . . .

She too gives *for.* She too, with open hands, gives (to) herself—
pleasure, happiness, increased value, enhanced self-image. But she
doesn't try to "recover her expenses." She is able not to return to herself, never settling down, pouring out, going everywhere to the other.
(87; trans. modified)

Once again, the practice of semi-reference is set to work detaching
"woman" from an actual referent and reattaching it to another, here to
the gift that does not return to the giver, in other words, to dissemination. But as we saw in the earlier passage, the logic of identity is also
working to counter the effort to pluralize or de-propriate the "proper"
of femininity. The consequence is a return of the feminine to itself,
which finally gives itself the gift of its own generosity, an "enhanced
self-image." Unlike in the passage we cited above from the same text,
however, this consequence is conceded at the outset when Cixous
writes, "Really, there is no 'free' gift. You never give something for
nothing." As these categorical assertions ought to make plain, it cannot be a question of distinguishing between gift and nongift, but rather
only between two ways of taking back the "gift," two ways, therefore,
of taking what one gives. If, however, there is no gift that is not already

a gift-for, that is, a giving-in-order-to-get-back, then what can it mean to write of "la femme," as Cixous does here: "She is able not to return to herself, never settling down, pouring out, going everywhere to the other"? And then to add, in another attempt to contradict the stated law of identity and of the nongift, "S'il y a un 'propre' de la femme, c'est paradoxalement sa capacité de se dé-proprier sans calcul . . . " (161–62) [If there is a self proper to woman, paradoxically it is her capacity to depropriate herself without self-interest] (87)?

What it *can* mean is a certain possibility of *thinking* the gift (and thus a woman "able not to return to herself") beyond or despite its impossibility in fact or in reality, beyond and despite the fact that "there is no 'free' gift." This fact or reality of the nongift comes down to and comes back to its subject, whether giver or receiver. So long as the gift is considered only in the form of gift-for-a-subject, then it can only be a matter of more or less taking, a matter of degrees of the nongift. In this regard, the "masculine" nongift would be but a version of the "feminine"—or vice versa. What would be a gift that returns to neither, to no subject, to no instance of appropriation? An impossible gift since, as Derrida has written in a recent essay that advances far onto the same terrain,

> Pour qu'il y ait don . . . il faut, à la limite, que [le donataire] ne *reconnaisse* pas le don comme don. S'il le reconnaît *comme* don, si le don lui *apparaît comme tel,* si le présent lui est présent *comme présent,* cette simple reconnaissance suffit pour annuler le don. . . . *A la limite, le don comme don* devrait *ne pas apparaître comme don: ni au donataire, ni au donateur.* Il ne peut être don comme don qu'en n'étant pas présent comme don.[11]

> For there to be gift . . . it is thus necessary, at the limit, that [the donor] not *recognize* the gift as gift. If he recognizes it *as* gift, if the gift *appears to him as such,* if the present is present to him *as present,* this simple recognition suffices to annul the gift. . . . *At the limit, the gift as gift* ought *not to appear as gift; either to the donee or the donor.* It cannot be gift as gift except by not being present as gift.[12]

The gift can never be (a) present, a gift as such, that is, it cannot present itself *for* a subject. As Cixous had intimated when she wrote "you never give something for nothing," the gift cancels itself out in the "gift-for" by which a subject capitalizes its loss. Derrida works through

---

11. *Donner le temps. 1. La fausse monnaie* (Paris: Galilée, 1991), 26–27; Derrida's emphases.
12. *Given Time, I: Counterfeit Money,* trans. Peggy Kamuf (Chicago: Chicago University Press, 1992), 13–14.

this aporia to the point at which the gift disappears with the very appearance of this subject. The gift is annulled

> dès qu'il y a un sujet, dès que donateur et donataire se constitutent en sujets identiques, identifiables, capables de s'identifier en se gardant et en se nommant. Il s'agit même là, dans ce cercle, du mouvement de subjectivation, de la rétention constitutive du sujet qui s'identifie avec lui-même. . . . La question du don devrait ainsi chercher son lieu avant tout rapport au sujet, avant tout rapport à soi du sujet, conscient ou inconscient. . . . On serait même tenté de dire qu'un sujet comme tel ne donne ni ne reçoit jamais un don. [38–39]

> as soon as there is a subject, as soon as donor and donee are constituted as identical, identifiable subjects, capable of identifying themselves by keeping and naming themselves. It is even a matter, in this circle, of the movement of subjectivation, of the constitutive retention of the subject that identifies with itself. . . . The question of the gift should therefore seek its place before any relation to the subject, before any conscious or unconscious relation to self of the subject. . . . One would even be tempted to say that a subject as such never gives or receives a gift. [23–24]

This "place" of the question of the gift "before any relation to the subject, before any conscious or unconscious relation to self of the subject," is what Derrida has been calling trace, differance, writing in the general sense: "il n'y a de problématique du don qu'à partir d'une problématique conséquente de la trace et du texte" (130) [that is why there is a problematic of the gift only on the basis of a consistent problematic of the trace and the text] (100). For a subject, the gift is impossible, but the *thinking* of this impossibility is opened up where an economy of the proper can only turn in its own circles:

> Car enfin, si le don est un autre nom de l'impossible, nous le pensons pourtant, nous le nommons, nous le désirons. Nous en avons l'intention. Et cela *même si,* ou *parce que, dans la mesure où jamais* nous ne le rencontrons, jamais ne le connaissons, jamais ne le vérifions, jamais ne l'expérimentons dans son existence présente ou dans son phéno- mène. Le don *lui-même,* nous n'oserons pas dire le don *en soi,* jamais ne se confondra avec la présence de son phénomène. Il n'y a peut-être de nomination, de langage, de pensée, de désir ou d'intention que là où il y a ce mouvement pour penser encore, désirer, nommer ce qui ne se donne ni à connaître, ni à expérimenter ni à vivre. [45]

> For, finally, if the gift is another name of the impossible, we still think it, we name it, we desire it. We intend it. And this *even if* or *because* or

to the extent that we *never* encounter it, we never know it, we never verify it, we never experience it in its present existence or in its phenomenon. The gift *itself*—we dare not say the gift *in itself*—will never be confused with the presence of its phenomenon. Perhaps there is nomination, language, thought, desire, or intention only there where there is this movement still for thinking, desiring, naming that which gives itself to be neither known, experienced, nor lived. [29]

It is to this possibility of the impossible, to the movement of thought, desire, and naming in the absence of an apparent phenomenon of gift, that Cixous's writing is given over. In *Limonade*, the writing finds an emblem in Kafka's gesture. His is an effacement that nevertheless inscribes itself with the lightest of touches. "L'ineffaçable de l'histoire, c'est l'effacement de F.: pour faire un geste aussi délicat, il faut être devenu aussi transparent qu'une libellule, aussi léger qu'une sauterelle" [What is ineffaceable in the story is F.'s effacement: in order to make such a delicate gesture, one has to have become as transparent as a dragonfly, as light as a grasshopper] (241). In rewriting this ineffaceability, Cixous transports the desired qualities of transparency and lightness on the syllabic wings or *ailes* of two names: *libellule, sauterelle*. It is a most delicate operation for it would disseminate the ineffaceable effacement throughout a text woven with the repetition of "ell."[13] Ell, as in the name of the beloved Elli, to whom the writer would send a first letter of love. But with that name, one reads—or rather she reads—the letter's forwarding to a general *elle (qui) lit*, she (who) reads. To Elli, to elle-lit, she would send, that is, give, with a gesture that repeats the transparency and the lightness of the grazing dragonfly and leaping grasshopper. A double gesture in one: addressed to Elli alone, but comprehended in a general address to every "elle (qui) lit." But how to give without weighing down with debt?

> Comment faire pour lui dire "je veux que tu te saches libre" sans que la phrase l'attrape entre ses pattes de mots, même pour la caresser et, dans son désir de lui confier sa bonne intention, l'oblige à freiner? . . . Et la question est: peut-on donner sans faire part? Comment faire part sans

13. There are other creatures on the list, *hirondelle, gazelle*, and *tourterelle*, but it also includes *aile, ocelle, femelle, jumelle, échelle, demoiselle, sorcellerie, patelle, étincelle, appel, dentelle, élégance* ("élégance de sauterelle," 262), *lamelle, cellule* ("C'est la cellule mélodique de tout un livre," 275), *frêle*, and the proper names Kohelet and Dominicella. One could also follow the other syllable 'li' toward the "Livre Ultime" and, of course, the first syllable of the ultimate sentence "limonade tout était si infini." As disseminated, disseminating points of the text, the syllables pinpoint the resistance to translation.

parole? Le silence aussi est de parole . . . Car penser les mystères du donner, qui sont aussi délicats que les ailes de papillon, demandait une délicatesse de même nature exactement. Rien que d'y penser lui faisait sentir son propre pesant. [18–20]

How can I say to her "I want you to know you are free" without the sentence catching her between its paw-like words, if only to caress her, and in its desire to confide in her its good intention, obliging her to slow down? . . . And the question is: can one give without taking part? How to let something be known without words? Silence is also speech. . . . For to think the mysteries of giving, which are as delicate as butterfly wings, required a delicacy of exactly the same nature. Just thinking about it made her feel her own heaviness.

In contrast to this heaviness, there is Kafka's effacement, his address to the other that manages to give without incurring debt. But how so, exactly? "Le merveilleux de cette histoire c'est comment F. arrive à donner, même si O. n'est pas en mesure de recevoir" [The marvelous thing about this story is how F. manages to give, even if O. is not up to receiving]. And yet "le don est bien reçu" (243) [the gift is well received]. It is received, and well received, because an incalculable difference opens up within the address, which sends it off beyond any possibility of return: "Le miracle avait déjà commencé à avoir lieu. Reste le trait de plus: l'effacement inattendu de l'effacement de F." [The miracle had already begun to take place. Remains the additional trait: the unexpected effacement of F.'s effacement] (ibid.). The effacement of the effacement, what we might call the splitting between its two faces, is a mark of which there is no author, no one to whom a debt is due. It is the uncalculated, incalculable chance whereby the general gesture is split by the grazing touch of a singular address. In that split moment, there is a gift that calls for no return, no gratitude, no recognition. The splitting cuts across, so to speak, the two sides to the encounter, as each is divided by the incalculable address; neither coincides with himself in that moment and from that moment, and this noncoincidence is the space of the encounter with the other.

For Cixous, this space of encounter, of writing, or of dissemination of the gift remains *impossible* not because it is wholly imaginary as some would have it, but because the noncoincidence with the other cannot be made present to a subject. Nor does this impossibility signal toward some utopian escape from the gravity of the world's affairs. For the gravest of questions in that world is still: what *takes place* in the approach to the other? Or, to put it in other terms, what gives there?

What gives beyond the calculations of exchange, the taking grasp of appropriation? What place is *given* that is not already taken back?

To give place is not an idiomatic English expression. To think its necessity requires an approach to the idiom of the other, to the untranslatability of the *donner lieu*, to that place-less place in which the impossible encounter takes place as a giving of place beyond or before any give-and-take. A place-less place or a silent word, unballasted of even the slightest weight, a breathless word, perhaps, *hors d'haleine*, extenuated from its effort of leaping at the impossible, à la *sauterelle*, of understanding (as we read in a phrase we will leave untranslated so as to give place to the other's breath and the other's name) "non avec des phrases de haute voix mais plutôt avec l'haleine du sang d'âme" (189).

MARY LYDON

Re-Translating no Re-Reading no, rather: Rejoycing (with) Hélène Cixous[1]

At Cerisy I was struck by the fact that women were speaking, for the first time so consistently, without taking the 'masculine position'— that is, they did not adhere to a discourse that was conceptual, philosophical, or academic. Apart from some exceptions (there are always exceptions) they were more direct, they were not defensive about their work or what they created. Here I am thinking of Hélène Cixous. The way she spoke was quite exceptional—I would even say independently of content.

—Serge Leclaire

Given the individualist orientation of Cixous's theory, it is perhaps not surprising that some of her students should present her politics as a simple prolongation of her persona.

—Toril Moi

Toi écrire? Mais pour qui te prends-tu? . . . "Pour personne." Et c'était vrai: je me prenais pour personne.
You write? But who do you take yourself for? . . . "Nobody." And it was true: I took myself for nobody.

—Hélène Cixous, 1976

1. My intention is to echo the title of Cixous's essay, "Sans arrêt non Etat de Dessination non, plutôt: Le Décollage du Bourreau," in *Repentirs* (Paris: Editions de la Réunion des musées nationaux, 1991), 55–64, translated by Catherine A. F. McGillivray as "Without End no State of Drawingness no, rather: The Executioner's Taking Off," *New Literary History* 24/1 (February 1993), 91–103. Inspired by a series of drawings in the Louvre, notably Rembrandt's "Beheading of John the Baptist," "Without End" brilliantly and lucidly expresses the desire for "the before of a book" ("l'avant d'un livre"), for "the forest that comes before the book, the abundance of leaves [*la foison de feuilles*] that come before the pages," that has animated Cixous's writing from the outset. Hence the tentative form of the title, which like a drawing in an artist's sketchbook, allows us to see the multiple lines of thought from which it emerged. Except where otherwise indicated, all the translations in the present essay are my own.

YFS 87, *Another Look, Another Woman,* ed. Huffer, © 1995 by Yale University.

I'm Nobody! Who are You?
Are you - Nobody - Too?
Then there's a pair of us
Don't tell! They'd advertise - you know!

How dreary - to be - Somebody!
How public - like a Frog -
To tell one's name - the livelong June -
To an admiring Bog!

—Emily Dickinson

Qui donc pourrait "se prendre pour" un personnage?
Who on earth could "take themselves for" a character?
—Hélène Cixous, 1987

Pas d'histoire sans M. Sans elle—Sans Marge pas de place pour la
scène des hommes.
No (hi)story without M. Without her—Without Marge no room for
the men's scene.
—Hélène Cixous, 1976

In 1986 Hélène Cixous published a volume of essays, written between 1976 and 1983, called *Entre l'écriture*.[2] As it strikes the Francophone ear, this enigmatic and virtually untranslatable title asks to be read between the lines, invites us, for instance, to take *entre* here not simply as a preposition ("between") but as a verb ("enter"), and consequently to read *Entre l'écriture* as though it were a stage direction; to translate it, by analogy with "Enter Hamlet," for example, as "Enter Writing." (Let me remark parenthetically that the ambiguity of *Entre l'écriture*, hence the difficulty of rendering it adequately in English, usefully illustrates the immediacy, the urgency with which the issue of translation, or better, translatability, asserts itself whenever Cixous is the subject. This is so to a greater degree in her case than it is for any other writer associated [as in the minds of her North American readers Cixous, willy-nilly, remains] with what we have come to call "French feminisms." Indeed it may well be the unique challenge her writing issues to translation that, more than anything, distinguishes it from the various other writing practices that have been grouped together under this rubric.)

2. Paris: des femmes, 1986. Subsequent references will appear in the text using the abbreviation *EL*.

The privilege Cixous has consistently granted to the imaginary and the body (a penchant which finds its happiest expression perhaps in her writing for the theater), not to mention the performative use she makes of her own compelling persona, would also favor a dramatic approach (the approach implicit in "Enter Writing") to what she authorizes us to refer to as her *oeufvre*.[3] It seems therefore quite appropriate to open this essay with a scene or tableau: the first tableau, let us call it, not just for chronology's sake, but to arouse the echo of one of Cixous's own titles, "The Last Tableau or the Portrait of God," and thus to draw attention, mimetically, to the degree to which echo no less than translation is an energizing force in Cixous's writing.[4]

Time: June 1975.

Place: Paris.

Scene: A makeshift lecture hall at 28, rue des Francs Bourgeois, where *la bibliothèque publique d'information* of the as yet unfinished Centre Georges Pompidou is nominally housed.

Enter representatives from the research collective on English poetics (*le collectif de recherche en poétique anglaise*) from l'Université de Paris VIII. All male, with one notable exception, they are scheduled to perform a joint reading of *Finnegans Wake*, pages 162–66, before the assembled company of the Fifth International James Joyce Symposium. The exception, "undistributed middle between males"—Joyce, as always has a word for it, *avant la lettre*—will turn out to be Hélène Cixous, whom I, like the majority of the audience (not many of us are French) am seeing and hearing for the first time.[5]

The entrance of this woman, immediately identifiable as a "cleopatrician in her own right" (*FW*, 166), a vision Joyce's phrase will subsequently serve to confirm, even as she assumes the role, or *personnage*, his words will have already evoked (but this is the very configura-

3. This portmanteau word which combines "oeuf" (egg) and "oeuvre" wittily acknowledges the important symbolic role of the egg (and consequently of hens and chickens) in the elaboration of Cixous's *oeufvre*. See especially 70 and 126 in *Entre L'Ecriture* for dazzling and quite untranslatable riffs on the *oeufvre* and what she calls the *oeuf d'art*, the egg/oeuvre d'art.

4. "Le dernier portrait ou le portrait de Dieu (1983) Inédit" in *Entre L'Ecriture*, 171–201. A translation of this essay under the title "The Last Painting or the Portrait of God" appears in Hélène Cixous, *Coming to Writing and Other Essays*, ed. Deborah Jenson, with an introductory essay by Susan Suleiman (Cambridge: Harvard University Press, 1991), 104–31.

5. See James Joyce, *Finnegans Wake* (New York: The Viking Press, 1939; rpt. 1947), 164. Future references to the *Wake* in the text will use the abbreviation *FW*.

tion of what constitutes an event, in Derrida's account) not surprisingly creates something of a stir. The curly black hair, cut close to
the contours of the shapely head, the long neck, the well-defined pro-
file, the large almond eyes, elaborately and skillfully made up, all these
highly distinctive features irresistibly and, as the maquillage and coif-
fure would suggest, consciously, recall Cleopatra as avatar of Nefertiti.
The costume, on the other hand, "a very 'dressy' affair" (FW, 166), is in
la dernière mode, hence unmistakably and stunningly Parisian.[6] It
consists of a full high-waisted frock in a rich dark brown or black
velvet, with an embroidered bodice and extravagantly puffed sleeves in
a gauzy white fabric: a dramatic and highly effective contrast, both in
colour and texture, to the rest of the outfit. Black high-heeled shoes
with a demurely retro strap across the instep and white stockings
complete the ensemble, which is as remote from the image of the
bluestocking or basbleu as its wearer, when she speaks, will prove to be
from what she will dub, deftly making the pejorative basbleu boomer-
ang, the "basbleurre."[7]

"Basbleurre," a characteristic example of Cixous's inspired neo-
Joycean neologisms, is designed to evoke the "babbler" (pronounced
with a French accent), the speaking subject as the product of a reductive masculine economy: the fallout, so to speak, of a relation to language that is based on the loss of part of one's originary substance,
hence the analogy to butter (beurre) which is produced by being sepa-
rated from milk, its consistency achieved at the expense of lactic flow.[8]
"Du lait au basbleurre," "From milk to basbleurre" (a word in which
butter, babble, Babel, bluestocking—originally a masculine item of
clothing, incidentally—lowdown [bas] and lure [leurre] are all operative) describes the cycle, the governing principle, of the masculine
economy according to Cixous. Readers of Lacan will readily detect an
ironic reference here to his claim that the emergence of the speaking
subject is contingent on the acceptance of castration, but "basbleurre"
may in addition be read as a thinking woman's riposte to the pejorative

6. The expression "la dernière mode" is an echo of Mallarmé's women's magazine,
La Dernière Mode. I argue that fashion has served writers in ways that are far from
frivolous in my "Skirting the Issue: Mallarmé, Proust, and Symbolism," Yale French
Studies 74 (1988): 157–81. An expanded version of this essay will appear in Skirting the
Issue: Essays in Literary Theory, forthcoming from the University of Wisconsin Press.
7. Cixous, "La Missexualité où jouis-je? 1976" in Entre L'Ecriture, 90.
8. "Consistency" here is meant to evoke that quality for which the discourse of the
basbleurre is most highly prized. The symbolic value of milk in Cixous's writing would
demand a separate, lengthy discussion.

basbleu.[9] Thus the term *basbleu* is effectively returned to sender via "basbleurre," a neologism that challenges the law of language and, thus, the very masculine economy that it ("basbleurre") is designed, mockingly, to represent, and of which it is the derisive emblem. (In the course of her presentation, Cixous will evoke what she calls "the young *missives* [letters and misses] from the unconscious of *Finnegans Wake*, who habitually, obsessively, sexpedite [sic] themselves to their dispatchers" ["jeunes *missives* de l'inconscient de *Finnegans Wake*, elles ont l'habitude, manie, de sexpédier elles-mêmes à leur renvoyeurs" (*EL*, 78)]. The neologism "renvoyeur," created by adding a supplementary "r" to "envoyeur" (sender) sounds what might be called (echoing "missive") a *dis*missive note, since "renvoyer" means among other things, to dismiss or to fire, a nuance I have tried to preserve with "dispatchers.") Thus by "sexpedit[ing] themselves to their dispatchers" the young missives at once assert their sexual difference and refuse to be dismissed: the strategy, precisely, of Hélène Cixous's unique missexual writing. But it is time to return to June 1975, and to 28, rue des Francs Bourgeois.

The members of the research collective have by now taken their seats on the platform and the reading is about to begin. At this remove I retain nothing of what any of the men said, however engaging it may have been, but even without recourse to the text, published the following year in *Poétique*, as "La Missexualité où jouis-je?" and subsequently reprinted in *Entre l'écriture*, though never to my knowledge translated (and for good reason), Cixous's performance of Joyce's "Marge" remains as vividly present to me today as when I first heard and saw it some twenty years ago.[10]

Since, unfortunately, I cannot reproduce the relevant pages from *Finnegans Wake* in their entirety here, much less attempt to explicate them (turn to Cixous for a brilliant reading), the following brief excerpt must suffice to provide a taste of Joyce's scene, in which Burrus and Caseous (alias Butter and Cheese)—one of the many pairs of warring brothers in *Finnegans Wake*—vie for Miss Marge's favor, which she however bestows, imperially, on a third party.

9. The term "bluestocking," defined as "woman having or affecting literary tastes and learning," derives in fact from a masculine item of clothing, as the *Concise Oxford Dictionary* (Fifth Edition, 1954) informs us: "Blue Stocking Society (in sense 'not in full evening dress') name given to meetings about 1750 at houses of Mrs. Montagu etc. to talk on literature etc. instead of playing cards; blue-worsted, i.e. ordinary stockings were worn by some of the men attending instead of black silk."

10. See *Poétique* 26 (1976): 240–49, and *Entre L'Ecriture*, 73–95.

Margareena she's very fond of Burrus but, alick and alack! She velly
fond of chee. (The important influence exercised on everything by this
eastasian import has not been till now fully flavoured though we can
comfortably taste it in this case. I shall come back for a little more say
further on.) A cleopatrician in her own right she at once complicates
the position while Burrus and Caseous are contending for her misstery
by implicating herself with an elusive Antonius, a wop who would
appear to hug a personal interest in refined chees of all chades at the
same time as he wags an antomine art of being rude like the boor. [FW,
166–67]

Making her entrance as a "cleopatrician in her own right" among
the males of the research collective, Cixous was quite clearly taking
herself for Margareen: not only *Marge la reine*, the imperial Margareena (though her certainly) but equally the peripheral Marge ("undistributed middle between males"), so that no less than her prototype,
her "misstery," "the secret of [her] imperial power," might be seen to
lie precisely "in the margin between Miss/and miss," "la marge entre
Miss/et miss (manquer)," between Miss and lack (*EL*, 91). Following
her own injunction to join forces with the letter to the point of em-
bodying it ("fais corps avec la lettre" [*EL*, 51]), Cixous, in a delicious
parody of the text at hand, *played* (fleshed out, in the strong theatrical
sense of the French *incarner*) her reading of it, showing, in the process,
exactly how one might stage the "entre," bring the marg(in) onto the
scene of writing (or reading, the two being always interchangeable for
her). Thus reading (writing) with Joyce, Cixous responded to the question she herself would raise, the question that in her view continues to
haunt the philosophy of Derrida: the question, that is, of how to incor-
porate the limit, "how to introduce the 'inter (the between)?' the
marg(in)?" ["comment faire entrer 'l'entre'? la marge?" (*EL*, 81)].

Far from underwriting the essentialism with which her notorious
endorsement of so-called "feminine writing" has since repeatedly
been taxed,[11] Cixous's reading of "Sweet Margareen," female (and
vegetable) substitute for the male characters (and animal products)
Burrus and Caseous, butter and cheese, drew attention rather to the
unstable underpinnings of what Derrida would later call "the law of

11. Catherine A.F. MacGillivray, in her excellent introduction to Cixous, *Manna:
For the Mandelstams, For the Mandelas*, trans. Catherine A.F. MacGillivray (Minneapolis: University of Minnesota Press, 1994), notes that the term "écriture féminine,"
though it has been so closely associated with her critical and writing practice, did not
originate with Cixous. See McGillivray, xliii.

genre": an instability that Joyce "looking wantingly around our undistributed middle between males" (*FW*, 164) had already introduced in the person of the "cowrymaid M" (a coinage one is tempted to imagine, à la Boticelli, as a kind of mock milkmaid on the half shell).[12]

Once she appears, though it will never be for more than a flash, Marge's effect, as Cixous's performance so successfully demonstrated, is dramatic. Thus in an uncanny (and hilarious) reproduction of the scene Joyce is describing and she is reading, the research collective, through the agency of Cixous/Marge, could be observed slowly to take shape, its male figures mustering a semblance of masculine solidarity, just as in *Finnegans Wake*, Cixous tells us, B and C top off their triangle, achieve closure when supplemented by A (Antonius) whom Marge the Cleopatrician brings into the fold by "implicating herself" with him. Thus she writes (reading Joyce):

> Enter the Cleopatrician.
>
> As Marge she strangely obliges the headless triangular figure made up of B and C to complete, to close itself. She triangulates them, then, with a. n. other [*avec de l'autre*],[13] but that other, - *A* is not her, it is under *A*, with *A*, in complicity with Antony that she binds the liaison. . . . It takes no less than three morsels of men for some modicum of man to manage to arise. She binds men together. It takes three sons to make a father. Or two plus A. . . . And it is she, as *Cléopâtre*, who has the key-of-the-father [*la clé-du-père*]. [*EL,* 89]

Readers of Freud and Lacan will recognize an old refrain here, though modulated into a different key, as it were. A long chapter might be written, for instance, on the implications of her teasing appropriation of Lacan's *Autre* (Other) with a capital "A," but Cixous's writing is attuned to its object, Joyce's text, that is to say to poetry, and hence avoids taking its pitch overtly from "a discourse that [is] conceptual, philosophical or academic," despite the fact that this discourse is

12. "Cowrie, -y, n. shell of a small gastropoid found in the Indian Ocean, used as money in Africa and S. Asia." (*Concise Oxford Dictionary*). In addition to "cowrie," the word "cowrymaid" contains "cow" which produces the association to "dairy" and hence to "dairymaid" on which "cowrymaid" was modelled to begin with. Joyce thus anticipates, in this single neologism, volumes of debate on the exchange of women, from Lévi-Strauss to Derrida. With regard to "the law of genre" see Jacques Derrida, "La Loi du genre," in *Parages* (Paris: Editions Galilée, 1986), translated by Avital Ronell as "The Law of Genre," *Glyph* 7 (1980): 176–232, rpt., *Critical Inquiry* 7/1 (1980): 55–81.

13. "a. n. other" (my translation for the partitive "de l'autre") was suggested to me by the convention followed in British newspapers for marking the place of as yet unnamed, because unselected, members of football teams, etc.

continuously present *en sourdine*, humming along, that is, with her music, for whomever has ears to hear. Thus, for example, *la clé-du-père* (molded on the name "Cléopâtre," with its *clé* and its *pater*) is a subversively "feminine" substitute (like *marge* vis-à-vis butter) for Lacan's *Nom-du-Père* (Name-of-the-Father). A brilliantly judged stroke, "Cléopâtre" gives a provocative new twist to Lacan's canonical formula, one that moreover opens the Freudian field to the neuter, the Miss, *das Mädchen*, the "slip of a girl" (*EL*, 87) on whose "implications," it is strongly suggested, the closure of the Oedipal triangle depends.[14] Cixous's brilliant set of variations and improvisations on the Joycean (and Lacanian) themes ("A capacity for improvisation should mark a reading process that is feminine," she will later write[15]) is an object lesson in how to get Marge on the scene, "comment faire entrer la marge." It is, moreover, a demonstration of how to do so by precisely *not* reducing her to an essence (like butter or cheese, both the result of condensation), but by insisting rather on her status as an emulsion (like margarine) hence preserving that ersatz quality from which, for Cixous, Marge's efficacy derives. Thus "Miss M," who as a "missage is never there, no sooner arrived is no longer there," would be "the letter [character and missive] of the Ersatz par sexcellence [sic]" (*EL*, 78–9), in other words the emblem (or embleM) of the text as it projects itself into the space and time of its writing.[16] That is why we must be careful not to make too much of Marge, not to essentialize her, not to "privilege marg(in), mistery," as Cixous puts it, "but [to] see there the incessant labor [*travail*] of the text, as it puts out new shoots, propagating itself, and flowering again, vying with, rivaling, its own reproductive élan [se replantant et refleurissant à qui mimieux]" (*EL*, 94).

14. "Le Champ freudien," the Freudian field, was the name given at Les Editions du Seuil to the series in which the writings of Lacan and many of his followers appeared. *Mädchen* (girl), like *Kind* (child) is neuter in German, Cixous's mother tongue (what she calls her "lalemande"), and she writes with a certain nostalgia of the period when she was the girl-child of a German mother, hence an *Es* (it) rather than a "she." "As *Es*," she speculates, "while I was still *das Mädchen*, I must have written without terror" (*EL*, 37).

15. Cixous, *Reading with Clarice Lispector*, edited, translated and introduced by Verena Andermatt Conley (Minneapolis: University of Minnesota Press, 1990), 4.

16. The privilege Cixous grants to the letter *M* throughout "La Missexualité" is a graphic demonstration of her poetics, which, like Joyce's, depends on hearing what is in letters. Thus playing on the homophony between *M* and "aime" (loves), she evokes that "extra, excessive, marginal M whom there is no doing without. That one loves [qu'on M] after all" (*EL* 80).

It is the *travail* of the text, its labor (the work of giving birth to itself) that is manifested in Cixous's writing, of which it is both the subject and the practice. This is nowhere more evident than in her reading of Joyce, where she joyfully joins in the process of the text as it reproduces, propagates itself, making it further increase and multiply, by miming it to the top of her bent ("à qui mimieux"). "Read," Cixous urges, "write the ten thousand pages of each page, bring them to light, increase and multiply and the page will multiply. But for that to happen, *read:* make love to the text" (*EL*, 34). Thus, in contrast to most of his male readers (including Derrida), Cixous does not feel compelled to engage in a trial of strength ("à qui mieux mieux") with James Joyce. Rather she invites Augustine Aloysius (Joyce's middle names) to play Antony to her Cleopatra, "A" to her "C," so that between them they may generate the current that will spark her virtuoso performance of "La Missexualité."

In Paris, in June 1975, that performance was indeed electrifying. I, at least, had never heard or seen anything like it, and though possessed of what I took to be a fully raised feminist consciousness at the time, had never imagined that "feminist" literary criticism could be practiced like this: that the "feminine" (for want of a better word) could thus infiltrate "conceptual, philosophical, or academic discourse," in order to emerge, dazzlingly, right in the middle ("en plein milieu") of it. "Milieu," Cixous would write, ever attentive to the graphic power of "mi" (half, mid, semi, but also musical note in the tonic solfa), as it moves along the chain "*mi*ss, *mi*ssive, *mi*stery, *mi*ssexualité," to unseat the binary oppositions on which gender and language, position and presence are said to depend. For *mi-lieu* evokes a utopian half, mid, or semi-place (*lieu*): the correlative, if one can imagine it, of "l'entre" and "la marge": of the "feminine." Looking back once more to 1975 one could say that the high-modernist milieu of Joyce studies became, momentarily, a "mi-lieu" (was breached) that "weird weekday" in June "(yet how palmy date in a waste's oasis!)" when, by Cixous's agency, Marge (re)appeared on the scene.[17]

But June 1975 also saw the reappearance of another female figure: one whose impact (for better or worse) was initially to prove more

---

17. These phrases are drawn from the celebrated passage in *Finnegans Wake* describing the hen Biddy Doran's discovery of the "litter" or "mamafesta" on the midden heap. The "palmy date in a waste's oasis" is the one on which "to the shock of both, Biddy Doran looked ad [sic] literature" (*FW*, 112). It should be noted, incidentally, that Derrida's *Marges de la philosophie* (Paris: Editions de Minuit) had appeared in 1972.

powerful, and certainly far more enduring than that of Sweet Margareena. I am talking of course about the Medusa, to whom by a remarkable coincidence, I was introduced, once again by Cixous, within a day
or two of my encounter with "la Marge."

Simone de Beauvoir et la lutte des femmes (Simone de Beauvoir
and the Women's Struggle), the now celebrated number 61 of the journal L'Arc, had just come off the press in June 1975. I ran across it by
chance, in the course of a hurried final inventory of the Paris book-
stores and snatched it up, in my enthusiasm for its subject, without
even reading the table of contents. (I had been actively involved for the
previous two or three years in feminist politics and had recently, like
thousands of other women in the United States, rediscovered Simone
de Beauvoir.) It was not until I was on the plane en route to Chicago
that I took L'Arc out of its bag and found, to my surprise and delight,
Hélène Cixous's name (which until a few days previously had been
entirely unknown to me) among the list of contributors. I turned at
once to "Le Rire de la Méduse" and thus read that now famous text for
the first time (more appropriately than I could have known) in Mid-
Atlantic, flying at twenty-seven thousand feet somewhere between
(entre) "Old Europe" as Rimbaud called it, and the New World.[18] What
better circumstances (with Marge still fresh in my mind) in which to
read sentences like this one: "These reflections," Cixous writes in the
third paragraph of "Le Rire de la Méduse," "because they advance into
a region that is on the brink of being discovered, necessarily bear
the mark of the meantime (l'entretemps) that we are living, the inbe-
tweentime when the new emerges from the old, or more accurately
the (feminine) new (la nouvelle) from the (masculine) old (l'ancien)"
("Rire," 39). Exciting as I found it, however, I could have had no idea
then of the impact Cixous's "mamafesta," to borrow another word
from Joyce, was to have, but it still pleases me to entertain the fantasy
that I may have been the first transatlantic reader of "Le Rire de la
Méduse," that I may have been the one who brought it to North America for the first time.

I cited "Le Rire de la Méduse" in a paper on May Sarton's Mrs Stevens
Hears the Mermaids Singing at the 1975 MLA; but since (though I did
not yet realize it) I would need to do a lot of reading in order properly to
read Cixous, the full effect upon me of Medusa, and to an even greater
extent, Marge, would only make itself felt, in classic Feudian fashion,

18. See L'Arc 61 (1975): 39–54. The opening sentence reads "I shall speak about
women's writing" ("Je parlerai de l'écriture féminine"), but see note 10 above.

with the belatedness or deferral (*Nachträglichkeit*) that allows previously unassimilated experience (with the acquisition of new knowledge) to be "incorporat[ed] fully into a meaningful context."[19] Thus it is only now, twenty years after the fact, that I am beginning to understand the significance of my precocious encounters with Cixous.

Although I read "Le Rire de la Méduse" in the wake of Marge, and was prompted to do so, in fact, by her, the apparent accessibility of this new text was so much greater, its overtly polemical stance (however unconventionally expressed) so much more readily assimilable to the feminist discourse with which I was familiar, that the laughing Medusa not surprisingly began to take precedence, in the months following my Paris experience, over the elusive Marge, who, infinitely more resistant to translation, slowly, imperceptibly submerged.

"Medusa eclipses Marge" would thus be an appropriate shorthand description of my initial experience reading Cixous. And not only mine, for I believe this experience to have been shared, consciously or not, by a majority of her early readers on this side of the Atlantic. Indeed it is tempting to suggest, on that score, that the reception given to "The Laugh of the Medusa" when it appeared in English in 1980, and its rapid translation into American feminist terms, resembled nothing so much as the reception given to psychoanalysis and its subsequent translation into American ego psychology. With regard to the latter, what got lost in the process (if we are to believe Lacan) was psychoanalysis' implication in language, and I would venture to suggest that equally, what disappeared in the translation of "Le Rire de la Méduse" (I do not mean only the rendering of the text into English, but rather its transfer and appropriation) was the element of linguistic play that had been (as it remains) intrinsic to the "feminine" as Cixous was attempting to represent it. On this view, the "feminine writing" seized upon so eagerly by the first generation of "The Laugh of the Medusa's" readers was arguably an impoverishment, a reduction (recall B and C) of the missexual writing practice for which a possible name would be—"Marge." The fate of the title of Cixous's essay provides a convenient example of what I mean, for to read "Le Rire de la Méduse" across French and English (à la Marge) would be to hear in it "The Rear of the Medusa," so that it becomes a cheeky riposte to Freud's "Medusa's Head," a quip which the monolingual "Laugh of the Medusa" is quite powerless to convey.[20] Freud's essay, though she never mentions it

19. See the article on "Deferred Action" in J. Laplanche and J. -B. Pontalis, *The Language of Psychoanalysis*, trans. Donald Nicholson-Smith (New York: Norton, 1973), 112.

20. "The Laugh of the Medusa," trans. Keith Cohen and Paula Cohen, was published

directly, is quite clearly—for whomever has read it, that is—both the stimulus and the target of Cixous's text, and her treatment of "Medusa's Head" is thus exemplary of the way she uses her "sources" (or as I would prefer to say, "reading") generally, and the effect that this use produces or fails to produce (if they do not recognize her references) on her readers.

The fact that "feminine writing" turned out to be so elusive a concept may be symptomatic of Marge's irrepressibility, her tendency to resurface, though submerged; and I wonder if "Le Rire de la Méduse," despite its air of being a radical manifesto, did not in fact represent for Cixous herself (no less than for many of her readers) a regression from the far more venturesome "Missexualité," with its daring attempt not only to represent but to preserve the synthetic nature of "la marge," of what we have no choice but to call "femininity."

That is why I believe, as my title aims to suggest, that retranslating Cixous means "rejoycing (with) her," recognizing that it is Joyce's example that has nourished her "extreme fidelity" over the last twenty years or more to a kind of writing that steadfastly refuses "the masculine position" (with all the risks, foremost among them the risk of being misunderstood, that such a refusal entails).[21] The challenge that Cixous, like Joyce, presents is that like Marge: "She doesn't explain— how she disjoins and conjoins the elements of multiple (hi)stories, how she recomposes, as margarine, herself a synthesis of oils" (*EL*, 91). This does not mean however that she does not explicate, unfold the texts she reads. On the contrary, like Marge she makes room for the men's scene, or as she often writes it *cène* (*Cena*, The Last Supper), so that, read with her, Freud, Lacan, Derrida, Heidegger, Blanchot, Kafka to name but a few of her "chastely tumescent troubadours," are reread, but differently.[22]

In addition to not explaining, Cixous does not often document the sources of her multiple (hi)stories, with the result that, as I already indicated, it takes a considerable amount of reading before one is able properly to read her. Thus, although I was familiar with Freud and Joyce

---

in *New French Feminisms*, ed. Elaine Marks and Isabelle de Courtivron (Amherst: University of Massachusetts Press, 1980), 245–64. See also Sigmund Freud, "Medusa's Head," in *The Standard Edition of The Complete Psychological Works of Sigmund Freud*, trans. and ed. James Strachey (London: Hogarth, 1955), vol. 18, 273–74.

21. "Extreme Fidelity" is the title of an essay by Cixous published in *Writing Differences: Readings from the Seminar of Hélène Cixous*, ed. Susan Sellers (New York: Saint Martin's Press, 1988), 9–37.

22. "Chastely tumescent troubadours" is the closest I can get, in English, to her "troubadours verginaux" (*EL*, 80), with its play on *vierge* (virgin) and *verge* (Penis).

in 1975, but not with Derrida, Lacan, or Heidegger, I remained deaf to many of the dominant themes in her music, unaware of the extent to which her compositions were, like Joyce's, *re*composed from a multitude of sources, literary, theoretical, philosophical, linguistic, and eventually, historical (Cliopatra being a later incarnation of the Cleopatrician): a synthesis of multiple languages and literatures.

Cixous reads Joyce (and other writers) in order to write *with* them, not *on* them, and this is where she departs most radically from a discourse that is "conceptual, philosophical, or academic." It is in recomposing existing inscriptions (the neologism being the extreme example, as it is the smallest unit of this practice) that she unsettles language, and to the degree that our relation to language has a bearing on sexual identity, the masculine/feminine polarity.

Thus she ventures to write, enigmatically and suggestively, that "M leads us to relate the status of (la) Marge to the operation of the text in general . . . what M and her remainders, sequels, and overflowings say is also the text. . . . But it is the text, as M, as that which cannot be dispensed with (dont on ne peut pas faire l'économie). And it is femininity. The femininity of the text of *FW*, the text-enigma as feminity. That which cannot be grasped, captured (l'imprenable)" (*EL*, 94). In other words, Marge's entry on the scene would be the entry of the "feminine," but the "feminine" as emulsion, that is to say, writing (*l'écriture*), and not essence, that is to say "Woman." It is therefore to the degree that "Enter Marge" and "Enter Writing" are interchangeable, that regardless of the gender of its producer, writing (*l'écriture*) is "feminine" for Cixous.

Cixous's readings are writings, as the publication over the past year or two of the volumes *Reading with Clarice Lispector* and *Readings: The Poetics of Blanchot, Joyce, Kafka, Kleist, Lispector and Tsvetayeva* testify.[23] That, in a word, is her most radical "missage" to those of us women scholars who still feel compelled to explain, in order not just to be understood, but to show that we understand. Perhaps what retranslating Cixous means is writing with her as she writes with those she reads, while remembering that the first among these was Joyce.

23. *Readings: The Poetics of Blanchot, Joyce, Kafka, Kleist, Lispector and Tsvetayeva*, edited, translated and introduced by Verena Andermatt Conley (Minneaplis: University of Minnesota Press, 1991.) These two volumes (which mark an important turning point in the reception of Cixous's work in this country) contributed significantly to the thinking that eventually gave rise to this essay. Verena Andermatt Conley was the first critic writing on this side of the Atlantic to address Cixous's missexuality. See her "Missexual Misstery," *Diacritics* 7 (Summer, 1977): 70–82

II. Other Realities, Other Fictions

NICOLE BROSSARD

The Textured Angle of Desire*

in every word, there is only
the meaning we prepare

No matter what meaning we give to the word feminism, we cannot
economize on what motivates it and what makes every woman apt to
become a feminist. You may think that each woman, educated or not,
is induced to lodge inside her skin and subjectivity, in the form of so
many contemptuous words and humiliating gestures, sufficient data
to initiate her revolt. On the other hand, it must be recognized that
each woman receives simultaneously the information necessary to
maintain her inferiorization and the disinformation indispensable for
her subordination. No woman gets used to violence, few women get
accustomed to scorn and insult, the majority of women become accustomed to dependency and accept patriarchal tradition as reasonable,
inevitable. Throughout the course of history, however, it can be as-
certained that despite the economic, legal, moral, and religious constraints assigning them to "second fiddle" and to self-effacement, women
have seized the opportunity to speak and have shifted into action. Each
time, they have done so in the name of life, sometimes in their own
name, demanding rights for their sex, not special rights, but equal
rights.

Now, the feminism we have been living in the West for more than
twenty years has given rise to a historical precedent in customs and
thought, because this feminism interrogates the imaginary, symbolic,
and psychological construct of those by whom the inferiorization of
women has been programmed. Moreover, by legitimating the singular

* Nicole Brossard, "L'Angle tramé du désir," in La Théorie, le dimanche, ed. Louky
Bersianik, Nicole Brossard, Louise Cotnoir, Louise Dupré, Gail Scott, and France Théoret (Montreal: Editions du Remue-Ménage, 1988), 13–26.

YFS 87, *Another Look, Another Woman*, ed. Huffer, © 1995 by Yale University.

and collective subjectivity of women, this feminism has permitted the flowering of their creativity, the affirmation of their identity, as well as making possible the establishment of solidarity. In other words, we can say that contemporary feminism, while undertaking the promotion of women and the extension of their rights, has also and *above all* become a body of thought, a morality, an ethics. This has come about by curious coincidence at the same moment as masculine philosophers and thinkers crown their books with titles such as *The Defeat of Thought, The Era of the Void, The Future of Negation, The Empire of the Ephemeral, The Death of Genre,* as if, having made the round of a garden laid out and cultivated by them, they are now becoming aware of its desolation and infertility.

My purpose is not so much feminism, though, as it is to understand how feminist consciousness works and to identify the difficulties it encounters according to whether it protests, asserts, or proposes. How does feminist consciousness *treat* reality so that we may inscribe our certainties and perspectives which form the thinking and creative subjectivity of an as yet unwritten world?

In response, it seems important to distinguish three elements on which the coherence of the work of feminist consciousness depends: motivation, decision, and concentration.

MOTIVATION

Motivation is defined as "action of forces (conscious or unconscious) which determine behavior." This is also the place to ask what is the source of our motivation, to identify the *motives* and the *mobiles*[1]

---

1. *Mobile* in the sense of affective motive is a neologism in English. *Mobile* has a long history in philosophic discourse from the *principium mobile* or "prime mover" of Aristotle and the Scholastics. The term was given renewed currency as affective motivation or desire by phenomenological studies of motivation as a translation for the German *Triebfeder* (spring setting in motion) for which André Lalande offers the English translation "affect" ("Mobile." *Vocabulaire technique et critique de la philosophie.* [Paris: PUF, 1962], 633). In German and French studies of motivation, "motive" is understood in a restricted sense as "the more reflexive determinant of action" in comparison with "mobile" as "the more passionate one" (Alexander Pfänder, *Phenomenology of Willing and Motivation,* trans. and ed. Herbert Spiegelberg [Chicago: Northwestern University Press, 1967], 13–14, note 8). Sartre's discussion of this distinction, in relation to how motivation in doing with regard to freedom puts being perpetually in question, offers as an example a "wrenching away from the self and the world" that is involved when a worker "posit[s] his suffering as unbearable suffering and consequently can make of it the motive (*mobile*) for his revolutionary action." The terms have been translated by Helen Barnes as "cause" ("*motif*") and "motive" ("*mobile*") (Jean-Paul Sartre, *Being and*

that generate and nourish feminist consciousness, as well as to understand how these latter organize the movement and the pertinence of our thoughts.

1. Motives

Philosophy teaches us that contrary to *mobiles* (affects), motives or reasons are easy to objectify and, consequently, to identify. To have access to them, it is enough to look about and gather documentary evidence. If you admit that motivation increases with the number of motives, you will agree that a feminist must constantly have her eye open, collecting material and bringing her knowledge into view. In fact, the past and present provide us with a quantity of *raw* information about what was and is the condition of women. Statistics, legal texts, TV newscasts, advertising, news stories, pornography: all are motives that daily sharpen our anger, our revolt, and strengthen our desire to act as well as the urgency of intervening. Other motives are found buried in history and literature: it rests with feminist consciousness to summarize and analyze them. These motives form an immense iceberg of injustice and violence: women see only the tip; feminists are able to evaluate its dimensions.

There is also another source of motives, those likely to orient our desire and inspire us. These are the words, writings, actions, and gestures of liberation accomplished by women throughout history. Closer to us, it could be said that each book written by a radical feminist, a lesbian feminist, or a radical lesbian is motivating material, supplies good fresh water for our mill.

2. Mobiles

Mobiles are distinguished from motives in that they are unavowed and unconscious, deeply intimate. As their name indicates, *mobiles* or drives move endlessly and travel through us as something unspeak-

---

Nothingness, trans. Helen Barnes. [London: Methuen, 1957], 436ff.). In the spirit of Spiegelberg's qualification of this as an "unhappily misleading" rendering (13, note 8), I have opted to reactivate and reinflect the philosophical term "mobile" in English. The suggested translations of André Lalande for *mobile* as "affect," or the terms "drive" or "impulse," which might follow from Paul Janet's description of *mobile* as "des impulsions de la sensibilité" (Lalande, 634), are problematic in English because of their imbrication in psychoanalytic discourse. Brossard is explicitly drawing on the philosophic and not the psychoanalytic analysis of "unconscious" (desiring) motivation. Trans.

able. In addition, it is more difficult for us to distinguish them among the throng of emotions and sensations we feel which, however, increase or diminish our motivation. So it is without our knowledge that they influence at one and the same time our energy, our affectivity, our subjectivity, which, of course, is not without consequence for our manner of investing and/or of disinvesting (in) feminism. Because they are unconscious, *mobiles* (the emotional) may also be qualified as personal and thus we cannot assess their real impact on our collective motivation.

You may think, however, that the solidarity of women, the pleasure we feel in being together, our identification with women, as well as the state of mind in which we immerse lesbian love constitute substantial *mobiles*. In another sense, we could say that the pain, suffering, and anger that come to us with the accumulated violence and scorn against the female sex and, consequently, against what we are mobilize in us the energy of a "sense of honor."

While motives refer to (f)acts, *mobiles* are intrinsically linked to faces,[2] roles[3] which, according to their affective and mental proximity, multiply fascination or menace, well-being or dis-ease—intimate faces and figureheads are never neutral: their proximity has the effect of inciting collusion or rejection, reconciliation or estrangement. In this, motives (in the public sphere) and *mobiles* (in the intimate sphere) manage, so to speak, our cautiousness and our boldness, our censures and our liberties, our reserve and our elation.[4]

THE DECISION

Concentration is what unites in one meaning, what calls forth the convergence of things. It can also be defined as an "application of any intellectual effort on a single object." Now if it is possible to say that we may be conscious of two things simultaneously (comprehension), it is not possible to assert that we can concentrate on two realities at the same time (perception). That, however, is what conditions the *radical ambivalence* and the *unspeakable certainty* of feminist consciousness when it seeks to articulate itself as a body of thought. It would also

2. Mother, father, brother, sister, lov(h)er, man or woman friend or enemy.
3. Heroine, hero.
4. According to the curve of events in a woman's life (childhood, loves, life in a couple, motherhood, friendships, work), one will see her motivation sometimes increase, sometimes decrease. This explains, among other things, the sudden defections and rallyings which are part of the contingencies of the feminist movement. It also explains the diversity of approaches and definitions given for feminism.

be well for us to give an account of what hinders the decision-making process and what encourages it.

The feminist diagnostic which concludes in the domination of women by men simultaneously brings about the valorization of women and discredits men and their institutions. Moreover, this diagnostic makes *effective* the *duality* of men and women and actualizes the atavistic *antagonism* which the idea of complementarity is unable to camouflage, complementarity in a patriarchal system being the equivalent of saying that the woman (complement) completes the man (subject).

1. Duality

The coexistence of two elements of a different nature is called duality. So the human species involves two groups, men and women. But where masculine thought has been able to make an economy of the duality of the sexes by the inferiorization of the feminine gender,[5] feminist consciousness cannot consent to such blindness in return. As well, while validating the existence of women and discrediting the logic of the imaginary construct of men, feminist consciousness is obliged to raise the question of differences in a series of prudent statements which, on the one hand, do not separate men form their human nature and, on the other, do not overvalue women. In short, it is through the very nature of its humanist claims that feminist thought is in some way compelled to grant to men not only ontological immunity, but also the consideration to which each human person has a right. This is not without consequence for the coherence of our purpose because where we are *morally* obliged to include and respect, we furiously reject those who are at the origin of our oppression, and scorn the arrogance, vileness, and hypocrisy they exhibit toward us. Our thought also gets lost by such inclusion and exclusion and hesitates to generalize even as it does to specify itself. In contrast, by refusing to *overvalue* women, feminist thought denies itself the representation necessary for all mythology, any imaginary, and, consequently, is incapable of reproducing itself. In this sense, feminist thought holds itself hostage: without cultural and institutional supports, without mythic space and anchorage in the

5. By refusing to live the duality of the sexes, that is, the inferiorization of women, men have been constrained to transfer it onto the antagonistic pairs body/mind, nature/culture, intuition/reason, always assigning the inferior place to the feminine which they then attribute to things.

imaginary, feminism can only be topical, that is, subject to the fluctuation of motives and *mobiles*. From this arises the feeling that feminism seems incapable of turning the corner with a second generation of women just as radical as the first.

Moreover, if one accepts that the knowledge and language we use are tributaries of masculine subjectivity alone, we have to recognize that in using them we work with instruments whose reliability is dubious and risk at every moment each utterance turning back on us. I shall give as an example the definition which the *Petit Robert* offers for the word feminist: "Relating to feminism. Ex.: feminist propaganda. Noun: Partisan of feminism."[6] Why then use the word *propaganda* when the word has a pejorative connotation and is used mainly to designate the diffusion of *false* information in order to influence opinion? Why use the word partisan in the masculine when it is very well known that feminists are, if not exclusively, at least in the majority, women? On the other hand, it will be argued that if feminism is a "humanism," it ought to be able to mobilize as many men as women and, consequently, the use of the word partisan in the masculine is justified. This, then, is an example that illustrates well the antagonism of men (propaganda), the comprehensive duality (feminism is valid for everyone), and the *general rule* that the masculine takes precedence over the feminine.[7] Therein is a semantic checkmate which only our determination can conjure away.

Thus I conclude that if it weren't for our *motivation* (anger against men, identification with women, sexual attraction and love between women), our feminist consciousness alone would never have been able to venture the assertions and propositions that have been ours for the last twenty years. This is to say that, although conscious of two things at a time, duality, we cannot economize on antagonism which allows us to find our polyvalence and to declare our difference in our own terms.

---

6. This negative definition is particular to French. *The Concise Oxford Dictionary* offers the following definition for "feminism": "Advocacy, extended recognition, of the claims of women. So _____ist n." Trans.

7. In the formation of plurals in French, the grammatical rule requires in the presence of a single word gendered in the masculine, within a group of numerically greater feminine entities, that the plural be in the masculine. So the pronominal plural for three hundred women and one man would be the masculine "ils," not the feminine "elles." Trans.

2. **Antagonism**

If our antagonism bears within it the terms of its own contradiction, what interest is there for feminists to take up again for our project the antinomic mode of a thought which blindly discredits and generalizes? Where misogynist antagonism has held women at a distance from their identity and integrity, can we think that a feminist antagonism would bring us closer? To this I would reply that, to the extent to which every process of opposition gives rise to its justifying and/or accusing counter view, the process generates *narrative*.

"The form of narrative," writes Roland Barthes, "is essentially characterized by two powers: that of distending its signs over the length of the story and that of inserting unforeseeable expansions into these distortions. The two powers appear to be points of freedom but the nature of narrative is precisely to include these deviations within its language."[8]

So oppositional relations, by increasing through tension the dimensions of "women's madness" and "men's reason," for example, or again of men's violence and women's gentleness, open up a way, in the narrative we are making, for a semantic virtuality favorable to a referential anchorage other than the one which until today has diverted our attention and so suspended our *judgment*. In fact, were it not for what subjective (diary, biography, letters) and fictional narrations of our lives expose to our consciousness, we would, for lack of another perspective, have no other alternative but to struggle with the antinomic and hierarchized pairs of the masculine imaginary construct.

To sum up, we could say that by finding a solution in narrative, the agonistic tension allows us to catch a glimpse of the polysemic images from which the scope of our choices and our presence of mind in the body of language follow.

CONCENTRATION

So that our thought is exerted in attentive listening to the narrative we carry within us and so that we can understand all the existential ramifications and the ontological implication, we must be able to focalize our subject of interest and our subject of identification in such a way as

8. Roland Barthes, "Structural Analysis of Narratives," in *Image/Music/Text*, ed. and trans. Stephen Heath (London: Fontana, 1977): 117.

to compose the image that makes us ONE (in the feminine),[9] to focalize the doubled image of a woman and a feminist, to focalize the fluid figure, close and distant, that speaks in us of presence. To focalize is to actualize our *pathos/logical* presence, that is to say, to make visible the logic of our passion, accepting in this way to diverge from the patriarchal norm until it is only a tiny insignificant point, a small scar on the back of the species.

Concentration results from the encounter of our mental and physical capacities. Concentration is the synchrony of desire and energy (she), a privileged moment in which knowledge, intentionality, and intimate certainties come together.

The Latin word *focus* gives birth to three words: foyer, fuel, and focal.[10] The first is associated with place, the second with energy, the third with point of view. So it could be said that the place from which one looks (distance), the intensity with which one picks up the object (speed), and the angle of view one extends toward the object (purpose) influence focalization itself.

Now, kept by men and their institutions at a distance from ourselves, from other women and from our history, and simultaneously brought closer to men by heterosexuality and its institutions, in what place, in what tree stump does feminist consciousness make a nest for its gaze? What distance must feminist consciousness cross in order to get closer to women, what energy is at her disposal, what types of interference does she encounter?

9. In French, Brossard writes "UNE," the indefinite article with the silent "e" ending of the feminine gender, referring both to women grouped together and the feminine gender of "image," to emphasize the constitution of a representation for women with the constitution of women as such—a singul*he*rity. This is Brossard's version of the problematic relation of women to the symbolic, of women and universals. Her position is somewhere between that of Irigaray, for whom an ethics of sexual difference would entail a new thinking of a symbology for women in the plural, and that of Monique Wittig, who advocates the necessity for a minority writer to make the minority point of view universal. One of Wittig's textual strategies for this is the use of the pronoun *on* or one, as she points out in "The Mark of Gender" (*The Straight Mind* [Boston: Beacon Press, 1992], 83). My emphasis on the mark of the feminine "e" in "one" is an attempt to combine the positions of these two French theorists whose work has been so important for Brossard. Throughout this text, there are similar double meanings conveyed through the third person feminine pronoun "elle" which, when replacing "concentration," "conscience" ("consciousness"), "decision" and "motivation"—all words gendered feminine in French—effect a convergence between these actions and women as subjects. I have tried to indicate this double play by introducing "she," but have more frequently used "it" to translate the pronoun in question. Trans.

10. The French words used by Brossard are *foyer, feu,* and *focal* (hearth, fire, and focal). Trans.

It is certain, for example, that lesbian desire synchronizes distance, energy, and motivation in a single reality and constitutes, properly speaking, the instantaneous focalization of image and presence. It cannot be said often enough to what point sexual desire multiplies energy, attraction, and motivation. But when among lesbians it is the *very* principle of pleasure itself which enables them to focus and hold their attention on women, must one think that this very principle of the (self)same has as a consequence the doubling of image and presence in female heterosexuality, distancing in the same instance the subject of interest, the subject of identification, and the subject of desire? Must we affix such a name to a context of distraction that makes one weep, suspends thought, invites melancholy?

In fact, what is at stake here is not so much what there is to reflect as what there needs to be in order to be reflected. Now, when being is in question, every woman must be able to disregard the masculine gaze, whether it is reproving or approving. Without this abstraction, there is distraction, that is to say a semantic event that severs painfully or that (g)ratifies (from being in) "good" sense. In the one case as in the other, there is a loss of concentration or the misfiring of a semantic ignition able to keep alive our attention on the feminine immanent and virtual, that is, on the spiraling curve of bodies heavy and aerial as ours are at the moment we enter into the imaged space of the self and its propositions.

This effort of concentration is required of us in particular because the *whole* environment is patriarchal: institutions, language, customs, and traditions. Everything that makes sense around us invalidates our presence or subordinates it to an identity, a cause, a first unity, whether this ensemble be the heterosexual couple, the family, the nation, the race, the social class, or even the profession. The vice of phallocentric form which consists of minoritizing, marginalizing women from reality or of incorporating them in a masculinized humanity makes it so that, in "that state," our thoughts are constantly displaced and postsynchronized.[11] Moreover, when speaking from the

11. Normally, we should have the right to expect that our acts of resistance would attract for us the same sympathies that any group working for its emancipation and dignity receives. Such is not the case, because, in the eyes of patriarchal society, women do not constitute a *minority* whose misfortunes can be circumscribed by a politico-historical chronology; women do not form a *nation* in the process of disappearing or extermination about which one could become scandalized or saddened at the eventual loss; women do not form a homogeneous economic *class* able to target its economic and political aspirations; neither do women form a *race*, because the uterus is not a distinc-

site of feminist consciousness we find at last the right tone, our voice is likely to be doubled by an effeminate voice that transforms the rhythm and timing.

Concentration is essential for the advent of our pluri-*elle* singul(h)erity, just as it is to the way we have of giving forms (thought) and customs (ethics) to our certainties, our intuition as yet unspeakable. Concentration is initiation to a thinking stance capable of getting us out of the binary and linear modes of masculine reason. Concentration is for us the wager of presence summoning hitherto unwritten metaphors.

In brief, where the motives and *mobiles* manage our motivation (movement), where duality and antagonism generate valuable narrative (our her/story, analysis, and version of facts), concentration produces presence, the sense and image of this ontological and poetic advent.

In conclusion, I will say that if the feminist struggle obliges us to think up strategies and to confront the weight of the real (organization, action, negotiation), feminist consciousness requires on its part a continuous movement toward the unknown, woman. Feminist consciousness links us creatively to the essential [*l'essentielle*] as in writing (her) consciousness commits us without respite to face the inner necessity that urges us to exorcize nightmares, to trace dream and utopia, to put color and sense into the most preposterous angles of desire, to braid language with ties so strong and slender that at times we will no longer dare to move for fear and joy.

It is with feminist consciousness that *moral* suffering has moved into our lives as an initiatory torment. This terrifies, exhausts. But it is also through feminist consciousness that the creative dimension of our lives begins, the sense and dignity of our lives, because breaking through the patriarchal sound barrier, feminist consciousness situates itself endlessly on the side of creation.

—Translated by Barbara Godard

---

tive racial characteristic. Although analogies of this sort are plausible, none is really workable. In fact, our struggle basically produces *movement*, that is to say "a changing of position in space as a function of time with respect to a system of reference." Now since this system was founded on the value power/domination, we are obliged to work urgently: to save democracy, to struggle against racism, to defend minority rights, etc. Our subject of interest subordinated thus to emergencies, it is very difficult for us to focus our attention.

LYNNE HUFFER

An Interview with Nicole Brossard Montreal, October 1993

In the city, the traces, leave behind the high stakes, nicole, without erasure.

—Nicole Brossard, *L'Amèr* (*Theseourmothers*)

Lynne Huffer: I would like to begin by talking about your work both as a writer and a feminist. Since the 1970s you have been a part of the feminist movement as a poet, novelist, editor, essayist. Could you put the history of these various activities in a contemporary context?

Nicole Brossard: The poet, the novelist, and the feminist are still very active. I am still trying to answer questions about what it means to be a contemporary subject in a civilization about to shift into another dimension. Very early on, I said that I saw myself as an explorer in language and that I was writing to comprehend the society in which I live and the civilization to which I belong. Actually, understanding what goes on means trying to process the double-time in which I feel I am living: on the one hand, a historical linear time-space with familiar patriarchal scenarios such as war, rape, and violence; on the other, a polysemic, polymorphic, polymoral time where the speed and volume of information erase depth of meaning, where science proposes itself as an alternative to nature, where reality and fiction manage exaequo to offer proof of our ordeals and of the most dreadful fantasies.

While scientific information and images of violence multiply to the point that ethics becomes a polymorphic version of virtual behaviors, I am still Nicole Brossard, born in Montreal, with a sense of the history of Quebec and of belonging in that French part of the North American continent. I am still the writer who cannot let go of the idea that literature is subversion, transgression, and vision. I am still the feminist who thinks women have been and are still marginalized by the patriarchal system. I am still the lesbian who enjoys the way desire shapes itself among women of *paroles*.

The radical feminist does not wish to repeat questions and answers she has given in her previous texts. I can only rewrite my obsession for

YFS 87, *Another Look, Another Woman,* ed. Huffer, © 1995 by Yale University.

language and for the enigma of creative writing. I also know that desire is definitely a key word for any kind of creative process and that collective dreaming is at the core of any political involvement. I also have in mind that keeping the focus on women's present and future is the most challenging feat.

LH: Let's come back to the subject of writing. Could you talk about your thoughts on fiction, in its etymological sense, as a sort of ruse or lie that transforms reality?

NB: Yes, I have often said "in reality there is no fiction." The dictionary associates fiction with faking, dissimulation, and lying. Fiction has always been opposed to reality, as being the fruit of our imagination, as if our imagination came out of the blue. We do not construct fiction differently from the way we construct our relation to reality. In other words, we behave (in terms of patterns) in fiction the way we do in reality. Fiction is not only about story-telling, it is also about the logic of the stories each person initiates in language. By logic I mean the coherence of a universe we construct with such materials as sensations, emotions, memory, knowledge, and beliefs which are at work subterraneously within our usual practice of language which is speech. Part of that logic comes along with the literary tradition we belong to, as well as from the language we use. Part of it is idiosyncratic. It is by becoming a feminist that I was forced to question the words fiction and reality. For it seemed to me that what women were experiencing was discarded into "you are making things up," fictions or lies. One can only think about the rejection into fiction of revelations about incest, rape, and so on. Sexual practice other than plain heterosexual penetration was also seen as fictive, "unbelievable." On the other hand, men's fictions about women always came out as being "true." I think that for a long time the word fiction was an underground territory for what society did not want to admit as being part of the real. Fiction is the hidden face of the unavowable as well as of the unexplainable. I think that by telling their reality, by bearing witness to their experiences, women have narrowed the territory of fiction, of lies about them. It seems now that reality, science, and fiction have proved equal in representing the unbelievable. What is fiction now that "reality shows"—those dramatizations of real stories about serial killers—provide all the details we wanted to know about sex, violence, and injustice? What is fiction when, through technology, a grandmother can bear and give birth to her daughter's child? Nevertheless, I see fiction as an open space for desire to figure out the narrative of all those permutations we are capable of in order to give meaning to our lives.

LH: In discussing theory and fiction in *Aerial Letter*, you say: "It is precisely where there is a referential illusion that theoretically women traverse the opaque reality of language and *le sujet fabuleux* we contain becomes operative." What is the relationship between fiction and this "fabular subject"?

NB: *Le sujet fabuleux* is constructed in fiction because it can only be developed in the unpredictable part of the narrative, where words and thoughts derive, blossoming with unexpected ramifications, and henceforth initiating threads of meaning that help us to protect the positive image each woman intuits of herself. This image is the fabular subject, but in a patriarchal society the image is seen subliminally. Writing and the referential illusion that it creates allow time to retrace and to focus on the positive image. It is through Man's fiction that we have become fiction; let us exit fiction via fiction. When you pass through written language there is more of an opportunity to deal with the symbolic or to make the symbolic act for you, to be able to question or to skirt around the given course of what seems to be the universal patriarchal symbolic order. Even by using the word "fabular," something already shapes itself into a proposition. Things (meaning, images, a sense of truth) happen in writing that would never happen otherwise. I will probably write all my life because the act of writing allows for an encounter with unusual images, unexpected thoughts; a new world is opened each time.

LH: Can you talk about the image of the hologram that is so important to your work?

NB: I have always been interested in everything that has to do with the eye and the gaze. When I first saw a hologram, in New York in 1979, I was absolutely fascinated by it. I started to read about holography and was totally taken by some of the vocabulary relating to it: real image, virtual image, reflection, wave length, holographic brain. Also by the fact that all the information about the image is contained in every fragment of the holographic plate. I related that information to the fact that sentences might also contain the whole of what is at stake in a novel. For me, the hologram became the perfect metaphor to project the intuitive synthesis that I had in mind of a woman who could be real, virtual, and symbolic. By symbolic I mean she who, by being other than the mother symbol, could alter the course of meaning, values, and patterns of relationship. The hologram is tied to the idea that somehow we women have to invent our own idea of woman in order to enjoy being a woman and to proceed as a creative subject in language. I often say that if each woman could project the best that she senses in herself onto other women, we would already have accomplished a lot. I, for example, have a tendency to project onto other women the image that they are writers, straightforward speakers, and so forth. With the metaphor of the hologram I was able to integrate reality (women characters living in Montreal, New York), fiction (construction of a space for them to exist beyond their status as characters), and utopia (projection of the desire for the female symbolic). There is utopia, celebration, and projection of a positive image of women in my books. I know that in the United States there is a debate about essentialism. I think feminists should be grateful to those feminist and lesbian writers who are criticized for being essentialist. Thanks to them, the feminist movement has developed beyond the issues of equality and equity into an important cultural and social movement. Fiction, particularly innovative fiction by lesbian writers and philosophers, was the site of an overflow that allowed energy to circulate among women, and that also permitted feminist discourse to open up questions beyond the ones raised in the nineteenth century. Without celebration, desire, radical statements, and lesbian desire, feminism could have been left in the hands of liberal lawyers, lobbyists, or civil servants.

LH: So you're suggesting that essentialism is a necessary risk.

NB: Absolutely. Somehow, I think there is a great deal of confusion between an essentialism that would refer to biological determinism and essentialism as the projection of a mythic space freed of inferiorizing patriarchal images. Usually the accusers associate mythic essentialism, which in fact is an ontological creation, with the biological one. This confusion is not only misleading but dull.

LH: Perhaps we can come back to what you were saying about projection—this new intervention of woman—and, in particular, a woman's gaze. In *Aerial Letter* you say that you write "with a woman's gaze upon you," and you continue: "A woman's gaze means: who knows how to read."

NB: Man's gaze—the father's gaze—certainly legitimates a woman writer; it might even inspire her to excellence, as long as the writing stays within the boundaries of patriarchal meaning. It can even allow her to challenge literary tradition, or to write pornographic texts; she can try, if she so choose, to compete with Henry Miller or the Marquis de Sade. But in regard to disobedience to phallocentrism, Man's gaze has proven to censure and silence women. It promises to retaliate.

I believe that a woman's gaze is the only one that can legitimate and challenge a woman writer to go beyond the description of her social experience. The gaze of the other woman is vital because it induces recognition, complicity, and possibly desire. The gaze between women breaks the line, the fluidity of a system where men and women are trained to direct their eyes on the capital M of man because we are thought to believe that M is humanity.

In "The Textured Angle of Desire" [in this volume], I remark on just how difficult it is to keep focusing on women, and that lesbian love is one of the elements that allows us to maintain this focus. It is difficult to keep the focus on women as a subject of interest, recognition, and desire because of our marginalization. She who chooses to live on the margins (by identifying herself as a feminist or a lesbian), but this time in full control of her choice, gives herself a chance to keep the focus.

For me, the loss of the gaze of the other woman is also related to the difficulty feminists have in reproducing themselves from one generation to another. In other words, losing the gaze and the focus, we always skip a generation of feminists.

LH: I find the idea of a woman's gaze very difficult to conceptualize, to the extent that the gaze itself is part of the constitution of masculine knowledge and desire. There is a philosophical relationship between the gaze and comprehension, between the gaze and amorous desire. All of this is based on the eye.

NB: It is true that the gaze itself is part of the constitution of masculine knowledge and desire. If you are not a voyeur, the gaze means that you are introducing yourself in another space which is not your own, but which can eventually become part of your world or yourself.

The woman's gaze is meaningful because it works at filling the gap between women. What women see between them is as important as what they see of each other and in one another. The back and forth of the gaze between women (writer and reader) textures the space between them and to me that creates a social semantico-imaginative environment where meaning can be debated. I am amazed how difficult it seems for women playwrights to create dialogue between women outside of the mother-daughter relationship. Most of the time, female characters will interact through monologues. Is it because of a feminist ethic that won't allow for power relations or hierarchical roles among women? The woman's gaze acknowledges the reality of the other woman. It makes her visible, present. I believe that it actualizes she who has more than a story to tell. By that I mean she who can play with me as well as with words.

LH: In concluding, I would like us to go back to an idea we started with: the importance of the place from where one writes. In *Aerial Letter* you talk about urbanity, and, more precisely, of "urban radicals," urban women who write and publish. Do you feel that there is still a *Qué-becois* specificity to this radical urbanity?

NB: It is strange, but I have always felt that speaking and writing about Montreal is making a statement about being a North American of French descent. It is also a way of valuing our own literature. For a long time in our literature, the city was associated with sin, depravation, a place where you lose your soul. So for someone of my generation, I guess it is easy to associate radicalism with the city. Somehow the city seems to organize a metaphoric network that integrates delinquency, belonging, movement, excitement, and excess. In a recent text, I was saying that I am an urban woman on the graffiti side of the wall, on the sleepless side of night, on the free side of speech, on the side of writing where the skin is a fervent collector of dawns. I am from the city; I've always lived there; and I love the city and the freedom it allows even if it is dangerous for women. So I'm an urban radical. It's also a metaphor for me to say: I am a girl in combat in the city of men.

LH: The fabular subject again?

NB: I guess so. Certainly one aspect of the fabular subject. *Urbaine radicale, sujet fabuleux, ma continent* are probably noticeable as expressions not only for the meaning they suggest but also for their linguistic fabric, a semantic mix which creates its own aura of resonance. But to come back to *la fille en combat dans la cité*, I guess she is the product of a choice that I make which is to stay in the *polis* in order to confront patriarchal meaning instead of retiring to the mythic island of the Amazons, whose subtext to me is peace and harmony, while the subject for *la cité* is the law (not harmony), the written word (not the song), and constant change. The mythic island is in me, in books, and in the women with whom I surround myself.

I am a woman of the here and now, fascinated with the virtual that exists in the human species. But have we women been damaged by men's way of ordering the world and proving their "humanity"? Because I want all the energy and creativity that women are capable of, I will stay in the city so the law can be changed. Of course, there is that possibility that the law will be changed into something else only when we are done with the written word, which is definitely a partner to patriarchy and history—history being the trajec*story* of desire. I guess it is difficult for me to stay on the island because I am a woman of the written word, nonetheless aware of the metaphoric network that comes along with it: individualism, and an endless process of desire and hope that often comes out as an excess or a quest for the absolute. For me, staying in the city means to be alert, vigilant, in order to discriminate between propositions for a future and procedures that would lead to catastrophe.

I think we now understand how the double constraint, the double-bind that women experience in a sexist, misogynist, and phallocentric society works. We now know that this double-bind immobilizes, demo-bilizes women.

LH: What you're saying reminds me of Monique Wittig's *Le Corps lesbien* [*The Lesbian Body*] where she also talks about this island sepa-rated from the continent, the "dark continent" of the patriarchal order. But it is not about finding the island and remaining there calmly and peacefully. What really remains is the tension between the island and the continent.

NB: The tension which is desire is creative, the tension of debate is also creative. I want women's creativity to sparkle throughout the city, in the university, on the radio, in books, in films.

I now feel that besides the creative tension of being *une fille en combat dans la cité,* there is also another tension which is the one I referred to in the beginning of this interview: a double-time where the sensation of the slowness of the act of writing and the sensation of speeding among images (virtual, fractal, or numeric) mix in such a way that the writer wonders with a sudden disquietude to what world she belongs; if she is drifting away from the shore or heading back toward the idea of a future, another shore.

—Translated by David Dean

MARYSE CONDÉ

No Woman No Cry[1]

In Morne Gabriel, Létitia was not well liked.

Yes, she always smiled at everyone as she said her hellos and good evenings. She knew just what to say to the afflicted, to those whom misfortune had struck. She was present at baptisms, at weddings, and at wakes. She even possessed certain infallible recipes which she shared readily. The rare few who frequented her house knew that she spoke little and listened generously, cutting short slander and putting scandalmongers firmly in their place. Marie Gracieuse, the Forget's third daughter, who came to wash and iron her laundry once a week, swore that Létitia kept a large prayer book on her bedside table. Everyone saw her get down on both knees at church every Sunday and on feast days, even if she didn't take communion. She lived alone, as she had ever since the afternoon she had reopened the door of her parents' house, which had been closed for so long that some had no memory of having seen it otherwise. The house lay between crowded clumps of banana trees, which had begun to grow freely, and under the shade of the flame trees from which, in season, blood-red petals would drop onto the Guinea grass growing on what was left of the lawn. No man had ever been caught stooping over and trying to make himself inconspicuous to go and slip into the warmth of her bed. The only man who visited her did so in broad daylight, about once a month, arriving on the express bus from Sainte-Fleur and leaving before evening. Who was he? She had never taken the trouble to explain, but even the most critical were forced to recognize a strong family resemblance in their faces.

1. Any English, French, or Creole words in italics are given as they appeared in the original. [Translator's note]

YFS 87, *Another Look, Another Woman,* ed. Huffer, © 1995 by Yale University.

In fact, there was absolutely nothing to be said against Létitia's conduct. Still, the black and secret water of her eyes seemed to hide unutterable memories. Her laughter, when it rang out, sounded modulated and troubling, like a saxophone. People calculated that she must not have been far from fifty, having already been a young girl when her parents left Morne Gabriel in order to seek their fortune, in vain, in France. Her body, clearly marked by her age, spoke of a former abandon, of extinct embraces and caresses which the law had surely not sanctioned and which the passage of time had rendered no less culpable.

So it is that when the evening hung its garlands of shadow on the trees, and spirits wandered in the forbidden territories of the imagination, everyone would try to pierce the mystery of Létitia's past. Made languid by the rum which they drank in abundance at the *Roses de Mélissa*, the men would shake their heads:

"What a woman she must have been in her day! What a woman!"

They said this without hate, simply envious of the treasures she had given to others, treasures which they would have liked to plunder themselves.

The same could not be said for the women.

Especially if their men left them night after night, in front of their American soap operas, and only returned a few hours before dawn, just in time to turn their noses to the wall and snore. Especially if they no longer had men, abandoned in mid-life by champions of dominos and dice. Especially if they had never had a man to begin with, and found themselves forced to play, day after day, the terrifying game of virtue.

Sister Rosa particularly hated Létitia. "Sister" was the name that had come to her because she used to wash the laundry of the nuns of Saint-Joseph de Cluny back when they had their convent at Braquemort, before they retired to the heights of Carmel. The name remained, now that she watched over the children at the school cafeteria, and it was accompanied by an unctuousness gained through her time spent in the milieu of the Church and by a perfect knowledge of hymns which made her invaluable at funerals and wakes. She hid her feelings toward Létitia beneath smiles, friendly words, and freshly-laid eggs offered over the bloodwort hedge. All the same, when she did speak to her, her deep and gravelly voice would stumble as it formed the words, as if the sound were bumping up against something which she would have liked to have said but was obliged to keep to herself.

Létitia was no fool, and knew how the people of Morne Gabriel felt about her. It didn't bother her in the least. It had been a long time since that sort of thing had caused her any pain. For her whole life, people had held her apart, outside of the circles they form, and she had always made her way in exclusion.

During the weekends she helped Monsieur Sosthène with the book-keeping of his store, and all the spare time she allowed herself to plant her Congo peas, to harvest her pumpkins, to read on her porch, to listen to music, to look after the child of a busy young neighbor from time to time, annoyed more than one individual. As did the sight of her, apparently serene, sitting in a corner of the back room of the store, glasses perched on her nose, her fingers tapping away on an electronic machine. So she was educated, then? Yes, you could tell from her way of speaking French, of avoiding the familiarities of Creole, of revealing armpits that were closely shaved and powdered with talc, and of never standing out on her doorstep like the other women, in disarray, with her nightgown hanging down below her robe.

However, more than any other, one detail of Létitia's life enraged the people of Morne Gabriel. This was her taste for long evening walks. She left the village at her feet and plunged into the heights of Bois Vert, her silhouette disappearing beneath the shelter of the tall trees. What pleasure did she find in stumbling over that thick, spongy soil, where roots slithered like sinewy serpents covered by clinging tree ferns? Did she like to breathe in that dull, damp air, heavy with the smells of decomposing life? If she ever found herself face to face with a vampire or a monster, then she'd ask herself what she had gone to look for there. But then it would be too late.

Sometimes, Létitia would linger so long that upon her return to Morne Gabriel, night would be lapping like a lake at the rooftops and drowning the houses with its rippleless water. Then her footsteps would echo on the road like the horseshoes of some nocturnal beast, and everyone would wonder:

"Where has she been to this time?"

After her days of solitude, Létitia needed this contact with the warmth and friendship of the trees. One of the men with whom she had lived had taught her to understand their language, to decipher their sighs and their cries of pleasure when the wind ruffles through their leaves, when the sun, warming their bark, works its way right through to their hearts and their sexes, and when the night comes in turn to pour its magic into their ears. That man had brought her many disappointments, but all she remembered were his lessons:

"They came with us from Africa or from India. Like us, they made the voyage down in the hold of a ship, and if they have accepted this exile, it is to comfort us in ours. We can ask them for anything. They offer everything."

* * *

That afternoon, Létitia had walked on as far as the village of Pâquette, a handful of black shacks floating on a green sea of banana trees, with a few families of the same color as the shacks. They were tireless workers, accustomed to hardship, and the women rose even earlier than the men, to feed the children. Létitia particularly liked the corner of the village that butted up against the side of the volcano, inaccessible behind its mists like a priestess in the depths of her cave. Turning away from the volcano, facing the mingled immensities of the sky and the sea, you could almost be convinced that nothing existed apart from those three elements, especially not the populous island, and that the world was still waiting to be born.

Unlike the people of Morne Gabriel, the people of Pâquette liked Létitia very much. They showed this by not shooting her the looks they reserved for strangers and even for the employees of the banana company who, season after season, came to weigh and carry off their harvest. Often, children would approach her and she, without disgust, would wipe their runny noses and pat the red peppercorns of their hair. Sometimes the women, with half a smile, would even offer her a good handful of fig-apples or some just-ripe bananas.

Létitia followed a path which ran alongside the banana groves and, after having snaked its way under the malimbé trees, came to an end at the top of a vertiginous cliff. She could see, covering the sides and bottom of the gorge, an impenetrable tangle of creeping vines, epiphytes, and the branches of trees hundreds of years old. A voice rose up from those depths, and it seemed to Létitia that it came from the island itself, that it was terrified by the highways, the marinas built for tourists, and the five-star hotels, its lament bursting forth in a thousand echoes.

Just as she was going to continue deeper into the trees, Létitia stopped and stood among the ferns. To her left, and a bit lower down, she had caught sight of a ribbon of smoke coiling around the leaves of a bush. That surprised her. It was coming from the spot where Lucien and Delphine, a couple of charcoal burners, had erected their shack of planks and sheet metal. They had raised their child there, a beautiful boy of two or three who would babble cheerfully as he watched the glowing fires lit by his parents. Sadly, as the result of a denunciation, Lucien had been arrested by the police and condemned to spend a year locked up in the Trois-Étangs prison. While waiting for him, Delphine, their son, and the new child that was growing in her womb all had taken refuge with relatives in La Désirade, and the shack had remained closed for the past six months.

Who, then, was living in it now?

Moving closer, Létitia noticed a man crouching down and fanning a fire lit between the stones of the fireplace. At first, all she could make out was the tangled blondness of his dreadlocks. Then he raised his head and she had a clear view of his face. He was young. He could have been the son she had expected for so long, before she realized that her body, so well-suited for love, was not made for maternity. She found him handsome, and the hostile, malicious gleam in his eyes made her feel uncomfortable. So she smiled at him and asked, in her most charming manner:

"*Ou sé moun Dominique?*"[2]

He shook his head and exclaimed with a strong accent:

"*Woman*, I'm American and I don't speak Creole!"

There was nothing more to say. Létitia was turning to leave, humiliated like a schoolgirl whom the teacher has ridiculed, when he called her back, asking in the same brutal tone:

"What are you looking for around here?"

She hesitated, then turned to face him:

"I'm not looking for anything. I'm just taking a walk, that's all. I'm from Morne Gabriel. . ."

"From Morne Gabriel?"

"Yes, it's good exercise for my heart, all those kilometers."

He sneered:

"For your heart? You talk like my mother. Every morning, she used to put on her sneakers and go. 'It's good for my heart!'"

Deciding to say nothing more, she turned and walked on, hearing him laughing behind her back.

Over the days which followed, Létitia often thought of "the American Rasta," as she had begun to call him. Like the rest of her generation, she had been fascinated in her youth by America. At the time when she was trying her hand, somewhat lethargically, at a degree in

2. "Are you from Dominique?"

mathematics, she had joined a group who flew off to America and scaled the Statue of Liberty and the Empire State Building, before dashing through Harlem and Coney Island. This visit had done nothing but whet her appetite for knowledge, for discovery. Back in Paris, in the cafés of the Latin Quarter where she spent most of her time, or in the waiting lines of cinemas, or in her room on the Rue Lhomond, ice cold in the evenings and with walls bare but for a crucifix nailed up by the nuns, her imagination, leaving her body behind like the shell of a *jan gage*[3], would fly off, taking that plane again, and she would find herself once more buried up to the knees in the snow on the sidewalks of Manhattan. Alas, this return was never more than imaginary and real life had tossed her elsewhere.

There were very few Americans in Guadeloupe, aside from the occasional tourist. What series of adventures had made that one end up in Pâquette? If, for some reason or another, he was searching for solitude, he could not have found a better place. And for what reasons was he searching for solitude? Létitia, usually so detached, could not stop herself from wondering, and then could not stop reproaching herself for wondering; all of which meant that her spirit did not stray too far from Pâquette, even if she was very careful not to wander in that direction during her evening strolls.

* * *

It was at that time that Hugo asked Létitia to live out her days with him.

They had first known each other during the brief time that Létitia had spent in Guadeloupe as a child. Before the mediocrity of his position and the difficulties that he had in feeding a family of six had pushed Létitia's father, the musician Aubert Garan, to listen to the gilded words of one of his friends and to leave and try his luck in France.

If only Aubert had gone alone! But he had refused to listen to anyone, and had not wanted to be separated from either his beloved Matime or his four children. No one who watched him climbing up the gangplank of the *Katoomba*, looking quite pleased with himself, needed the gift of second sight to predict the continuation of his story. Poverty in a house in Aubervilliers. Premature death in a hospital, and, to finish things off, four orphans whom Matime bled herself dry to raise.

3. Character in Antillean mythology. [Translator's note]

Then Hugo and Létitia met again in Paris. Hugo worked at the Hôtel-Dieu as a nurse and came around on the weekends to warm himself up with the pork curries that Matime prepared with the powder her sisters sent her. Hugo called her "Aunt Matime" without anyone knowing if she really had a right to that name, and the youngest children called him "cousin."

Then, Hugo and Létitia fell out of touch for almost twenty years, until she found him again in the cardiology department of the hospital in La Pointe.

Ever since then, they had shared a bit of their solitude and spent the last Sunday of each month together. Hugo, divorced, lived alone, his three children having chosen to settle in France close to their mother, a Frenchwoman. Létitia did not seem to have any attachments.

When they were together, it was Hugo who would speak: of Paris, which had been transformed without his knowledge, like his own children, who had become indifferent, even hostile adults, preoccupied only with their mother; of his years in Algeria, where he had fought in the war, the bloody smell of which could still wake him up at night; of the years which had crept up on him without warning—wasn't he soon going to be fifty?—and it was Létitia who would listen, standing massive in front of the Creole stove, preparing the meal that later they would slowly eat under the passion fruit vine.

Sometimes, he would interrupt himself and look at her:

"It's strange that with the life you've led, you know how to cook so well!"

She would laugh, not at all annoyed:

"What do you know about the life I've led?"

He would grumble:

"People talk, people talk!"

She would laugh again, and then insist with a sort of pride:

"People know nothing about my life. No one knows a thing about my life. Not a thing!"

That Sunday, Hugo showed up with a handful of arums, sickly pink at the ends of their stiff stalks, and arranged them in a vase himself. However, he could not bring himself to reveal his plan until the end of the meal, when, a slice of sapodilla skewered on his dessert fork, he asked:

"Wouldn't it be better if we were to live together?"

She remained silent. He continued:

"If you want to go to city hall, we'll go. But didn't I always hear you say that you don't believe in marriage?"

She said only:

"Why this, all of a sudden . . . ?"

"It's not all of a sudden. I've been thinking of it for quite a while, even if I haven't said anything to you!"

Suddenly passionate, he added:

"You know, I'm still in perfect working order. There are women who could assure you of that."

She looked him over, his face slashed by the years, his neck furrowed with knotty veins, rising up powerfully above his collar, his throat and the triangle of fuzzy gray hair just visible through the opening of his shirt. Why, at that precise moment, did she have to remember the sinuous slenderness, the burnished torso of the "American Rasta"? She recoiled slightly and murmured:

"Aren't we related?"

Once again, he shook his head:

"Not a drop of blood in common! When the idea first came to me, I looked into it. It was your mother's father and my father's father who were such close friends that they thought of each other as brothers, and that closeness was passed down to their families. But one was from Port-Louis, while the other was a native of La Pointe."

She got up to get the coffee cups and said, in a very quiet voice:

"Listen, we'll talk about this next time."

He tried not to smile. He knew her; she was whimsical, unpredictable. But she hadn't brushed him off. The battle was half won. So, just as he was leaving for the bus stop, he allowed himself to place his mouth on hers and to caress the flesh of her neck, soft, warm, and lightly creased.

When she found herself alone, Létitia sat down in front of the mahogany table in the dining room. As if in a crystal ball, images of the past floated up to the shining surface of the wood, spreading out, gathering together, shimmering for a moment before disappearing.

Hugo! How ironic! The very man she had desired so ardently when they were young and living in Aubervilliers! But back then, he had eyes only for his blond conquests, whose merits he praised feverishly to her brothers, Élie and Georges. She could always hear them laughing and whispering in their bedroom on the second floor. Létitia's older sister Estella, who, in spite of the airs she put on, also had quite a crush on their "cousin," would rage:

"As soon as they set foot in France, they think of nothing but those white whores. And as for us, proper young ladies of their own color, we're left on the shelf."

Saying this, she would glare at Létitia so as to make it clear that she did not include her in this category of "proper young ladies." Matime, carefully ironing shirts which her sons would return to her stained with lipstick and reeking of women, would sigh:

"God is good! One day, you will find the man you deserve."

It took Estella almost thirty years to find the man she deserved! And that isn't to say that she followed him willingly to Abidjan when he moved there. He may have been a doctor with a perfect education, but Bernard Amazouan had nothing in common with the image of Prince Charming so dear to the fantasies of her Antillean girlhood. So black and with all that kinky hair! For her part, Létitia, who recognized all this, wondered why such an elegant and cultivated man would make such an effort to acquire an imitation, a fake jewel that no one else wanted. Really, love must be blind!

Estella had had it all, her ceremony at Saint-Germain-l'Auxerrois, her reception at Ledoyen, and her honeymoon in Italy! Then, bringing along her helpless old mother, she flew off to Abidjan.

It was there that Matime had died!

The two sisters saw each other again on that occasion. In spite of her grief, Estella could not keep herself from showing off the two cars in her garage, the ten rooms of her villa, her three sons raised in the American way, with lots of cereal and apple juice.

A few days before Létitia's scheduled date of departure, Estella entered the room where her sister, paralyzed with grief and remorse, could not bring herself to face the cruelty of another day. She flung the windows wide open to get rid of the smell of smoke and alcohol, and stood there for a long while, saying nothing, motionless, looking out on the panorama of the lagoon where the dead bodies of branches and tree trunks floated among the water lilies. Then she turned and fixed Létitia with her inflexible gaze:

"Stay with us here! Believe me, it's for her, for her that I ask this. She was always so worried about you, I'm sure that shortened her life. I can't even count how many times I found her crying because of you! But God is great, He will judge us all. You're old enough now, you must understand that the time for foolishness is over. What you need is some order in your life, and a good man by your side! With his connections, Bernard can find you a job in no time. As for the rest, well, you always did know how to handle men. . . ."

If she had had her wits about her, Létitia would have refused with all her strength the life Estella was offering her. But her senses were dulled by the pain she felt at not having held Matime one last time while begging her forgiveness; by her despair at the idea of leaving her mother there forever, lost in that foreign cemetery; by her fear of picking up the dirty threads of her life in Paris. She accepted, and that acceptance had meant disaster.

Disaster.

Létitia bent forward, leaning her elbows heavily on the table. On its polished surface, the images of the past began to spin, to spin wildly as if caught in a furious maelstrom, while all the old scars and wounds reopened and the blood dripped through her fingers that were clutched tightly at her chest.

Disaster.

Suddenly she noticed that night had fallen and that she was sitting in a pool of shadows. She stood up and went to turn on the lights. At that moment, a figure appeared in the doorway. She had thought of him so often in the preceding days that at first she thought he was a hallucination, a vision plainly reflecting her troubled spirit. Then she realized that he was really standing there, in flesh and blood, the American Rasta, wearing torn jeans and a leather jacket studded around the collar with stars and buttons. He smiled, and that furtive smile, full of malice, made all the images of violence associated with America pass through her head. She became frightened and said curtly:

"What do you want?"

As he closed the door behind him and took a few steps forward, she thought of all the neighbors who had seen him enter her house and of the rumors that must have been flying through the village. Dropping his backpack on the table, he laughed:

"You were a whole lot friendlier the other evening!"

She repeated:

"What do you want?"

He shrugged his shoulders.

"Nothing! I wanted to talk. It's been a long time since I've talked to anyone. You know, the people in Pâquette . . . they're not exactly great conversationalists. . . ."

She decided to try to calm her fears. Controlling her voice, she offered:

"Do you want something to drink?"

He pouted:

"What do you have? Rum, I bet, and I hate rum!"

She turned toward the sideboard, and suddenly he was on top of her. Terrified, she pleaded:

"I don't have anything. No jewels! No money! Nothing!"

He smiled his unsettling smile:

"That's not what I came here for, *woman!*"

* * *

The people of Morne Gabriel were hardly surprised when the American Rasta, whom they called simply "the Rasta," left Pâquette and went to live at Létitia's house. They had always known that Létitia wasn't a proper lady, and that one day she would be at the center of a scandal of the highest magnitude, a scandal never before seen, never before heard, a scandal that would stay forever in their memories.

The women began to slip out to visit Mme Forget, the mother of Marie Gracieuse, so as to gather the juiciest details of that sinful life, details they later reported to their men, who discussed them somewhat enviously at the *Roses de Mélissa*. Marie Gracieuse went on for days about how the Rasta spent his time lying in bed, naked under the sheets, enveloped in the smell of the brown cigars he was always smoking; or about how, with Létitia's help, he emptied bottle after bottle of whiskey—and she didn't let her half go to waste, oh no, far from it! Everyone agreed that if it weren't for her family's desperate need for the 1,200 francs Létitia paid her every month, promptly and in cash, a young girl like Marie Gracieuse should certainly stay away from such a place. It is not good to be exposed to vice: sooner or later, it contaminates you.

Without question, in all of Morne Gabriel, the most offended was Sister Rosa.

* * *

The first few days, Létitia lived with Ron as with some unknown animal, clearly vicious and cruel, whose fatal bite she feared at every moment. Even the pleasure he gave her, which she found irresistible, seemed destined to consecrate her humiliation, to drive her right to the edge of terror and defeat.

Then, everything changed.

One night, she opened her eyes to see him standing next to the window, staring at the blond moon above the black trees. On his face was an expression of such adolescent pain and confusion that all her fears dried up at once, replaced by an immense desire to comfort and help him. Feeling her eyes on him, he turned and came to sit on the edge of the bed:

"I think I'm going to go back up to Pâquette. I've been enough bother as it is."

She could think of nothing to say. He asked her:

"Why didn't you call the police? I forced you at the beginning."

She shrugged her shoulders:

"I've always thought that I should get out of trouble on my own."

Suddenly, he collapsed on her chest and blurted out:

"You're a good woman, you know! A good woman!"

Carefully she stroked his cheek, which she was not surprised to find sticky with tears. She murmured:

"Tell me. . ."

But he shook his head furiously:

"No. There's nothing to tell."

From then on, he became the son she had waited for, and what went on between them was no longer so serious, giving rise to no more guilt than those imaginary acts of incest committed by all sons with their mothers, before they truly become men. Since his stomach was in knots, she fixed him small plates of food and fed him by mouthfuls. Since he wrapped himself in that filth which, she knew, sometimes serves as a cocoon for grief, she pushed him under the shower and washed his shivering body. She tried in every way possible to keep him away from the backpack from which he drew his deadly sustenance, distracting him by making herself by turns a storyteller, a singer, even a dancer. She asked him nothing more, since he did not want to confide in her, but contented herself with the scraps of information he let fall. His father and his mother were legal advisers at a firm in Los Angeles. He had been spoilt. Linguistic vacations in Paris. Snowy vacations in Montana. Seaside vacations in St. Barthélemy. Then, the machine that lobotomizes the children of the bourgeoisie had jammed. Everything revolved around a brother whose story involved more than the usual family abuses: had he killed himself? been killed? died from an overdose? from AIDS? was he in prison? Létitia couldn't quite figure it out. She felt helpless, and with her imperfect knowledge of the facts, all she could do was echo the same ineffectual words that Matime used to repeat endlessly—"take your life into your own hands," "bury yourself in your studies, that's all that counts!", "find someone who'll make you forget all this," "you have your whole life ahead of you"—realizing with anguish that love has no remedy to offer. He huddled up next to her, repeating:

"They won't get me. They won't get me!"

* * *

Anselme, the police superintendent, looked with some annoyance at the two men, the two women, and the young girl—practically a child, really—sitting on the other side of his desk. He knew Sister Rosa, since in a small community like Morne Gabriel such vipers rarely pass unnoticed, but thank God! he had never had to deal with her. Irritated, he grumbled:

"There's nothing I can do about it. Taking a young lover isn't a crime. . ."

Sister Rosa's icy glare made him add quickly:

"Unless, of course, a minor is involved. And as for this Rasta, do you think we arrest people just like that? We need proof!"

Sister Rosa spat, her eyes narrowing with hate:

"What more proof do you need?"

At this, she pointed to the young girl to her right, visibly uncomfortable and not at all proud of the role she was playing:

"She saw it! Tell him what you told us, Marie Gracieuse!"

Marie Gracieuse complied in a voice so barely audible that Anselme had to lean forward to catch her words. After she fell silent, he said nothing, and sat watching a hummingbird courting a hibiscus flower in the garden. Sister Rosa shouted at him:

"What more do you need? Do you want him to start selling his drugs to the children at school?"

The hummingbird, being drunk with love, flew off toward another flower. Sister Rosa practically screamed:

"Didn't they say on television just the other day that some cocaine smugglers were arrested in Marie-Galante? How do we know that he's not one of them, come to hide out at her house?"

Since Anselme was still saying nothing, she threatened:

"And if you don't want to do anything, I'll go talk to the Mayor, in person, and we'll see what he thinks about all this!"

Beaten, Anselme scratched a few words on his notepad and asked Marie Gracieuse:

"In a backpack, you say?"

* * *

After everyone had come and told him what was going on, down to the last detail, Hugo did not set foot in Morne Gabriel for six solid months.

He was outraged. How could she do such a thing to him? He was a good catch, dammit, with his head nurse's salary . . . not to mention the money he made making house calls after six, pedaling around on his old racing bike—even at his age he didn't need a car! He could have chosen some young thing to spice up his old age! At the same time, he was suffering, for he had always had a weakness for Létitia, ever since the time she used to watch him at the house in Aubervilliers, caressing him with her brazen eyes, challenging him: "What are you waiting for?"

But that was just it: back then, she frightened him. He didn't trust her, knowing that she would not be the reliable companion a man needs, a woman who would give you children, do the cooking, and cry hot tears when you cheated on her. Afterward, when she started going from man to man, he felt the satisfaction of a seer whose predictions were coming true. Finding her again in Guadeloupe after all those years, growing old alone, he decided that she had been punished enough and that she was at last the kind of woman he wanted. Apparently, he had been mistaken!

Nevertheless, at the end of six months, Hugo, tying his tourniquet around the arm of one of his patients or sticking the needle of a syringe into another's bottom, was seized with such a desire to see Létitia, to hear her voice and her laugh, that he could not wait for the weekend to go up to Morne Gabriel, and right in the middle of the week he leapt onto the six-thirty express bus. A little before nine, the bus dropped him off in front of Madame Mondépé's shop, and he walked up the main road, trying not to pay attention to the men and women who came out of their houses and, at the sight of him, turned into pillars of salt under the bright sunshine.

Even from a distance, Létitia's house struck him with its air of desolation. The garden, once so carefully tended, planted with all the different rosebushes she had bought from the priest in Goyave, had been abandoned. Weeds and Guinea grass had invaded the flower beds, the neighbors' puppy had burrowed holes in the small lawn, and overripe oranges lay rotting at the base of the trees.

Hugo crossed the living room, in which the furniture, covered with sheets, drifted like icebergs. He walked through the bedroom, cluttered with glasses and empty bottles, into the kitchen, devoid of smells and warmth.

Létitia was sitting outside under the passion fruit bower, her hands crossed over her knees, staring off into space. When he called out to her, she turned toward him a face so ravaged that all the reproachful speeches he had prepared during the trip flew out of his head. Her eyes were like two wells of unfathomable suffering. He sat down next to her, as silent and compassionate as if he were at a wake, and took her weak and lifeless hands in his. After a few moments, she cried out in a strangled voice:

"He was my child and they took him from me. There was nothing I could do for him."

Quickly, he said:

"Your child? Does that mean that you didn't . . ."

Then he felt ashamed of the question he was going to ask and fell silent, holding her hands more tightly.

She continued:

"I took him to the airport when they deported him, and since then, I've had no news, not one letter, not one phone call. I just wait and wait."

He murmured:

"That's normal. He's gone back to his country, to his family. He's trying to forget the nightmare he had in Guadeloupe!"

She shook her head violently:

"No, no! That's not it at all! He wanted nothing to do with his country, or his family. I'm afraid something has happened to him. . . ."

At this point, she burst into uncontrollable tears. Quiet for a moment, he pulled her toward him and softly stroked her neck, her shoulders, her tangled hair:

"You know, that's what they are, children. Anguish, worry, ingratitude! Look at me and my children. Do they care about me? Do they write to me? Do I know what has happened to them? We still have a few good years of life left to live. Let's take advantage of them, and think about ourselves. Go wash your face, change your dress, comb your hair, and pack a few things. While you're doing that, I'll close the doors and the windows. We'll catch the express bus at noon. I fixed up my parents' house myself. You'll see how well we'll live there. Think about us. That's all that counts!"

She sobbed for a long time, endlessly it seemed, curled up against his chest. Periodically she murmured angry words, as if she were revolting against this final blow of a destiny that had never been kind to her, that had on the contrary wounded her, made her bleed at will. Finally, gradually, she calmed herself and stood up, swaying as if already old age had beaten her forever.

When she got up to the front door, she stumbled, almost fell, barely regained her balance, and turned toward him to ask, in a voice charged with disbelief:

"Can it be true? You want me . . . still?"

Torn between the anger and shame he felt at his own weakness and a sense of pity and immense tenderness, he said roughly:

"Go get dressed, I said!"

After she had disappeared into the house, he stayed huddled in his chair for a long while, imagining the shocked amazement of the people of Morne Gabriel when they saw them crossing the village, she leaning heavily on his arm, he guiding her as he would from then on. For the rest of their days.

The sound of a donkey braying rose up from a neighboring field, a sure sign that noon was not far off. He arose in turn and went into the house.

—Translated by Karl Britto

ASSIA DJEBAR

The White of Algeria

INTRODUCTION
By Clarisse Zimra

In 1993, the French city of Strasbourg, in association with the University of Strasbourg, the Cultural Ministry of the French government and of the Common Market, sponsored its annual series of symposia, films, and round tables at the Center for European Literatures. As implied in the official title, "Le cri du monde" (The World's Scream), its theme was dedicated to the defense of artistic freedom around the world; its aim was to bring about, at long last, Herman Broch's old dream of the 1940s, a "Parliament of Writers" to act as the conscience of the Western world. This time around, the meeting focused on Sarajevo and the violent disintegration of Eastern Europe, "an obsession with identity, only achievable through ethnic, cultural, and linguistic cleansing, to which Bosnia has become the ghastly emblem, as well as the laboratory."[1]

The presence among the participants of writers from the Maghreb, Assia Djebar and Mohammed Dib among them, was no accident. Their country is now on the brink of a civil war; its borders have been closed. Open season has been declared on all dissenters by both sides, a repressive but semi-secular government battling religious fundamentalism. Intellectuals, journalists, artists, writers (and women) are now *personae non gratae*. Thousands have been murdered.

Algeria may well be the next ghastly laboratory of identity politics. Djebar's essay singles out the official "Arabization policy" that has systematically distorted her country's long and complex past, one that goes back all the way to the autochtonous Berber resistance to Egyptian encroachment; and one that would now deny the "Algerianity" of writers who chose not to write in Arabic, herself included. Since the 1962 victory against the French masters, a

1. Christian Salmon, "No to Speechlessness," *Le cri du monde,* special edition of *Carrefour des Littératures Européennes de Strasbourg* (4–8 November 1993), 2.

YFS 87, *Another Look, Another Woman,* ed. Huffer, © 1995 by Yale University.

new kind of cultural imperialism has erased all other political, linguistic, and cultural contributions to what might have been the only successful multi-ethnic, multicultural national revolution on the shores of the Mediterranean.

Jaded revolutionaries, grown fat on oil royalties and foreign aid, attempted to sweep under the rug the problems raised by the decomposing economy they mismanaged. Their decision to give a free rein to religious fervor, and to pro-mote teachers and intellectuals trained in Middle-Eastern countries as a coun-terbalance to the pull of the West and the calls for a more open society among European-trained intellectuals, misfired. On 4 October 1988, in the streets of Algiers, the army opened fire on a sea of young civilians protesting the recent rise in the price of bread. Hunted down alleys by tanks, thousands were injured, thousands more tortured—many disappeared while incarcerated. The official count at the end of the first day was of six hundred dead—that is, for those whose bodies could be found. Djebar has commented on this as the shattering events that precipitated the writing of *Loin de Médine* in a 1993 *Callaloo* interview.

Although these riots were the culmination of a series of tough factory strikes, the October march managed to regroup a motley alliance of idealistic students, committed democrats, lukewarm religious believers, and at least eight different women's associations. The blood bath played into the hands of the hard-core fundamentalists. Three years later, in December 1991, the FIS (Front National de Salut or National Front for Salvation) cleaned up at the polls. In an unprecedented unconstitutional move, and with the backing of frightened secular moderates, the regime declared the elections null and void, and put the country in the hands of a Security Council. After a few months of tentative thawing, the replacement president was murdered while attending an official function in June 1992, his execution broadcast live on television. While it is tempting to speculate that his assassins, who claimed allegiance to the FIS, were religious fanatics, a cynic might find it equally compelling to conclude that they were egged on by military hard-liners. There has been ever more violent repression, torture, and execution from both sides. As of Septem-ber 1994, an estimated 10,000 people have been killed, according to the state-run news agency.

"The White of Algeria" takes up the problematic and tangled connection between writing and saying the individual self, writing and expressing the collective self (*parole* vs. *écriture*) in a repressive state. Algeria, once in the throes of a revolutionary war against the French masters, is now in the throes of a civil war against itself (the self-cannibalistic immolation, *auto-dévoration*, that ends the essay). In the current power struggle, physical and cultural vio-lence has been aimed at the women who continue to march. In the first months of 1994, twenty-seven were killed, often stabbed, or their throats cut, for not wearing the veil. The youngest was fourteen; the oldest, ninety-four. In retalia-tion, secular, anti-FIS groups have attacked veiled women. Although the European media have commented abundantly, American press releases have been few. Thus, in an essay ostensibly intended for a European audience, Djebar need not specify her subtext: in the ever-repressive Algerian state, women are now targets of choice, because they've always been the culture's symbols of choice.

That Djebar would couch her response to the current events in her country under the twin symbols of the Woman (covertly) and the Berber (overtly) is deliberate. "The White of Algeria" pointedly yokes Apuleus, the North-African writer born in the Numidian capital of Ciria (modern-day Constantine) in 125 AD, but writing in the language of the Roman invaders, to the modern-day, Arabophone Kateb and Berberophone Mammeri, who practiced the language of the French invaders. In a bold countermove shored up by its authentic past, Djebar claims for Algeria a larger literature, and a wider homeland that would encompass not only the "treasures" and "jewels" of classical Arabic poetry; not only the "suffused iridescence" of the folk dialects and the oral tradition; but the sons and daughters of colonizers as well. Her reclaiming Camus and Roblès as part and parcel of the Algerian landscape, not to mention Derrida and Cixous, is thus truly provocative, given the officially sanctioned short-term historical memory, in the teeth of both stubborn Kabyle endurance and female autonomy.

Nevertheless, one must be careful not to oversimplify. Although female resistance to the fundamentalist platform has been documented in the western press, there is plenty of evidence of vigorous female participation in the FIS as well. Some are younger scientists educated in Arab universities, who may resent their lack of access to the West (Western-trained Francophone or Anglophone intellectuals have tended to belong to the middle and upper classes). Some may well find in their sanctioned public participation in the ongoing political and social debate that the FIS provides them a forum long denied by the "back to the kitchen" policies of aging erstwhile revolutionaries. Be that as it may, Algerian women have always been the ideological refuge of last resort. Where the eraser effect of French colonialism was particularly brutal (and efficient), and by the very virtue of their enforced isolation, women were entrusted with preserving the last cultural values and the last shreds of dignity of a dispossessed people. Thus, in the ideological war now waged along with the economic one, Woman has become the ultimate pawn.

Both a mourning celebration of departed friends (Kateb, Mammeri, Djaout) and a grieving for a suicidal nation, "The White of Algeria" marks a turning point in Djebar's career, because it is the first time she has come publicly, in voice as well as in print, to an openly political position regarding current events in her country (although she has, of course, done so in her novels and indirectly in her interviews). She indicts the official governmental policy that would render the complex and multilayered ethnicity of past and present-day Algeria into a single entity. But she also indicts a whole generation of writers and thinkers, herself among them, who have not spoken soon enough and loudly enough. Not anymore.

"Le blanc de l'Algérie," a title that puns simultaneously on "white," "blank," and "void" (three possible meanings of the French), was presented at the week-long meeting of world writers at the Center for European Literatures in Strasbourg. Then writer-in-residence at the Center, Djebar was part of a distinguished roster, from Nobel Laureate Octavio Paz to the United States's own Susan Sontag and Toni Morrison, brought together to address the questions of world-wide freedom of expression and political censorship. She served on the steering committee calling for an International Parliament of Writers. The manifesto was signed by two hundred of them.

In the original French, the essay appeared in *Carrefour des Littératures Européennes de Strasbourg*. It was translated by their in-house translator, Andrew Benson, for use during the meeting. I have added footnotes to this version, graciously sent by the editorial team of *Carrefour* with Mr. Benson's permission.

* * *

Algeria today . . . in the wake of a series of murders of writers and intellectuals that was triggered, it seems, in response to increased repression—the only policy anyone can find to brandish against a religious fundamentalism set on taking power whatever the cost; in the face of these convulsions which are plunging my country into a war that dares not speak its name and that again could be euphemistically referred to as "events"[2]; in this return of violence and its anaesthetizing vocabulary, what is this "white" (the whiteness of dust, light without sun, dilution, etc.) and why bring it up here?

Rather than simply inscribing my comments in the wake of those made on this tragedy by sociologists, historians, political scientists, and even pamphleteers, I can find no other way to express *my own* unease as a writer and an Algerian than by referring to this color, or rather, this non-color. Kandinsky said that "white, on our soul, acts like absolute silence." Here, by means of this reference to abstract painting, I am setting off a discourse that is, in such circumstances, somewhat off-center.

Irreversibly, the edges of the chasm are gaping, pulling into the abyss not only some of the boldest intellectuals, but, according to

2. The euphemism used by the French government and media reporting on a national liberation struggle (1954–1962) they did not want to dignify with the name of "war." Djebar uses the allusion sarcastically, as does Dib in the poem she includes later.

the luck of a bloody lottery, some of the meekest as well. Indeed, the violence so unleashed, in its blind acceleration certainly accentuates the vanity of the spoken word, but also its necessity. Any word (*parole*) that would not primarily be one of passion, and that, groping about in the dark for the limits of its reach, could remain aware of its own fragility and even of its inanity comes too late. But, beneath the leaden sky where it unfurls, let such a word come out of its hiding place to set traps and ambush all ambiguities; to wit, the fact that the media take-over of any intellectual resistance (one remembers before 1992 the media transforming a few fanatics of God [*fous de Dieu*] into a spectacle) only ended up in a thickening white noise, the blank zone of the projectors, widening the desert (here I am only referring to Algerian intellectuals on the verge of the dizzying abyss and not, of course, to the solidarity, in France and elsewhere, which is trying to organize itself).

For I am haunted, personally—in the calm before the storm—by the long and abiding state of morbidity in which Algerian culture has lingered: discourse secreting and fomenting the latent brew of discord—not because of the emptiness of political speech which wasted little time in degenerating into a mere bandying of words and the recital of socioeconomic findings trapped within their own science. No!

It has often seemed to me that, in an Algeria that has increasingly become culturally fragmented (and where the traditional sexual segregation has tightened all the screws), words (*paroles*) have, of necessity, lost their edge even before they could sharpen themselves by their own flickering light.

And yet, I am moved only by that need for words (*paroles*) with which to confront this imminent disaster. Writing and its urgency.

Writing about an Algeria teetering on the brink and for which some people are already preparing the white shroud.

I lived in Algeria as a university academic for much of the thirty years of independence; as such, I tried to fight, like my peers, and before long, to little avail, against the setting up of an educational system whose absurdity—no, worse than that, whose imbecility—in the sense of inherent and irremediable weakness—sent so many young people headlong into a distressing cultural underdevelopment, one that fed itself, true, on a hunger for social justice that was being simultaneously sharpened and frustrated. Their numbers have been growing because of an unbridled population boom deliberately encouraged by the state.

Now that the three knocks have already sounded on the stage of this drama (or this tragedy), it would be useless to indict a policy that preached from on high a massive, cut-rate Arabization, backed by elites more often than not graduated from the Sorbonne, and not just any Oriental universities or medieval "zaouias." And all the while, such a policy claimed a desire for modernity, when it only meant technology!

Long before the Islamic fundamentalist danger flared up, fanned by all these winds of popular dissent, long before it turned oppressive, some dissident intellectuals had denounced the pseudopopulism of a self-congratulatory authoritarianism that was using the wealth from our nationalized oil to shore up its self-serving image.

My intention, more limited in scope, is to throw light on the cultural, there to focus on the fatal point where the inevitable failure anchored itself.

Throughout the seventies, Algeria polished up its official image as a representative of international third-world politics, while in its own market towns and villages, in every lower-class district (already mired in the twin sicknesses of unrest and poverty), everything relating to communication—or the word (parole)—was progressively sealed off. Inexorably the poison seeped in—what I do not flinch from calling a "war between languages."

Algerian literature—from Apuleus in the second century to Kateb Yacine and Mouloud Mammeri, our contemporaries departed in such untimely fashion—has always inscribed a linguistic triangle:

—A first language of rock and soil, let us say sprung from the original language, the Lybico-Berber which for a while lost its written form, except among the Touaregs.[3]

3. Traced as far back as 1200 BC, when they tangled with the Egyptian pharaohs, the Berbers are part of the motley grouping of original people along the Mediterranean shores. (The Arab invaders from the East did not settle in earnest until the eighth century AD.) They shared a linguistic base and a common writing system with the Semito-Phoenicians, leaving some stone monuments inscribed with these "Lybico-Berber" characters.

Although varieties of the Berber language have survived and are thriving in North Africa in oral form, the written version had all but disappeared in the twentieth century, kept barely alive in the transcription system of the Nomadic Touaregs of the Sahara, who may now number well over a million.

—A second language, that of the prestigious outside, of the Mediterranean or Eastern or Western heritage, reserved, it is true, for literate minorities: in the past, for a long time, it was an Arabic kept in the shadow of official French; a French now marginalized when it is used to creative ends, but valued at school only as a "language of science and technology."

—The third partner in this "ménage à trois," the most visible, dominant, public language, the language of power: that of diatribes but also, in written form, the medium of scribes, lawyers, and notaries. This role has been filled by different languages throughout our history: Latin until Augustine; Classical Arabic in the Middle Ages; Turkish, which, during the "Kingdom of Algiers," took over administrative and military usage. Then, after 1830, French entered the stage, dressed in a colonial uniform; now, the so-called "modern" Arabic taught to the young under the pompous, ahistorical term of "national language." (To be logical, our "national language"—or that of a reborn postcolonial Algerian State—was Turkish for three centuries, and Arabic only for the last three decades. This Arabic may be "classical" but it is limited and soulless. The Nation, though, like all nations, enriches its language with the swelling of its verve and sap, in the bad times as in the good.)

As for the "war between languages" mentioned above, I came to experience it personally only gradually at the university. At first, I underestimated its quasi-neurotic symptoms: that certain academics, spouting a grotesquely pompous jargon of scholastic Arabic, devoid of any real thought, as soothing and meaningless as Church Latin, should suddenly decide, long after the war of independence, to become born-again aggressive nationalists, waging war against the French language, and, if need be, against the "West"; there was a comedy of human stupidity, which sooner or later, it seemed to me, would inspire an Algerian Flaubert or Gogol.

To sum up, this drive for institutionalized mediocrity worked on two fronts: for example, promoting the "national language" in the media meant, first, authoritatively restricting the living space of other languages, cutting off programs in French and Berber from television and radio, like so many limbs. The second tier of discordance in this sterilizing monolingualism, the diglossia of Arabic (that vertical variability of structure that could give school children a precious mental agility), was handled the worst by far when compared with other Arab educational systems, undoubtedly because of a massive importation of

Middle Eastern teachers, and, above all, because of a ban on the popular culture that feeds on a dialect suffused with the iridescence of regional variations, a dialect subtle in its innate power to convey contention, irony, and dreams.

Thus, denying a whole people their genius went hand in hand with being suspicious of that minority of writers who express themselves in French and who, against the odds, or, for lack of better, in exile, managed to continue to produce.

Jacques Berque, who recently declared that "Islamic fundamentalism" wants to claim modernity while rejecting its intellectual substructures, says of Algeria and its linguistic choices that it is living a situation that has never existed in any of the twenty other Arab countries, those that also had to face diglossia, with the presence of one or two second languages. He concludes that Algeria has been good at turning a potential source of superiority into a major problem!

Following the—prestigious—example of Georges Bataille who, on the day war was declared in 1939, began his work *Le Coupable* ("I am beginning because of the events but shall not speak about them . . ."), perhaps it is time for the few writers occupied with questions of "Algerianity" [*algérianité*] to tackle texts they may feel constrained to write, no longer in memory of a colonial past in which their childhood took place, but in the light of the present threats on the land of their ancestors, even if they have left it behind.

I use the word "Algerianity," a far broader notion than the "Algerian identity" recorded on official papers; just as in the past it included Camus and Roblès alongside Ferraoun and Kateb, it would now link Derrida and Mohammed Dib, or Hélène Cixous and myself.

Writing Algeria as territory. The desert of writing (*l'écriture*), "that which, from the indefinite white which starts out, reconstitutes the margin," in the words of André Dubouchet, speaking in 1986 in Hölderin's house in Tübingen.

And what of the white of Algeria, "out of tune, out of sorts [*désaccordée*], as if by the snow"? I am coming back to it.

I appear to have lingered over the ruins of deliquescent knowledge, whose pathetic failure ought to have acted much earlier as a warning of an explosion, that of October 1988. Six hundred young corpses in the sun—the future bled white—were not entitled to the least liturgical mourning in any of the three languages, or in a symphony of all three together: where was poetry to be found, then? Where, its summits?

Where, its abysses? Aphasia was no longer condemnation but a mask pulled over a decomposing face. . . .

Kateb Yacine, whom I saw in Brussels one month later, was quiet, determined to be quiet. When he made up his mind, a bit later, to return to exile to write, to write of his rage no doubt, he was struck down by leukemia, the white disease.

The "opening" which followed on the political front allowed a multiparty system and, it was hoped, democracy: it turned out to be fragile and fit only for buffoons. Then, after the murder of the head of state, with everyone watching live, one Monday in June of 1992, things accelerated in a chain reaction.

Two weeks before Tahar Djaout[4] was murdered, when I was paying public homage in Paris to Mohammed Dib, I expressed my anguish over the deadlock in which the noncommunicable—the white blankness, as it were, of Algerian misfortune—plunged first and foremost our writers into an abyss:

> The proud ally of the wind, you say
> The bird traveler, yes, that land of Algeria,
> The proud ally, barefoot in the sand, hair like brushwood
> and stomach rounded, Algeria of the shadows
> She fed those angel faces arising in full sunlight, over there
> She kholed their cold eyes with a dancing anger
> Rouged their cheeks with solitary boredom
> Reddened their mouths with screaming silence
> Thirty years on, words come full circle in a heavy sky
> and return to their source
> They explode, sedition of space:
> "events," state of siege, riot police, outlaw
> and the victims of chance, wide-eyed, and tears
> It all comes back—but in a pitiful inversion.

In fact, during the bloody days of October, the insomnia that plagued me in the middle of Algiers, with its curfew, where tanks threaded through the streets, led me to begin a text called "Deserted Algiers,"

4. Born in 1954, and trained as a mathematician, he was one of the younger generation of Algerian intellectuals. Of probable Kabyle ancestry, he was murdered by Fundamentalist sympathizers on 26 May 1992. He had published poems and novels in France. His last publications were *Les Vigiles* (Seuil, 1991) and *L'Exproprié* (Majault, 1991). His short and gifted life qualified him for almost all of the unforgivable sins on the FIS list: writer, journalist of avowed secular bent, trained and published in the West, and with homosexual leanings. His paper *Algérie-Actualité* had published excerpts of Djebar's last and controversial historical meditation on the life of the Prophet, *Loin de Médine.*

never finished; my anger, when I reread the translucent poetry written by Dib (appealing for a "beyond-powerlessness") found, thanks to the silence of that friendship, a sort of outlet.

I realized that the desert could seize our words (*parole*) from within.

Algeria left untranslated: the outstanding works of the most important "national" writers (Kateb, Dib, Ferraoun, Mammeri) translated almost throughout the world, were left untranslated into the "national language" for thirty years! All they were reluctantly allowed was the academic readership at university, but confined to the "foreign languages" department! From time to time, they were anthologized in some dreary secondary-school readers.

More serious still: the treasures of oral literature in the delicate dialects—the living breath of the Algerian people over centuries— were equally excluded; a few were, sometimes, transcribed. One never tired of harking back to yesteryear's manly struggle, but no attention was paid to the treasures expressing courtly love, or nostalgia, jewels that ran the gamut from deeply felt mysticism to voluptuous and tender beauty. Living Algerian Arabic, a language for doves and poets, but not for the new civil servants.

As for Berber, it was banned very early on at universities (if you wanted to study it, you had to go to Naples or Aix!) and persecuted even in primary schools, fueling the fire of discontent leading to the Kabyle crisis in 1980.[5]

Each language, then, was confined to its area, regional or social— condemned to a ghetto—while in between them lay a no-man's-land. Wan whiteness crept in, like a lonely wind or frost.

The worst occurred during the mid-1980s. The tap controlling the consumption of live images was opened fully (nonpictures for the most part), allowing in French television or, more accurately, American series dubbed into French. At the same time, a decision was made to end—under the pretext of saving money—the circulation of any press which expressed opinions from elsewhere, thereby starving researchers and real readers—a minority, it's true—to whom books were as vital as food and drink. In universities, a stop was put to the teaching of the main European languages—apart from French and English—

5. A probable reference to the strikes and street riots in the city of Azazga, in Greater Kabylia, triggered around the visit and subsequently banned public lecture on Kabyle language and culture by Mouloud Mammeri.

putting a whole section of the Algerian memory out of reach—all that lies in Spanish, Italian, and Turkish archives.

This means that a whole treasure has been put out of bounds, including *Nedjma* and *The Stranger*, but also *Nausea*, Kafka's *Letter to His Father*, and *Dr. Zhivago*, because they have not been translated into the "national language": blacklisted—rather, white-listed or whitewashed in the dirty white of tacit, lazy censorship. In fact, I think it is really the brighter-than-white shine of the ring around the bull's eye. These works, which might have sparked interest in young minds, had to be kept out of reach. So that they do not fly off and reach the point of no return: the inquisitive, questioning reader who, in their mirror, would have felt less deprived.

Between creator and reader, whether in French, Arabic, or Berber, stretched the inner border of a "new" Algeria, i.e., one fragmented, sealed off from any thought nurtured somewhere else and drained of the sap of its scorned roots. Held in that tight grip, Algeria was unmoored and delivered, wide-open, to the peddlers, to all kinds of "media" of all persuasions, as well as the warped zealot.

In this "unsaid" of the cultural desert, you could begin to hear, underground, the barely audible crackle of the current fissure.

The white of silence and that of the page waiting in vain for an original text and its translated double, at the risk of being somewhat betrayed.

The white of writing, in an untranslated Algeria? For the time being, Algeria, writingless, despite all the actions of writing, despite its angers and groans; alas, for the time being, a bloody but writing-less country (*sang-écriture*).

How can we mourn our friends, our colleagues, without beforehand saying out loud why yesterday's funeral took place, the funeral of the Algerian dream? The white of dawn—between the colonial night and the rising day? "White square on a white background," like a Malevich painting, exclaiming, at the turn of the century: "But this desert is brimming with an objective sensitivity that pervades everything!"

In the brilliance of that desert, in the retreat of writing in search of a language outside languages (*hors les langues*), endeavoring to scrub out, in ourselves, all the furies of collective self-devouring, to find that place "from within-among words" (*en dedans de la parole*) that remains our one and only fertile homeland.

—Translated by Andrew Benson

CLARISSE ZIMRA

Disorienting the Subject in Djebar's
L'Amour, la fantasia

Over eighteen years ago, something happened that changed our
scholarly landscape forever. Within a few months of its controversial French publication in 1975, Hélène Cixous's "The Laugh of the
Medusa,"[1] an ebulliently optimistic manifesto that dared both men
and women to write their bodies "otherwise," had found its way into
Signs, an American journal.[2] Five years later and within weeks of
each other, assessing the progress of what had then become a full
fledged countermovement within discourse theory, both *Yale French
Studies*[3] and *Signs*[4] devoted an issue to French feminists in translation, as opposed to the occasional articles that had cropped up here
and there across the academic horizon. Acknowledging its debt to an
earlier issue of *Feminist Studies*, *Signs* offered four essays: Kristeva
("Women's Time"), Cixous ("Castration or Decapitation"), Irigaray
("And the One Doesn't Stir without the Other"), and Fauré ("Ab-
sent from History"). These had been seminal texts in Europe, and the
editors hoped that these translations would, across national boundaries, refine our understanding of "the precise relation of women
to history" (1), a relation described as simultaneously sexed and gendered. Although "marked by genuine frustration," primarily at "the
density of the French material . . . its penchant for ultimately un-

---

1. Hélène Cixous, "Le rire de la Méduse," *L'Arc* 61 (1975): 39–54.
2. Hélène Cixous, "The Laugh of the Medusa," *Signs* 1/4 (Summer 1976): 875–93.
3. *Yale French Studies* 62 (Autumn 1981). This issue was edited by Colette Gaudin,
Mary Jean Green, Lynn Anthony Higgins, Marianne Hirsch, Vivian Kogan, Claudia
Reeder, and Nancy Vickers.
4. *Signs* 17/1 (Autumn 1981).

YFS 87, *Another Look, Another Woman*, ed. Huffer, © 1995 by Yale University.

translatable word play," the *YFS* team rising to the challenge nonetheless concluded:

> Feminism, then, far from bringing to literary criticism the assurance of a unified ideology, introduces on the contrary, a different deconstructive twist into existing critical approaches: it adds new force to the recognition that reading is always rereading.[5]

From the "natural" crossbreeding between complex continental positions with their impeccable theoretical constructs, on the one hand, and, on the other, the sturdy determinism of Anglo-American pragmatic historicism, a new method was to be born that would translate almost immediately, perhaps even effortlessly, theory into praxis.

The task has proved somewhat more daunting than anticipated, and it is commendable that *YFS* should now re-open the question. With the accurate, 20/20 vision of the backward glance, and sporting the few bumps and bruises of life in the academic trenches, we've learned *not* to take for granted any of the conceptual categories with which we must work, all the while aware that work with them—as well as against them—we must. If French Feminism, in its gendered linguistic assault on the legacy of Eurocentric Enlightenment Humanism, had taught us little else, it would have taught us plenty.

So, if one now wonders whether such a stance still has anything to teach the rest of us, one must remember that, thirteen long years ago in *Yale French Studies*, Gayatri Spivak, taking on Kristeva's simplification of Chinese womanhood, and warning against Irigaray's potentially "idealistic subtext of the patriarchal project,"[6] had already demonstrated that deployment of discourse always entails a restrictive ideological foundation, whether self-consciously so or not. Domna Stanton's no less crucial warning, the witty "Difference on Trial" essay, would follow in 1986, excavating the increasingly dissymmetric blind spots of the Great Mothers.[7] Such sane assessments demonstrated that one could appropriate the French Feminist move as a reading method that was history-specific.

Out of the theoretical thicket, one road back to scholarly sanity may be to insist on meticulously honest textual, if not literal, reading; a way to stay, if for the moment, the choreography of Same and Other unfolding in the poststructuralist, postcolonial, postmodernist, post-

5. Gaudin et al., "Introduction," *Yale French Studies* 62, 13.

6. Gayatri Chakravorty Spivak, "French Feminism in an International Frame," *Yale French Studies* 62, 183.

7. Domna K. Stanton, "Difference on Trial" in *Poetics of Gender*, ed. Nancy K. Miller (New York: Columbia University Press, 1986), 156–81.

everything space. This need not imply that one comes to a definitive and essential textual truth, but, rather, to a specifically grounded and firmly circumscribed one. "French Feminism" (the handle has conveniently covered a variety of diverging positions) was always more strategy than methodology. Thus, to the Foucaldian-Derridean-Lacanian question, "who speaks, here (and for/instead of whom)," one can now respond "who reads, from where, and with whom."

WHO READS HERE

The present essay, itself an attempt at reading literally, started with the rather simple observation made by Assia Djebar during the course of a six-hour-long, largely unpublished, 1992 interview.[8] Commenting upon the publication of *Loin de Médine*,[9] a work that had put her in hot water with Islamic fundamentalists, who accused her of pandering to the expectations of the former masters, she volunteered that the language of the colonizer was no longer an issue for her: "En écrivant *L'Amour, la fantasia*, j'ai définitivement réglé mes comptes avec la langue française. Les peintres furent mes intercesseurs." [In writing *Fantasia*, I settled my accounts, once and for all, with the French language. The painters were my intercessors.] The term "intecessor," one who intervenes *with* someone, as well as *on behalf of* someone else, shifts simultaneously in opposite directions through ambivalent registers: either that of an accredited, trusted mediator who speaks for someone; or, perhaps one who, secretly and speciously, presumes to speak "instead of" those who cannot, or may not, speak for themselves. The deployment of the term thus invests the liminal, transgressive space where subjectivity is to be negotiated, as well as the space where it may find itself infinitely (re)negotiable.

The position is fraught with ambiguities, as one can see in Djebar's opening remarks to *Femmes d'Alger dans leur appartement*,[10] "among my books, the one most in dialogue with [French] feminism":[11]

Ne pas prétendre "parler pour", ou pire, "parler sur", à peine "parler PRÈS DE, et si possible, TOUT CONTRE: première des solidarités à

8. All private interviews henceforward are referenced as "unpub." A small portion of these six hours was translated as "When the Past Answers Our Present," *Callaloo* 16/1 (Summer 1993): 115–31. Unless otherwise indicated, all translations in this essay are mine.

9. Paris: Denoël, 1991.

10. Paris: des femmes, 1980.

11. I had phrased my question thus: "Was your choice of a maverick (at the time) French feminist publisher deliberate?"

assumer pour les quelques femmes arabes qui obtiennent ou acquièrent la liberté de mouvement du corps et de l'esprit. ["Ouverture," 8]

Not to claim that one can "speak for," or worse, "speak on/about"; barely perhaps [that one may] speak in CLOSE PROXIMITY, and if possible, PHYSICALLY UP CLOSE: the first solidarity to claim among the few Arab women who are enjoying or have acquired freedom of movement for their body as well as their mind. [Djebar's emphasis]

To acknowledge the limits of the empowering voice is to discover the limits of all representation, since voice can stand for self. As I have argued elsewhere,[12] the 1980 collection resists the iconic representation staged in Delacroix's hypostasis (women as Woman, Woman-as-Algeria, Algeria-as-Woman, Woman-as-the Other's other). The painting on the cover is textually redoubled by the framing *mise en abyme* of "Ouverture" and "Postface" (See Figure 1). The pictorial frame and its verbal double push against such limits, playing on the ambiguities of the in/authentic, in/authentified pose—what I have called the "posing effect." Who are these women, *really,* who may or may not have been the lawful wives and servants of this Algerian *chaouch*? How much "authenticity" could one have expected of a colonial (and colonized) subaltern ordered by his French superior to allow a foreigner and an infidel into his home, and forced to serve as interpreter for these silent women?[13] Djebar herself, using Delacroix's notebooks and documents from his contemporaries, stresses that the visit took place only "after lengthy discussions" needed to wear down the reluctance of this native employee (168). Can the "language" of the Other, verbal as well as pictorial, intercede for a Self hitherto silenced and cloistered? I wish now to consider how this resisting scriptive strategy, grounded in

---

12. "Writing Woman: The Novels of Assia Djebar," *Substance 69. Special Issue: Translations of the Orient* (Winter 1992): 68–84.

13. Malek Alloula, *Le Harem colonial: Images d'un sous-érotisme* (Paris: Slatkine, 1981), has documented that many of the photographs sent home by various colonial agents, soldiers, or travelers, were "posed." Quite a few of these "authentic Algerian ladies" were impersonated by their own servants, or by their Jewish neighbors, whose faith did not impose the same restrictions on representation. Much the same situation prevailed with Delacroix, who acknowledges freely in his own journals that, when he could not get Moslem women to pose for him, he resorted to Jewish "stand-ins." In pose, clothing, and ethnic types, the 1837 "Noce juive dans le Maroc" ('Jewish wedding in Morocco') shows close similarities to "Femmes d'Alger"; the painter himself makes the point in the notes he contributed to his own catalogue: "Les Maures et les Juifs sont confondus" (Moors and Jews are mixed [that is indistinguishable one from the other among the wedding revelers]); reproduced in *Eugène Delacroix: 1798–1863. Mémorial centenaire de l'exposition*, ed. Maurice Serullaz (Paris: Musées nationaux, 1963), 105.

1. Eugène Delacroix, "Femmes d'Alger." Reprinted with the permission of the Musée du Louvre. Copyright photo R.M.N.

a historical fact, first developed from the 1980 *Femmes d'Alger*—the work that stresses the ambiguities of the posing effect—to shape *Fantasia*,[14] the 1985 novel that finally succeeded in appropriating such ambiguities to "unvoice" the silenced master.

We know, from her published interviews, as well as from the famous semi-autobiographical opening of *Fantasia*, that the question of language has never been simple for Djebar. Witness the explicitly emblematic scene, the oft-cited description of the little girl, solemnly walked to her first day at school by her own father, an Algerian schoolteacher in the French school and a colonized subject himself, who delivers her to the intercession of the Other's language. The alien language was conceived by them both as liberating ("Il y eut d'abord

14. (Paris: Lattès, 1985).

ma sortie au dehors" [First, there was for me the very act of going outside]];[15] literally, because it made possible her physical escape from the female confinement upon puberty; and culturally, because it gave her an epistemological weapon against the cloistering brothers. As the first intercessor standing for the Father, the French language made possible the escape *out* of cultural confines.

Not too surprisingly for those of us familiar with the polysemic layering of a writer for whom to write is, always, to recontextualize the construction of subjectivity, the term "intercessor" comes back at us from the other direction in *Fantasia*, there to generate a much different signifying system: that of activating an exploration *into* cultural memory. The term describes the nineteenth-century French officer in charge of mopping up operations against the rebellious people of the hinterland, among whom lived Djebar's maternal ancestors, first trapped, then burnt alive in the underground caves where they had taken refuge:

> Au sortir de cette promiscuité avec les enfumés en haillons de cendres, Pélissier rédige son rapport qu'il aurait voulu conventionnel. Mais il ne peut pas, il est devenu à jamais le sinistre, l'émouvant arpenteur de ces médinas souterraines, l'embaumeur quasi fraternel de cette tribu définitivement insoumise. . . .

> Pélissier, l'intercesseur de cette mort longue, pour mille cinq cent cadavres sous El Kantara, avec leurs troupeaux bêlant indéfiniment au trépas, me tend son rapport et je reçois ce palimpseste pour y inscrire à mon tour la passion calcinée de mes ancêtres. [93]

> Freshly up from his promiscuous descent among the smoke-charred bodies in their tatters of ashes, Pélissier writes his report [inscribes his relationship], one he would have liked to write as expected. But he cannot; forever transformed into the sinister, yet moving surveyor of these underground native cities, he has become the quasi-fraternal embalmer of the definitively unconquered tribe. . . .

> The intercessor for the long dying of one thousand and five hundred corpses (lying under El Kantara, whose cattle endlessly bellow their agony, Pélissier now hands me his report and I receive it, palimpsest on which I shall, in turn, inscribe the charred martyrdom [passion] of my ancestors.

French and male, the intercessor writes his *report* across the liminal space between conquerers and conquered, there to inscribe a *physical*

---

15. Succinctly so described in the essay "Du langage comme du butin" ('Language, my war booty') *Quinzaine littéraire*, (16–31 March 1985): 25.

relationship—the French term, "rapport," signifying both the linguistic account and the physical intercourse. Boldly calling it "promiscuous," Djebar's text "genders" this verbal/physical act of writing the conquest, eventually to deploy it along a signifying chain of intercessive acts.

In attempting to compose the *pro forma* ("conventionnel") report expected of an officer in hostile territory, Pélissier inadvertently sent a graphic document that nearly finished his career. Literally walking among these dead, he finds himself compelled to inscribe into presence this Other whom official military reports erase: these bodies will not be silenced. Still, the sliding signifier of a Christian-inflected (and inflicted) martyrdom—"passion" in the original—will not come to rest on this agonistic act of Moslem resistance. If the officer cannot bring himself to write the required report, neither is he able to acknowledge collective responsibility: the French subject will not question the *mission civilisatrice* and his paternalistic compassion keeps the Other subjugated. In the crypt turned mausoleum, he deciphers well enough the hieroglyphs of these tattered corporeal ashes: his revulsion betrays him. But he cannot give them their own voice: representation fails him. This very failure is recorded in the silences of his own colonial palimpsest, as Pélissier engages the "paleographic strata" (93) on which the charred bodies have left traces of their own presence. His palimpsest in turn empowers a writer, who is neither French nor male, to claim the role of an intercessor who will plunge back into the subterranean cave of collective memory, there to retrieve the plural palimpsest she'll call *Fantasia*.

Many pages later, a similar failure closes the novel, giving us a possible representational paradigm:

> Eugène Fromentin me tend une main inattendue, celle d'une inconnue qu'il n'a jamais pu dessiner. . . .
>
> . . . au sortir de l'oasis que le massacre, six mois après, empuantit, Fromentin ramasse dans la poussière, une main coupée d'Algérienne anonyme. Il la jette ensuite sur son chemin.
>
> Plus tard, je me saisis de cette main vivante, main de la mutilation et du souvenir, et je tente de lui faire porter le "qalam". [255]

> Unexpectedly, Eugène Fromentin offers me a hand, that of an unknown woman he was never able to sketch. . . .
>
> Upon leaving the oasis still reeking from the massacre of six months earlier, Fromentin picks up from the dust the severed hand of an anonymous Algerian woman. Later, he throws it away.

> Much later still, having seized this living hand, the hand of mutila-
> tion and memory, I try to make it hold the "qalam."

By the end of the novel, the intercession has again moved in the other
direction. The disempowered colonizer (Fromentin) becomes indebted
to the intervention of the once-colonized (Djebar) to make meaning of
their mutual confrontation, as the reader realizes that the voiced representation to be "sketched" by the ritual *qalam* is, of course, the novel
we have just read and are going to reread intercessionally.

These two moments of textual and intertextual intercession—one
failed, one retrospectively successful, yet in dialogue with each
other—constitute Djebar's invitation to read "with" her and "up
close." Her staging of colonial power as a failure in representation
makes us aware of the contested construction of subject-position in
the shuffling and reshuffling of competing yet mutually imbricated
versions of the past that are, also, *visions:* hence, in the concluding
lines of the prior paragraph, the dynamic, if not synergetic, conflation
of image and word, painted representation that could not occur with
silenced voice that could not be written/yet has just been written.
Pélissier, movingly if unwittingly, bears witness as "quasi-fraternal
embalmer." But Fromentin, the representative of an Orientalist aesthetics confronting the rawness of conquest, is rendered twice impo-
tent, as a painter and as a writer. Djebar challenges us to rethink the
relationship between the written and the visual, as a metaphor for the
tangled relationship of the subject self and the subjugated self; a divided self constituted within the violence of the colonizer's language
and its double, the violence of his visual tradition.

The dual metaphor disrupts the colonial master narrative on several levels. One, it destabilizes the position of the sovereign subject in
the field of vision, forcing us to consider who is watching whom. Two,
it undermines the programmed binary relationship of Orientalism, by
excavating the conditions of its production: composed after the fact,
those paintings on whose vision *Fantasia* "signifies" (in Henry Louis
Gates's use of the term), are an imaginary restaging of an imaginary, if
not phantasmatic Other. And three, it articulates the inextricable
connection of such a vision to the written text of violence, the gory
archives of the conqueror for whom, Djebar has said, "to write is to
kill":

> I had to settle my quarrel with the language first. That's when I under-
> stood that the French language, for me, had nothing to do with Sartre or

Camus. The French language for me is the language of those people coming into my land with the colonial conquest. Those first few official conquerors—they came, they killed, they conquered. They write and kill as they write—*in the very act of writing.* (Djebar's emphasis).[16]

Silenced and blinded by an experience he cannot comprehend, the artist can neither sketch/trace ("dessiner") the severed hand, failing to identify it as the same hieroglyphic "trace" as the soldier's charred tatters, nor write (for/with) it. Djebar focuses our attention on this one moment of epistemological aporia in the colonizing subject. A constitutive part of her "intercessive" strategy, this faltering moment situates subjectivity, textually, at the tensive intersection of the written and the painted, on the one hand; and on the other, epistemologically, at a specific point in history: the years of conquest.

From within the very space of a binary and monological Orientalist representation, governed by the hierarchy of Same and Other, *Fantasia* weaves a structure that is palimpsestic (implicitly dialogical and three-dimensional), as well as intertextual (explicitly dialogical as well as multifaceted).[17] This perpetually unbounded narrative modulates the coming to awareness of a self-reflexive subjectivity with regard to the question of female empowerment (giving voice to the silenced women of the crypt, uncovering the covered/veiled women of the tribe, a constant dual thematics with Djebar). It is a strategy that triangulates plural vantage points among noncentered subject positions, situating them firmly within a crucial historical moment, that of "the first Algerian war."[18] In dismantling male-grounded textual poetics, Djebar repositions the colonized female object as the resisting subject of the gaze/voice, who may free herself from the cloistering brothers (as well

16. "Woman's Memory Spans Centuries," interview with Clarisse Zimra, *Women of Algiers in their Apartment* (Charlottesville: University of Virginia Press, 1992), 184.

17. The operative metaphor here has to do with a synergetic restructuring of space. Proud of her narrative structuring—"in my craft, my forte, I think, is structure: first, I construct/erect" ('dans tout ce que je fais mon point fort, je crois, c'est la structure: je construis d'abord')—Djebar has commented on her "architectural imagination" as "what is left of my youthful urge to become an architect" ('c'est ce qu'il me reste: jeune, j'aurais voulu devenir architecte'; unpub. 1992).

Of course, Delacroix and Fromentin are not the only "intercessors." To name a few: Bonnard (window as liminal framing); Picasso (revisioning Delacroix and Matisse); and, in the matter of the title, one intercessor Djebar identifies (Beethoven) and one she does not (Adorno). Space being limited, this essay is a preliminary version of further research in progress.

18. The second is, of course, the war of national liberation that formally ended in 1961. *Fantasia* is, among many other things, a parabolic rewriting of "the second Algerian war."

as the cloister/crypt), by means of, as well as against, the intercession of the Orientalist Masters.

IN THE VERY ACT OF WRITING

At the very moment when the French army is practicing tribal geno-cide, Eugène Fromentin "authors" North Africa as Ancient Greece in his description of *fantasia,* for *Une année dans le Sahel* (A Year in the Sahel):

> *Réduite à des éléments tout à fait simples,* à ne regarder dans cette mise en scène surabondante qu'un seul groupe, et dans ce groupe qu'un seul cavalier, la *fantasia,* c'est à dire le galop d'un cheval bien monté, est encore un spectacle unique. . . . La Grèce artiste n'a rien imaginé de plus naturel et de plus grand. . . . [D]e ce monstre aux proportions réelles, qui n'est que l'alliance audacieusement figurée d'un robuste cheval et d'un bel homme, elle a fait l'éducateur de ses héros, l'inventeur de ses sciences, le précepteur du plus agile, du plus brave et du plus beau des hommes. [Emphasis mine][19]

> *Reduced to its simplest elements,* watching in this super-abundant staging only one group, and in this group only one rider, the *fantasia*—in other words, the gallop of a well-mounted horse—is still a unique spectacle. . . . In all its arts, Greece could not imagine anything more natural or more grand. . . . [From] this well-proportioned monster, which is but the audaciously represented alliance of a robust horse and a handsome man, Greece formed the teacher of her heroes, the inventor of her sciences, the preceptor of the most agile, bravest, and hand-somest of men.

This is the Centaurian beast whose hooves, moments later, will crack open the forehead of the noncompliant woman, a scene with which Djebar chooses to end her own *fantasia.* The "spectacle" of male valor is not a make-believe "staging" at all, but the ritualized murder of Woman in the patriarchy. Likewise, other references in Fromentin's journals purge the human element from the "silent land." Then comes the ur-moment of Orientalism, Fromentin's first encounter with the desert in *Un eté dans le Sahara* (A Summer in the Sahara).

> On se demande, en le voyant commencer à ses pieds, puis s'éntendre, s'enfoncer vers le sud, vers l'est, vers l'ouest, sans route tracée, sans inflexion, *quel peut être ce pays silencieux, revêtu d'un ton douteux*

19. *Oeuvres complètes,* ed. Guy Sagnes (Paris: Gallimard, 1964), 354–55.

qui semble la couleur du vide; d'où personne ne vient; où personne ne s'en va et qui se termine par une raie si droite et si nette sur le ciel. [*Oeuvres* 126–27; emphasis mine]

Seeing it start at one's feet, then stretch out, plunging toward the south, the east, the west, without trace of a road, without any inflection, one wonders *what this land can be, silent, clothed in a doubtful hue that seems to be the color of the void; from which no one comes, toward which no one goes,* and which ends with so straight and sharp a line against the sky.

Compare this to Hegel's sovereign disregard for the presence of the Other on the historical shore, of which I need only quote the most famous sentence:

From the earliest of historical time, Africa has remained cut off from all contacts with the rest of the world; it is the land of gold forever pressing in upon itself, and the land of childhood *removed from the light of self-conscious history* and wrapped in the dark mantle of night. [Emphasis mine][20]

The trope of absence that presides at the birth of the modern colonial discourse, blind to its own hegemonic premises, implicitly harks back to the founding text of Western philosophy, Plato's *Dialogues*, a text that never elucidates "the Pleasant Bend" in the Nile but enfolds the Other in a discrete hint of cannibalism.[21]

Similar remarks dot the journals of Fromentin's master, Eugène Delacroix, with whom all of Fromentin's work is in dialogue. On 4 June 1832, the very month when he is to be admitted to a native home, Delacroix writes to Auguste Jal, art critic and confidante:

Les Romains et les Brecs sont là, à ma porte: j'ai bien ri des Grecs de David, à part bien entendu, sa sublime brosse. Je les connais à présent; les marbres sont la vérité même, *mais il faut savoir y lire,* et nos pauvres modernes n'y ont vu que des hiéroglyphes. [Emphasis mine][22]

The Greeks and the Romans are at my front door; they make me laugh aloud at David's Greeks—but not at his sublime technique, of course. I know them now as they are, and our marbles [i.e., statues] reproduce

---

20. *Lectures on the Philosophy of World History,* ed. J. Hoffmeister (London: Cambridge University Press, 1980), Vol. 1, 173.

21. "Phedrus," in *The Collected Dialogues, Including the Letters,* ed. Edith Hamilton and Huntington Cairns (New York: Bollingen Series 1963–66): Vol. 1, 503.

22. *Correspondance générale,* ed. André Joublin (Paris: Plon 1935), 330.

them, in truth, *provided one knows how to read them,* and our poor moderns have only been able to see a few hieroglyphs.

After the famous visit, he concurs: "C'est beau! C'est comme au temps d'Homère! La femme dans le gynécée s'occupant de ses enfants, filant la laine ou brodant de merveilleux tissus. C'est la femme comme je la comprends" [How beautiful this is! This is Homer's age! Woman within the gyneceum, taking care of her children, weaving wool or embroidering marvelous cloth. Here is Woman as I understand her].[23] Writing to his father some fifteen years later, Fromentin has learned his lesson well: "Pour ma part, je ne peindrai jamais rien qu'en toute sincérité d'esprit; et comme après tout je ne veux relever que de mon propre sentiment, je ne toucherai pas du doigt à ce beau pays d'Afrique, *avant de me l'être approprié"* [As for me I shall paint only that which I can paint with the utmost sincerity of spirit; and since, after all, I want to be indebted only to my own emotions, I shall not put a finger (i.e., lay a brush) on this beautiful land of Africa, *before I have succeeded in appropriating it* (18 August 1847; *Oeuvres* 1253; emphasis mine)].

Against the lethal effacement of/by the Other, Djebar mounts a two-pronged attack. First, as we have seen, she juxtaposes the exotic visions against the colonizers' own records, the archival texts. Their contradictions engage each other until they produce the final moment of aporia that clenches the failure of the West's moral imagination. Next, she deconstructs the pictorial. The specific trigger for this dual re/visioning is autobiographical. Her first physical encounter with "Femmes d'Alger" is off camera, an intensely private, intensely empowering moment:

> En entrant dans la salle, j'ai été saisie, assaillie physiquement comme sous le coup d'un choc, tellement le tableau est immense. Et puis surtout . . . c'était mes aieules que je voyais, là, devant moi, pour la première fois. *Elles sont dehors. Elles me sont rendues. Et elles me regardent.* [Unpub. 1992; Djebar's pause and emphasis]

> Entering the room, I was stunned, physically assaulted as if hit with a blow, so huge is this painting. Above all . . . these were my fore-mothers whom I was seeing, right in front of me, for the first time. *They are out(side). They are rendered unto me. And they are looking at me.*

---

23. *Eugène Delacroix,* ed. Serullaz, 201. Not surprisingly, the original is relentlessly "impersonal." The pronoun ("c'est"), as well as the generic use of "la femme" (impersonal in intent) erase the human time and place, the Algerian specificity of the encounter.

For this daughter, who has just stumbled into the Louvre gallery where the canvas occupies an entire wall, the foremothers are no longer passively "exhibited" as bejewelled objects, but actively "sprung out" by their daughter's active engagement. The echo of an earlier pronouncement ("Il y eut d'abord ma sortie au dehors" [First, I was sprung outside]) is not fortuitous: like writing, painting the body operates the forbidden breakthrough from the confinement of a society that precludes both. These women are subjects of their own gaze and—the tense shift from past to present is crucial—present to each other and to her. Effortlessly, almost instinctively, the "colonial" historian caught in the imperial drive of Western aesthetics resists it to her own ends, demonstrating that vision is always a recontextualization. With Djebar—Maghrebian, Muslim, and woman—the "Orient" calls on the "Occident" to validate itself.[24] The resulting "intercession," the moment of triangulation, challenges the dual hegemonic discourse that cloisters and mutilates from within—that of the Islamic brothers who extoll the return to tradition—as well as that which maims from without, the representation of a monological, liberal West that reifies Islam's Woman on canvas, the better to bewail Islam's reification of women. Since the late 1970s, the years of her personal engagement with French feminism and, in particular with her first film, *La Nouba des femmes du monde Chenoua* (1979), Djebar has embarked on a gendered redefinition of public and private space by way of a representational negotiation of bodily space and bodily display that reinscribes Woman as subject back over the Orientalist palimpsest. There is no question that, while much of the impetus has come from her practical dialogue with world feminists, the project has been neither reactive nor derivative.[25]

On 19 June 1845, one hundred and eighty foot high flames engulf fifteen hundred victims in the subterranean caves. A bare few months later, Fromentin will come over for his grand tour. This is the time when, flush with the success of the first "Femmes d'Alger" (exhibited

24. An Arabic speaker may hear yet another semantic glide. "Maghreb," the name for North Africa, means "land to the West." It was bestowed by historians based in Damascus—a neat demonstration, if we still needed one, that the distinction between Orient and Occident is not based on geography.

25. She argues vigorously, in the 1992 interview "Woman's Memory," that Western feminists have had as much to learn from their "other worlds" sisters as the reverse. In the seventies, she was also engaged in experimental theater work in Paris, and in promoting the French translation of a work by a kindred spirit, Egyptian firebrand and ex-minister Nawal el-Sadawi's *Woman at Point Zero*, to which Djebar also wrote a preface.

in 1834), Delacroix has been simultaneously preparing both a second version (to be exhibited by 1847), and the famous "Odalisque," icons wherein the native body speaks the colonizer's desire. Recontextualizing the iconography, *Fantasia* reminds us that this prescribed representation hides a much less honorable reality: the "charred tatters" of corpses ordered brought up by Pélissier, to be "exhibited" in the colonizer's archives, as they are in his paintings: "Les corps exposés au soleil, les voici devenus mots. Les mots voyagent" [Exposed to the sun, the bodies become words. And words travel] (89). Against the Golden Age image of the sheltered gyneceum, "Woman as I understand her," speaks the severed hand that stays the brush/pen of the artist. This hand functions as the floating metonym of a sacrificial intertext, that of the mutilated body. In perfect circularity, mutilation and torture open the eponymous first short story of the collection, *Femmes d'Alger;* mutilation and dismemberment end the novel. These images are intended to dis/orient the exotic representation of Islam's Woman, as well as break the taboo of a Moslem culture that eschews any foregrounding of the personal.

Djebar's pointed choice of titles and covers must therefore be deciphered each alongside the other. While *Femmes d'Alger* "signifies" on Delacroix's painting of the same name, the mysterious female inner space of "the harem" and its prurient undertow, *Fantasia* takes on Fromentin's expanding on Delacroix's glorification of Maghrebian reality as "virile," the outer space of the rogue warriors. In its sexualized difference, the glide from Delacroix to Fromentin marks an Orientalized misperception of which Djebar is only too aware, and which she seeks to dismantle:

> Le monde qu'il a découvert au Maroc et que ses croquis fixent, est essentiellement masculin et guerrier, viril en un mot. . . . Mais passant du Maroc à l'Algérie, Delacroix franchit une subtile frontière qui va inverser tous les signes et être à l'origine de ce que la postérité retiendra de ce singulier 'voyage en Orient'. [*Femmes,* 168]

> The world discovered in Morocco, what his sketches have seized, is essentially a masculine and warrior world, in a word, virile. . . . But, as he moves from Morocco to Algeria, Delacroix crosses a subtle frontier that will invert all signs and become the very origin of what future generations will remember of this singular 'voyage (in)to the Orient.'

Delacroix's painting, "Femmes d'Alger," fixes forever in Western consciousness the "singular" vision of the conquered land as Woman; a semantic shift facilitated by the fact that, in the French language, Morocco is masculine and Algeria, feminine. The multilingual reader may hear a different context, since in Arabic "Morocco" is also called "Marakesh," which is feminine. Yet a logical problem remains: why a painting by Delacroix on the cover of a book that engages Fromentin's reluctance to engage? And why not select, for the cover, the sketch of a *fantasia*, whether by one or the other, since they both made them? In an unguarded moment, Djebar conceded that it was an unpremeditated choice ("c'est venu comme ça," unpub. 1990).

I would like to argue that it did not "just happen." *Fantasia* sports on its cover a Delacroix painting—"The Abduction of Rebecca"—that depicts the kidnapping, followed by the off-camera cloistering and rape, of a prone female body spread out against finely crenelated, fiercely burning walls. Clearly identifiable in other Delacroix works, this is the famous Moroccan fortress of "Mekinez" (Meknes), thus by Djebar's own definition, a foregrounding of the "virile." All three existing versions, (1846 Salon, 1856, 1859 Salon), illustrate a scene from Walter Scott's *Ivanhoe*, although Scott's novel provides no description. The second version, used on the cover, shows a telling difference in focus. The walls have been clipped off, so that attention is fully centered on the abduction in progress; and, in case we missed the point, the abductor's hands are now firmly crossed over the woman's pelvis.

According to his journals, between successive versions of "Rebecca," Delacroix worked on the second "Femmes d'Alger" (begun shortly after the first "Rebecca," in 1847), to be exhibited at the 1849 Salon. Thus, all of the versions of "Femmes," "Fantasia," and "Rebecca" are connected in concept. The pose of the famously compliant "Odalisque," for instance, is the reversed mirror image of one of the models in "Femmes d'Alger." Why choose Delacroix, indeed, in a text predicated on Fromentin's reluctance to paint the gruesome atrocity of female dismemberment?

First, because the relationship between these two constitutes a primer of Orientalist iconography; they paint/write each other's vision, their hall of mirrors reflecting contemporary attitudes toward the exotic object. Delacroix paints as Fromentin crosses the seas to write home about it; as if each conceptually redoubled the other. When, in both *Sahara* and *Sahel*, Fromentin stages the *fantasia* murder, it is with characters inspired by Delacroix's own posed women, down to the color scheme of their clothes, as he himself specifies twice (*Oeuvres*, 288 and 1254). Second, because of the topic. The Knight Templar stands as the West's last defense against Islam. Islam's imaginary violence against *this* fetishized female body displaces, in the Western viewer, the on-going violence against *that* land, the better to deny it.[26] Delacroix's "Femmes d'Alger" stages the forced invasion of this colonial gaze, a fetishizing of the female body on display that Djebar's textual re/vision engages in *Femmes d'Alger*. "Rebecca" makes explicit the graphic violence hitherto implicit in the fetishizing gesture against body and land, a gesture just as graphically countered by the subject-tropes of *Fantasia*. The pictorial structures the *mise-en-abyme* display of each text, as well as their relationship to each other. Accidental as it may have been, the choice of Delacroix's "Rebecca" on the cover of her novel constitutes Djebar's challenge to read otherwise the "virile" valorization of *fantasia* in its most lethal patriarchal subtext: the appropriation of the female object by the West *and* the East. (See Figure 2)

BODIES BECOME WORDS

Brutally real in the many actual dismemberments reported in the colonial archives; invasive in the pictorial rape fantasy; less brutal but no less invasive in the pictorial harem fantasy: Man's appropriation of Woman persists by way of a phantasmatic sign—that of the mutilated body.

It is a familiar imagery in the Djebarian corpus. Already coded in the sexual realm, the botched abortion of the first novel (*La Soif*), it has been carried over in the torture scenes of every subsequent work but one: from *Les Enfants du nouveau monde*, to the first short story in the collection of 1980, "Femmes d'Alger," by way of *Les Alouettes naïves*.[27] In that novel, the blurring of the two codes, love and war, was implied in the erotically charged refusal-surrender of the first wedding night:

26. I am using Laura Mulvey's recent reworking of specular Freudian categories, "Some Thoughts on Theories of Fetishism in the Context of Contemporary Culture," *October* 65 (Summer 1993): 3–20.

27. *La Soif* (Paris: Julliard, 1957); *Les Enfants du nouveau monde* (Paris: Julliard, 1962); *Les Alouettes naïves* (Paris: Julliard, 1967). Even so, the lone exception, *Les Impatients* (Paris: Julliard, 1958), is a thematic sequel to *La Soif*. Although not as graphic, the appropriation and disposal of the female body is played out in the familiar cloistering scenes; be they in the old, traditional house which the westernized heroine flees, or with the possessive fiancé to whom she flees: he locks her up in her room, calling her "ma belle cloîtrée" ['my beautiful cloistered lady'] (212), an obvious indulgence of the harem fantasy.

2. Eugène Delacroix, "L'Enlèvement de Rebecca." Reprinted with the permission of the Musée du Louvre. Copyright photo R.M.N.

> lame de couteau dans la laine de l'abandon . . . tout à fait au fond, pourtant, comme une bête hurlant le refus, la révolte aveugle, le durcissement dressé: 'Non!', un corps peut-il hurler 'Non!' en son profond, et que ce soit pourtant un don? [*Alouettes*, 178]

> a blade knifing through the soft wool of her surrender . . . deeper within her still, an animal screams her revolt, blind refusal of stiffened spine. 'No!' Can the body scream 'No!' within and yet surrender?

By the historical last days of national liberation, the blurring had turned love into war at the novel's concluding paragraph: "Car je sais à l'avance—vieux préjugé?—que la guerre qui finit entre les peuples renaît entre les couples" ('For I already know—an ancient prejudice?— that the war that has just ended between [two] peoples is being reborn within the couple' [*Alouettes*, 432]). Prescient words written around independence: a decade later, Algeria would reinstate Islam as state religion, and embark on an ever-accelerating attack on women's rights.

Written soon after, the well-known frame of *Femmes d'Alger*, its preface and postface, constitutes Djebar's wry nod to French theory, "my *own* kind of feminism," an acknowledgement that is also a distancing.[28] The frame interpellates the female subject within the Islamic patriarchy, while the short stories, in turn, dismantle both Delacroix's Orientalist paintings and the monological obsession within his and Fromentin's journals. Borrowing from and rewriting of/over the Other's text, Djebar's strategy makes possible the surfacing of a female subject hitherto suppressed, cloistered, "veiled"—Woman *qua*

---

28. "Woman's Memory" (176; Djebar's emphasis). While she freely professes her admiration, Djebar has long been skittish on the subject of her precise relationship to French feminists, part of a long-standing refusal to be stereotyped. Her preface to *Women of Islam*, a Unesco-sponsored photo-essay published in the 1950s and all but untraceable now, was never published in the original French, and translated without her. She once claimed to have misplaced her manuscript deliberately, "irritated as I was to find myself, as always, in the position of 'the token Muslim female'" ('comme toujours, je me retrouvais la musulmane de service, et ça m'a agacée' [unpub., March 1980]). The famous "Ouverture" of *Femmes d'Alger*, on which much of her feminist reputation rests in the English-speaking world, was twice translated without her permission: J. M. McDougal, "A Forbidden Glimpse, A Broken Sound," *Women and the Family in the Middle East*, ed. Elizabeth Warnock-Fernea (Austin: Texas University Press, 1984); and Lee Hildreth, "Forbidden Sight, Interrupted Sound," *Discourse* 8 (Fall 1986–87): 39–57. The first attempt contains glaring errors, bewildering omissions, and whole snatches are missing; the second is much closer in tone to the original. Nonetheless, the situation which had left her wary was not remedied until I talked her into collaborating with the University of Virginia team for the translation of *Women of Algiers in their Apartment*. Despite her protest of inadequate linguistic skills, she did proofread it meticulously (and even corrected, with profuse apologies but firm intent, a couple of passages).

body, sign in a system that has assigned her a silent object position. In this context, Woman's freedom can only come through the transgressive body; which is to say, when the body freely unveils itself ("naked," as the Algerian vernacular calls the woman who does not wear the veil).[29]

The movement from *Femmes d'Alger* to *Fantasia* reinscribes the female body as transgressive in both the Orient and the Occident: posed, painted and celebrated, *because* it can be tortured, butchered, and dismembered. This is the specular tragedy of an Other/ing vision that kills, deployed in semiotic equivalence, the violence that mutilates. In *Fantasia*, the body becomes autonomous subject-sign, articulating the transgression for which the severed hand serves as synecdoche. The hand emasculates a painter who runs away from his own entry into colonial history, thus making possible the granddaughter's intercession. Again, I cite this passage about the severed hand:

> Eugène Fromentin me tend une main inattendue, celle d'une inconnue qu'il n'a jamais pu dessiner.
> . . . au sortir de l'oasis que le massacre, six mois après, empuantit, Fromentin ramasse dans la poussière, une main coupée d'Algérienne anonyme. Il la jette ensuite sur son chemin.
> Plus tard, je me saisis de cette main vivante, main de la mutilation et du souvenir, et je tente de lui faire porter le "qalam". [255]

> Unexpectedly, Eugène Fromentin offers me a hand, the hand of an unknown woman he was never able to sketch.
> . . . upon leaving the oasis still reeking from the massacre of six months earlier, Fromentin picks up from the dust the severed hand of an anonymous Algerian woman. Later, he throws it away.
> Much later still, having seized this living hand, the hand of mutilation and memory, I try to make it hold the "qalam."

The tense shift is telling, here, and the French original much more powerfully affective: "je me saisis" (simultaneously grasp/clasp/seize and hold fast to, in a motion that affects myself). Both hand and woman being in the feminine, one stands for the other: the painter could not sketch it (the hand)/her (the woman). The original uses the present

29. The veil has been "fetishized" in both Islamic (Alloula, for instance) and Western discourses, whether of the liberationist kind (Fanon), or the paternalist kind (Tillon). This is the essentialist urge against which other worlds theorists warn us (Mernissi, Ahmed, Malti Douglas, Spivak, to name a few). To avoid the pitfall, I consider it as a rhetorical trope tightly circumscribed by Djebar's own historically-grounded textual strategy.

perfect ("il n'a jamais pu dessiner"), a form that signals that an action, triggered in the past, still operates, is "alive" ("vivante") in the present. English expects a compact preterit ("he never could sketch"), because both painter and model are dead, and the opportunity forever missed. Djebar's own tense shift (literally, "he has never been able") prolongs a moment that resonates into our reading present.

In "clasping" so passionately both hand and *qalam*, Djebar activates other cultural grids as well. For only men may hold the *qalam*, sacred stylus with which the faithful copy the Qran. The transgression of the daughter who, appropriating the male instrument, gives back to her foremothers the right to their own gaze/eye (I), at last exorcizes the implied vernacular obscenity (naked woman reduced to her genitals, in Algerian slang, "eye" being also the contemptuous term for female genitalia). Reinscribing these bodies as subjects, Djebar gives them back their own erotic autonomy, a transgression of the highest order.[30]

It is that very transgression on which Fromentin reports. His diaries romanticize several versions of a factual *fantasia* murder. Thinly disguised as an autobiographical dalliance in *Un été dans le Sahara,* then expanded in *Une année dans le Sahel,* they feature a painter, an obvious cross between Delacroix and Fromentin, and a Berber beauty by the name of Haoûa whom, Fromentin admits, he has modeled after Delacroix's famous "Women of Algiers" (*Oeuvres,* 1254). This first tale of transgression dovetails with another: the rape and murder by the conquering French army of two young "Naylettes" who had welcomed in their home a friend of Fromentin's. They die, one of them still "clasping" a button torn from the attacker's jacket. Unable to bear its touch and unwilling to write its story, the friend shows this button to Fromentin—a first doubling of the painter's own experience. This is further redoubled by the transgressive act of the twentieth-century daughter, who holds out to us this text of the *qalam* that equates, in its signifying chain, button, severed hand, and Woman's murder. The mutilated hand of memory becomes the fetish that insists on its autonomy, synecdoche of an avenging body that "speaks" to us at the end of a gendered chain of dis(re)memberment.

Between these two colonial moments, the rape-murder of the

30. One does not have to go very far to see in this threatening eye a variation of the Medusa figure, of which Cixous has made so much. Indeed, Djebar's careful montage of some of the Eurocentric continental premises against a relentlessly *Algerian-based* history of conquest serves to remind us that, even if the global persecution of women by the patriarchy exists, it is the specific modalities that we must attend to.

Naylettes and the mutilation-murder of the female whom he could not sketch, stands the figure (and masterful figuring) of Haoûa, the free woman. Here, Fromentin—and Djebar with him—weaves together the strands evoked by the enigmatic, silenced, or dismembered females, and the rogue warriors of the *fantasia* scene. Haoûa pays with her life for befriending the outsider (as had the young Naylettes), for going "alone" to the *fantasia* celebrations; in short for "circulating," Djebar's recurring term for a physical as well as a spiritual freedom that includes autonomous sexuality.[31] Her jilted lover runs his galloping horse straight into her. Djebar uses Fromentin's own words from *Une année dans le Sahel*, first verbatim, in a preface to her own book that is both foreshadowing and warning: "Il y eut un cri déchirant—je l'entends encore au moment où je t'écris—puis des clameurs, puis un tumulte" [There was a heart-rending scream—it still rings in my ears as I write to you—then loud cries, then a commotion]. She then repeats them, as an intercessive variation, in her own concluding words:

> Dans la gerbe des rumeurs qui s'éparpillent, j'attends, je pressens l'instant immanquable où le coup de sabot à la face renversera toute femme dressée libre, toute vie surgissant pour danser! Malgré le tumulte des miens alentour, j'entends déjà, avant même qu'il s'élève et transperce le ciel dur, j'entends le cri de la mort dans la fantasia. [255]

> Within these spreading clamors gathering speed, I expect/await with a sense of foreboding the ineluctible moment when the kick of the horse's hoof into her face shall trample down any woman who stands up free, any creature alive who insists on dancing. In spite of the commotion among my surrounding kin, I already hear, even before it has spurted forth and rent the unyielding sky, I hear the scram of death within the fantasia.

In a further act of signifying, she calls the palimpsest book that brings back this death into our living memory, "l'amour, la fantasia." For "l'amour" (love) and "la mort" (death) are close phonetic clusters. Woman's body speaks with a terrifying voice.

31. For the male patriarchs, Haoûa is indeed "alone" at the *fantasia*, because she eschews overt appropriation: although accompanied by a female friend, she is without a male protector. Her easy hospitality for the French traveler, as well as the "female dancing friend," connect her to the "two Naylettes," themselves small-time courtisanes and members of the Ouled-Nail tribe. The connection brings into *Fantasia* the semic trace of *Les Alouettes naïves* (the term "innocent larks" being the French corruption of the tribal name), the first fusion of love-as-war, Eros as Thanatos, in the Djebar corpus.

To say that Djebar claims to write as a woman (she has done so repeatedly herself in just about every published interview), is not necessarily to conclude that she believes in a bio-essentialist fallacy "made in Paris." Her refiguring of the pictorial convention born at the very time of conquest (France invades Algeria in 1830 and Delacroix visits soon after), represents a literal attempt to think the Orientalist self through to (and into) the historically grounded present of the post-liberation, yet all too patriarchal state. Triangulating among inherited Western images and Western texts, her overt use of clearly referenced colonial sources and archives (the professional habit of the practicing historian she still is) forces us to pay attention to the fact that she writes as an Algerian. Further, she does so at a particularly conflicted postcolonial moment of nation formation in her country. If Woman remains the key trope in her corpus, it is because women in Algeria are still the front troops of a new social order that may never come to pass.[32]

32. While we were setting up an interview for inclusion in this issue as agreed, Djebar's brother-in-law and childhood friend, Abdelkader Alloula, a respected theater director and playwright, was murdered in Oran, and Djebar cancelled the interview, "unwilling to talk politics but unable to think of anything else." She has since informed me that upward of fifty prominent professional women, many of whom she knows, are in hiding in Algeria, never sleeping in the same house twice; and that twenty-five young Algerian women have been murdered within the past ten months by Islamic fundamentalists for going about "uncovered." Even the usually sedate *Le Monde* notes that FIS sympathizers (Front Islamique de Salut/Islamic Front for Salvation) now roam the streets, demanding that young women wear the *chador* (not a part of Algerian tradition, but a significant tilt toward Iran), some of them mounting guard in front of schools and universities, openly displaying knives (*Le Monde hebdomadaire*, 24 March 1994, 3). Western-trained professional men and women have been clandestinely trickling into Europe, some with just the clothes on their back. She begged me to remind her American readers ("il faut le dire, il faut le savoir" [it must be said, it must be made known]), that, of all the groups opposed to the FIS that have gradually fallen silent in Algeria, only women's groups courageously continue to march, without police protection or government acknowledgement—a fact even *Le Monde*, commenting on "the Islamic night that is decending upon Algeria," finds appalling.

III. Rethinking (French)
Feminism

SARAH KOFMAN

The Psychologist of the Eternal Feminine (Why I Write Such Good Books, 5)[1]

Suppose that an ideal reader of Nietzsche could some day exist. In affinity with Nietzsche's lofty perspective and "his" style, this reader would have to read his writings as he himself reads texts: as an honest and veracious philologist, able to read between the lines, looking, like a Janus, prudently before and aft, with reservations, with delicate eyes and fingers, meticulously, and, like a goldsmith, taking his time: the good reader, like the good philologist, would, above all, be capable of reading *lento*, in complete contrast to today's modern readers, busy and hurried, slaves to the needs that dictate the apportioning of their time.[2] The slow reading taught by philology is the counterpart of a slow writing, which does not economize on deciphering the hieroglyphs that comprise the long past of human morality, nor on all the serious, dull work on documents, for which the "gay science" is only the reward. "Finally, one writes so slowly" because writing is a reading which, beneath all the superficial layers of varnish and the transvestisms, aims to decipher the original text of all genres, all moralities, all religions, of culture in general: *homo natura*.

Nietzsche—this "teacher of slow reading," who stood aside, took his time, became slow, silent, and careful—would indeed have "merited," in return, a "philologist" as reader of his writings. But what his own profound readings actually taught him was that there is no good fate—a kind of Providence that would ensure that "good" books fall

1. This article is a translation of "Le psychologue de l'éternel féminin (Pourquoi j'écris de si bons livres)," in *Explosion II. Les enfants de Nietzsche* (Paris: Galilée, 1992).
2. See *Daybreak*, "Preface," ¶5, and also the "Preface" to the 1986 edition. Also, in my *Explosion I* (Paris: Galilée, 1992), see, among other chapters, "Voies de traverse."

YFS 87, *Another Look, Another Woman*, ed. Huffer, © 1995 by Yale University.

into the hands of "good" readers; the *fatum libellorum*[3] reserves for them, rather, the opposite fate, and the good fortune of finding an appropriate reader is never, for the author, the certain reward of virtue or merit; it is a stroke of luck. And in this epoch of hurried men, it was actually misfortune that smiled upon the man who—wanting to be the "Horace" of his century, like the Latin poet he took as his model and admired above all others—deserved to find readers who knew how to read him.[4] Lacking a true philological reader, Nietzsche is forced to reread his own texts, to decipher them, and despite the repugnance of his proudest instincts, to present himself by posing to his own writings the question he poses to the writings of others: "Who is speaking?" The response of the good reader (himself) is that in his writings, an unparalleled psychologist makes himself heard. A psychologist in the new sense that Nietzsche gives to this term in *Beyond Good and Evil*[5]: a psychologist of the depths, whose idea—which had not yet dawned upon anyone else—was to turn psychology, understood as morphology and as a general theory of the will to power, into the queen of the sciences, for whose service and preparation the other sciences exist (whether philology, which teaches how to read between the lines; physiology, which promotes the acceptance that the only reality is the body—understood as a collective of many souls; or medicine, which inaugurates a generalized symptomatology, diagnosing texts as healthy or sick). This new psychology, conceived as a path to the essential problems, should replace the old form, which has remained superficial because it is infested and corrupted by moral prejudices. It is primarily practiced by philosophers who, dismissing the prejudices of common sense, have the presumption to believe that they are free of them: "The power of moral prejudices has penetrated deeply into the most spiritual world, which would seem to be the coldest and most

3. See Nietzsche, *Philosophy in the Tragic Age of the Greeks*, and, in my *Nietzsche et la scène philosophique* (Paris: Galilée, 1986), "Le complot contre la philosophie."

4. See *The Twilight of the Idols*, trans. Walter Kaufman, in *The Portable Nietzsche* (New York: Viking Books, 1954), "What I owe to the Ancients," ¶1: "To this day, no other poet has given me the same artistic delight that a Horatian ode gave me from the first. In certain languages that which has been achieved here could not even be *attempted*. This mosaic of words, in which every word—as sound, as place, as concept—pours out its strength right and left and over the whole, this minimum in the extent and the number of the signs, and the maximum thereby attained in the energy of the signs—all that is Roman and, if one will believe me, *noble par excellence*. All the rest of poetry becomes, in contrast, something too popular—a mere garrulity of feelings."

5. *Beyond Good and Evil*, trans. Walter Kaufman. (New York: Vintage Books, 1966), ¶23. Numbers in future citations of this work refer to sections.

devoid of presuppositions, and has obviously operated in an injurious, inhibiting and blinding and distorting manner" (§ 23). Playing on the homophony of the words *Hohltöpfen* and *Kohlköpfen*, Nietzsche makes fun of the empty heads of these ham-fisted philosophers, these cabbage-heads, who, under the sway of morality, that sorceress (*magicienne*) who rules them without their knowing it, constantly make faux-pas and naive mistakes. The supposed men of the *Begriff* keep making *Fehlgriffen*, to the great joy of he who, in *Beyond Good and Evil*, calls himself the spoilt child of philosophy.[6]

As a good psychologist, Nietzsche makes a list of the *mille et tre* most common philosophical mistakes (mishandlings),[7] revered by all as truths: the belief in the opposition of values, the metaphysical prejudice par excellence (*Beyond Good and Evil*, § 2); for example, the belief in the opposition of egoism and nonegoism, by which behavior of the first kind is disqualified as immoral, while the latter is valued above all else. Not only is this opposition false, but the two terms, judged to be antithetical, suppose a common postulate: the existence of an ego that, in the first case, puts itself before others, and in the second, sacrifices itself in a "selfless" way. Now the "ego" is a pure, mystifying fiction, a "higher swindle" of the weak who need to believe in antithetical values, in the existence of "good" and "bad" subjects or free "egos" who are responsible for their acts. In fact, the "ego" is not an origin, but the superficial result of a certain hierarchization of forces acting in the depths. Because the "ego," according to the "bad" grasp that the weak have on it, is a fiction, these two terms, "egoistic"/"nonegoistic," are psychological misinterpretations.

Another mistake, which has been held to be a self-evident truth by philosophers at least since Plato, is that the end of all human endeavor is the pursuit of happiness—a misinterpretation for which, once again, the weak who raise their sickly perspective as an absolute, are responsible. Under the name "happiness," they seek, and can only seek, the absence of suffering, repose, nothingness. Their disloyalty, upheld by the philosophers, is to "forget" that a living being who is truly living, wants not happiness, but power, the increase and surpassing of oneself.

Another prejudice, which is shared by all philosophers up to Kant,

6. On the faux-pas of the philosophers, which Nietzsche scrutinizes as a child watches the unavowed "crimes" of his parents during the primal scene, see my *Nietzsche et la scène philosophique*.

7. In French, there is a play on the words "*méprises*" and "*mal prises en main*," stemming from the verb *prendre*, to take or grasp. [Translator's note]

is that "happiness," supposedly pursued by all, is the reward of virtue. Kant himself only differed from his predecessors in that he saw this proposition not as an analytical judgment, but as a synthetic a priori. The consideration that virtue and only virtue conferred, not happiness, but worthiness of happiness, led him to set forth his three postulates of practical reason: the existence of a free, responsible subject; the immortality of the soul; the existence of a just and retributive God. In fact, these postulates are nothing more than the demands of the weak, who need them to fulfil their "duties" and to frighten and give a bad conscience to the strong. The opposition of "pleasure and displeasure," which the old "psychology" accepts as self-evident, supposes that pleasure is the satisfaction of a need whereas, of course, it is immanent to the living being's exercise of its power. As such it is proportional to the resistance encountered and surmounted, and thus to the "displeasure," which is not its opposite, but one of its necessary ingredients. In order to bear "suffering," the weak individual who cannot will it, forges the fiction of "sin" for which it is a punishment, while pleasure is the reward of virtue.

Behind the "psychological" opposition of pleasure and displeasure, one can devine, once again, that of good and evil, the moral opposition, the fundamental prejudice of philosophers, which, by infecting and falsifying it, corrupted the whole of psychology and turned it on its head. Under the seductive sway of morality, this Circe of humanity and the philosophers, psychology found itself transformed with the wave of a magic wand. Whereas the Homeric Circe was able to seduce Ulysses' companions and so turn them into swine, the philosophers' sorceress (*magicienne*)[8] works in the opposite direction: she idealizes everything, conferring a divine and noble origin on that which, to borrow its own terms, has its origins in the "low" which it disqualifies,

8. See *Daybreak*, trans. R. J. Hollingdale (Cambridge: Cambridge University Press, 1982), Foreword, § 3: "But morality does not merely have at its command every kind of means of frightening off critical hands and torture instruments: its security reposes far more in a certain kind of enchantment it has at its disposal—it knows how to 'inspire'. With this art it succeeds, often with no more than a single glance, in paralysing the critical will and even in enticing it over to its own side; there are even cases in which morality has been able to turn the critical will against itself, so that, like the scorpion, it drives its sting into its own body. For morality has from of old been master of every diabolical nuance of the art of persuasion. . . . For as long as there has been speech and persuasion on earth, morality has shown itself to be the greatest of all mistresses of seduction—and, so far as we philosophers are concerned, the actual *Circe of the philosophers*."

by opposing it in tragic mode[9] to the sublime world of morality which it invented.

Contaminated by this formidable seductress, by this insidious woman who was able to devise more than one strategem and more than one strategy for triumphing over the strongest victims, moralized and moralizing psychology—and for Nietzsche, this is the height of the absurdities and astounding misinterpretations it enunciates— proclaimed that love should be something "unegoistic," that it requires oblation and sacrifice: a proposition which reveals a complete mystification and occultation of the true nature of love and the true relationship between the sexes.

Presenting himself, like Socrates, as an expert in love, as a veritable defender of women, and as the first psychologist who has been able to understand them "in truth," countering the *mistakes* of the psychologists and philosophers who lacked the virility to know how to *handle* them, Nietzsche lingers, at greater length than over the other misinterpretations, on the one they committed in regard to the nature of love, and assigns himself the task of correcting it. The first condition of love is, of course, that one *be able* to love, which implies not some mad abstraction of one's desires and impulses, of "oneself," "being selfless" or taking refuge in the ethereal sky of a delusive ideal, walking on one's head as if in a camera obscura, but, on the contrary, having both feet firmly planted on the ground, and sitting firmly on oneself (*auf sich sitzen*). In commanding disinterest, "morality" gives an imperative which no one can obey, because one must only do what one can do, and love cannot be cut off from its roots in the impulses, from all interest. *Who*, in any event, would want an ethereal love? Women, good little women, at least those who, by the sensitivity of their ears, are Nietzsche's allies, would certainly send packing any lover who claimed to be objective and "disinterested": they would probably find uninteresting a man who, like Kant or Schopenhauer's lover of art,[10] declared that he sought from them a pleasure that was "disinterested," in other words, without interest for their existence and cut off from all the impulses.

Much keener psychologists than the philosophers, women share an affinity of the ear with the only true psychologist who, as a disciple of

9. On the "tragic opposition," see my "Nietzsche et Wagner," *Furor* 23 (May 1992): 3–28.

10. It goes without saying that Nietzsche does not accept the "disinterested" nature of aesthetic pleasure either. See his *On the Genealogy of Morals*, trans. Walter Kaufman (New York: Vintage Books, 1969), third essay, § 6.

Dionysos,[11] this equivocal god, both masculine and feminine, whose duplicity he has inherited, addresses them as Dionysos speaks into the little ears of his fiancée: unlike the philosophers who despise (*mépriser*) them, or make only mistakes (*méprises*) regarding them, he claims to be the only one who really knows them. And who loves them, as the affectionate diminutive by which he designates them on this page connotes: good *little* women (*Weiblein*). For, as we know,[12] the women Nietzsche loved had to be "tender little women," full of malice and grace, affectionate and playful. Nevertheless, like all diminutives, the expression "good little women" is not without irony and ambivalence; it also "belittles" women who, for many misogynists, do not reach the same heights as men. Yet it seems that Nietzsche only adopts a superior tone toward them the better to denounce this tone of superiority. For he affirms that women are in fact more intelligent than men and far more formidable: far from wanting to belittle them, it is to defend himself against the inordinate fascination they exercise, as from their love, that he speaks of them pejoratively. For unlike the pseudopsychologists, and thanks to women, whom he was capable of hearing, Nietzsche claims to be more expert in love than anyone: he knows that it is inseparable from cruelty, from the savagery of the beast of prey, from malice and a subterranean and insinuating ruse. He defends himself against the love of women out of a fear of being torn to pieces by them, as, according to Euripides,[13] Pentheus was torn apart

11. See *Beyond Good and Evil*, § 295 and in *Explosion I*, "The last disciple of the philosopher Dionysos."
12. See *Explosion I*, "Intermezzo."
13. See *The Bacchae* in *Euripides V, Three Plays*, trans. William Arrowsmith, (Chicago: University of Chicago Press, 1959) 1098–1148, particularly: "Then Agavé cried out: 'Maenads, make a circle about the trunk and grip it with your hands. Unless we take this climbing beast, he will reveal the secrets of the god.' With that, thousands of hands tore the fir tree from the earth, and down, down from his high perch fell Pentheus, tumbling to the ground, sobbing and screaming as he fell, for he knew his end was near. His own mother, like a priestess with her victim, fell upon him first. But snatching off his wig and snood so she would recognize his face, he touched her cheeks, screaming, 'No, no, Mother! I am Pentheus, your own son, the child you bore to Echion! Pity me, spare me, Mother! I have done a wrong, but do not kill your own son for my offense.' But she was foaming at the mouth, and her crazed eyes rolling with frenzy. She was mad, stark mad, possessed by Bacchus. Ignoring his cries of pity, she seized his left arm at the wrist; then, planting her foot upon his chest, she pulled, wrenching away the arm at the shoulder—not by her own strength, for the god had put inhuman power in her hands. Ino, meanwhile, on the other side, was scratching off his flesh. Then Autonoë and the whole horde of Bacchae swarmed upon him. Shouts everywhere, he screaming with what little

by the Maenads. Indeed, in love, women become veritable Maenads, the frenzied followers of Dionysos' cortege, who, possessed by the god, abandon themselves to the worst excesses, losing all control of themselves and ceasing to recognize the conventional, Apollonian limits dividing humanity from animality: the sway of the god or of passion brings down all the artificial barriers, permitting the return of a natural "savagery" which explodes with a violence that is all the stronger because it has long been repressed: thus Agavé tears to pieces the body of her own son, taking him in her delirium for a mountain lion.

However, unlike the Maenads whom they incarnate, when they love, women retain a civilized, amiable, and agreeable air: one must be a good psychologist, like Nietzsche, to unmask, beneath the veneer, the malice and cruelty of living beings who, when necessary, do not hesitate to satisfy their need for vengeance. Then, like birds of prey swooping down, nothing can stop them. Because she is more "natural" or more alive than man, woman is more malicious, more cunning, cleverer, gifted with a more devious intelligence (with this *Klugheit*,[14] which Nietzsche—who is related to them in this—claims is one of his own characteristics). A *"good"* woman (not to be confused with a "good *little* woman,") is a degenerate: her goodness can only be a symptom of sickness, of the weakening of the natural savagery of her instincts. A man who is wise will prefer to keep his distance from her. One must also be wary of the women whom, in distinction to those he terms degenerate or lost, Nietzsche calls *well turned out:* those who figure the perfect and natural type of woman, the Eternal feminine, of which, appropriating for himself a claim made by Strindberg, he claims

---

breath was left, they shrieking in triumph. One tore off an arm, another a foot still warm in its shoe. His ribs were clawed clean of flesh and every hand was smeared with blood as they played ball with scraps of Pentheus' body.

The pitiful remains lie scattered, one piece among the sharp rocks, others lying lost in among the leaves in the depths of the forest. His mother, picking up his head, impaled it on her wand. She seems to think it is some mountain lion's head which she carries in triumph through the thick of Cithaeron. Leaving her sisters at the Maenad dances, she is coming here, gloating over her grisly prize. She calls upon Bacchus: he is her 'fellow-huntsman,' 'comrade of the chase, crowned with victory.' But all the victory she carries home is her own grief."

14. In this he is also related to Jews. Nietzsche may perhaps be borrowing from Lessing's *Nathan the Wise* the two characteristics of the Jew, *Weisheit* (wisdom) and *Klugheit* (cleverness), in order to play on them in his own way (see *Why I am so wise* and *Why I am so clever*). Unlike Nathan, who is named wise and clever by the people, Nietzsche, in a provocative gesture, attributes these "qualities" to himself.

to be the first psychologist. In an earlier version, he states that: "The judgment which he brings to bear on the 'Eternal feminine' is the measure and probe of a psychologist." Nietzsche's judgment is thus deeper, more radical, more detached than any other judgment, and notably, than that of the Parisian pseudopsychologists who, because they fail to use a typological and historical method, by a sort of generalized induction or metonymy, elevate their perspective on the nineteenth-century *parisienne* to an absolute. Because she is a sick, degenerate, or lost woman, they render women "as such," in general, the weaker sex. This claim is contested (according to Nietzsche, who puts his trust in Bachofen) by history and ethnology: "There are—or there have been—almost everywhere, forms of civilization in which it is *woman* who is dominant."

"Woman" as "weaker sex" is not an essential determination of woman, but a historical event that threatens to have become definitive and to constitute henceforth the feminine "type" par excellence: "It is a significant event, it is, if you will, a *decisive turning-point* in the destiny of humanity that woman has definitively become the underdog, that *all the instincts of submission have triumphed in her and have created the feminine type.*" Thus, Nietzsche appropriates the expression "Eternal feminine" only to demystify it, since, as an unparalleled psychologist, and thanks to his genealogical and historical flair, he was able to detect, beneath this pseudo-eternity, a historical creation. It is the triumph in "woman" herself of a certain type of instincts over others that were once dominant (which nevertheless continue to exist and are ready to unleash themselves all the more savagely precisely because they have been dominated and appear to have disappeared) that signs the creation of "woman." Woman's ruse is to foster the belief that she is and always has been, effectively and exclusively, the weaker sex, to conceal the complexity of her instincts. Her "malice"—her sudden transformation into a Maenad—is all the more unforeseeable and frightening for men.

At this decisive turning-point—the moment in which woman becomes "Woman" in all her complexity—she also becomes, for the psychologist, an interesting being, an enigma to decipher. For, by her ruses and stratagems, characteristic of the weak, she becomes unpredictable, duplicitous, she begins using devious ways of seducing men, of tearing them up and definitively triumphing over them, the "stronger sex." "It is only from this moment that woman becomes something enchanting, interesting, complicated, cunning, a subtle lace of impossible psychology: in it, she ceases to be boring." The strong are uninteresting:[15] for the keen psychologist, that nutcracker of souls, they are far too simple, too direct, too boring. "Power is boring. One need only look at the Reich." It is the "becoming-Woman" of woman that made life on earth interesting: if "God" created woman, Nietzsche says elsewhere, it was to rescue man from boredom. But God has been dead for a long while: the myth of the "creation" of Eve signifies that it is men themselves (and the women who are in league with their interests) who, at a given moment when it was entirely in their interest, created woman as the "weaker sex" or Eternal feminine, transforming her into an interesting enigma: "Would life on earth be possible if woman hadn't become a genius of conversation and grace, if she hadn't become Woman?" But for this, one must be weak, a genius of malice and even somewhat of a Maenad. Weak and malicious: the two apparently antinomic terms do not exclude each other, since feminine "malice" marks only the "return" of the strong and "virile" instincts which, though suppressed, continued to exist in her. Indeed, they seem all the more savage for having been "dissimulated" by women in the interest of their cause, their pretended weakness, and because they act deviously and by surprise. Only the Judeo-Christian perspective, maintaining that with the creation of woman, evil and sin enter into the world, condemns feminine "malice."

Nietzsche's greatest objection to the Christian heaven, is, on the contrary, that the angels in it are bereft of all malice, therefore boring, asexual. They lack "virility" or this femininity which ultimately also supposes virility, since woman is only woman in virtue of her sexual "complexity," and the victory within her of submissive instincts which dissimulate the existence of her "virile" dominating instincts. These were once in her—though no "her" as yet existed—the masters, and stealthily continue to affirm their will to power: "maliciously"— as though to "avenge" themselves for having been subjugated by the weak and reduced to acting or reacting like the weakest among them. Women should be grateful to Nietzsche for being so well understood by him, and even if he is wary of their "love," which he has been able to unmask in all its cruelty and ambivalence (for there is no sensuality without cruelty), they cannot but love, with a quite maternal tenderness, a man who is so closely related to them. For the women who have

15. Nietzsche notes that it is only when man is transformed by the ascetic ideal into a "sublime miscarriage" (*Beyond Good and Evil* § 62) that he becomes an extremely "interesting animal" (*Genealogy of Morals*, first essay, § 6).

turned out well (*wohlgeraten*) are, first and foremost, mothers. To be "saved," cured of the "weakness" which has triumphed in them—to be cured of their "femininity"—they need a child, and man, as Zarathustra said, is only ever a means for them: "Everything about woman is a riddle, and everything about woman has one solution: that is pregnancy. Man is for woman a means: the end is always a child."[16] This is what Freud too, in different terms, would say: for woman, the child is always a child-savior who cures her of her femininity, since, in the Freudian version of things, he is the substitute for the penis which nature and her father refused to give her.[17] But the child is the remedy, not to women's native deficiency (as Freud would have it), but to their "acquired" weakness, the response, not to the repression of an originary "virility" within an individual history of the libido, but to what will prove to be a decisive event in the destiny of humanity: the triumph in woman of the instincts of submission over those of domination. The child is the only salvation.

Nietzsche rejects all other means: for example, those preached by "feminist" women who call themselves emancipated and who, because they are completely lacking in psychological finesse, readily call him (like Freud) a misogynist. These women do not love him, but then for him, they are not really women—they are abortive (*missratenen*) women who lack maternal fiber. *Lost* women—lost as women and lost because they reject the only means of salvation at their disposal (and in this they are unlucky [*verunglückten*] women): childbirth. As he says elsewhere, they prefer making books to making children,[18] and in their case this is a symptom of perversion and degeneracy. But far from recognizing this, they call themselves progressivist, believing themselves superior to other women, while, by their perverse conduct, they seek to *belittle* the general condition of women out of resentment for those who have turned out well (*wohlgeraten*). Those who seem to be fighting for women's liberation are actually women's worst enemies. Their attacks on men are merely a tactic, a devious strategy on the part of those who cannot give birth, used to attack those who can. The women who play at being "beautiful souls" are simply pathological

16. *Thus Spoke Zarathustra*, "Of little old and young women" and "On child and marriage."

17. See, among other texts, *Female Sexuality*, and my *The Enigma of Woman*, trans. Catherine Porter (Ithaca: Cornell University Press, 1985).

18. Freud makes the same critique of the emancipated woman in *The Taboo of Virginity*.

cases. Their claims are diagnosed by the doctor Nietzsche as symptoms of a physiological disequilibrium. However, to avoid falling into a "medi-cynism" that, with impudence and vulgarity, would revel in the idea that the true motivations of all conduct supposed to be elevated or sublime, lie in the belly—or in the womb—Nietzsche does not enter into the scabrous details, but limits himself by displacing the question from the physiological to the typological, diagnosing "ill health," indeed, degeneracy, whenever a "woman" claims to fight against men for the salvation of women, notably by demanding equal rights. Such a demand is always a symptom of weakness, since it implies as its condition a misunderstanding of hierarchy, the negation of differences, and a will to reduce the stronger to the weak, forcing them to relinquish at least a part of their power: "Neither God nor master"[19] could be the slogan of these emancipated women whom, for this reason, Nietzsche calls the "anarchists of the world of the Eternal feminine," and whose deepest motivation lies not so much in the womb, as in the desire of the weak for vengeance against all that is strong and powerful.

The "true" woman has no interest in equal rights or indeed in the world of law at all: she knows that the state of nature, which is a state of war to the death between the sexes, accords her, and not man, the highest rank. Contrary to what Darwin—another bad philologist and psychologist—thought, the state of "nature" guarantees without contest the victory of the "weaker sex" over the stronger. As Rousseau had already claimed in Book 5 of *Emile*, equality of rights between men and women could only rob those who are the real women of their power, their phantasmatic all-powerfulness. They would cease to be queens or goddesses,[20] to be obeyed at the least word, the least gesture. For Nietzsche, they would lose what characterizes their strength: the enigmatic character that they gave themselves by creating the type of the Eternal feminine with its contradictory characteristics. By agreeing to enter into the world of law, and by demanding equality a fortiori, they would

19. In *Beyond Good and Evil*, § 22, Nietzsche demonstrates that the concept of the "law of nature" is only a physicist's interpretation resulting from bad philology, sanctioning the democratic instincts of the modern soul. Universal equality before the law is "a fine instance of ulterior motives, in which the plebeian antagonism to everything privileged and autocratic as well as a second and more refined atheism are disguised once more." "Neither God nor master" is the wish that Nietzsche, as a good philologist, deciphers beneath all proclamations of demand for universal equality before the law.

20. In *Totem and Taboo*, Freud shows that it is only when women lose the power accorded them by their sons after the murder of the father of the primitive horde, that they are, in compensation, transformed into great goddesses and acquire a fearsome phantasmatic power.

cease to be cunning birds of prey who subjugate and fascinate. With the savagery of a beast showing all her claws (hand and foot, says the German, *mit Hände und Füssen*), the woman worthy of her type—of the type she created for herself—defends herself against all ideas of right (this masculine invention for ensuring the reciprocal respect of the strong and, by making them relinquish some of their power, avoiding a fight to the death).[21]

Woman, like life or nature, demands, *wants* war: the war between the sexes in which she is sure to triumph. Contrary to what a naive and superficial psychology might suppose, this war or mortal hatred between the sexes, in which each of them, by diverse, more or less devious strategies, attempts to triumph over the other, is not opposed to love, but is rather its most natural principle. The true psychologist or philosopher, freed of moral prejudices and complicitous with the good little women, knows that love, cut off from hatred, which is its principle, and from war, which is its means, is a word forged by the beautiful souls, the better to dissimulate, behind the gracious games and tender sentiments that they push to the fore, the ambivalence and cruelty that are inherent to it. The definition of love proposed by Nietzsche aims to translate it back into nature, as perhaps only Mérimée, in his *Carmen*, had previously done. In *The Case of Wagner*, Nietzsche had already paid homage to the man who so well discerned the ambivalence of love, and the inevitable tragic humor which is its result.

> Love translated back into *nature*. Not the love of a "higher virgin"! No Senta-sentimentality! But love as *fatum*, as fatality, cynical, innocent, cruel—and precisely in this a piece of nature. That love which is war in its means, and at bottom the deadly hatred of the sexes!—I know no case where the tragic joke that constitutes the essence of love is expressed so strictly, translated with equal terror into a formula, as in Don José's last cry, which concludes the work:
> "*Yes. I have killed her*
> I—*my adored Carmen!*"[22]

21. See *The Genealogy of Morals*, second essay, ¶ 11. Nietzsche specifies there that the laws created by the strong "can never be other than exceptional conditions, since they constitute a partial restriction of the will to life, which is bent on power, and are subordinate to its total goal as a single means: namely, as a means of creating greater units of power. A legal order thought of as sovereign and universal, not as a means in the struggle between power complexes but as a means of preventing all struggle in general—perhaps after the communistic cliché of Dühring, that every will must consider every other will its equal—would be a principle *hostile to life. . . .*"

22. *The Case of Wagner*, in *The Birth of Tragedy and The Case of Wagner*, trans. Walter Kaufmann (New York: Vintage Books, 1967), 158–59. Senta is a character in Wagner's *Flying Dutchman*.

Mérimée—and Bizet who set his *Carmen* to music—discerned in love this indissoluble union of opposites in the same (which Freud would later call ambivalence) which, far from being the dialectical reconciliation of opposites in a third term, suggests a logic of supplementarity, that of life, which admits of neither morality nor logic. All the misinterpretations of love, its idealization of "pure love," stem from the metaphysical belief (which goes hand in hand with logic and morality) in opposites. Wagner himself did not escape the naivete of creating heros whose love presents itself, contrary to all "true psychology," as disinterested ("oblative," say the old manuals); heroes who appear even to sacrifice their own advantages for the sake of the beloved. And yet, in a symptomatic and revealing manner, they also hope to "possess" the object of their love and to be loved in return. Behind the display of disinterest, this love obeys the same mercantile logic[23] as all other human relations, as all human "affairs": a logic not of the free "gift," which could be symbolized by the phrase of Goethe which Nietzsche recalls— "If I love you, is that your concern?"[24]—but of the *reciprocal* gift which, as such, ceases to be a "gift." The love of God, which men have deemed to be in the image of their own, itself obeys this mercantile logic; God becomes menacing when he is not loved in return—"in exchange."[25]

23. It should not be forgotten that in the final analysis, this logic refers to the will to power and *agon*. For to "weigh," "measure," "calculate," establish equivalents and "exchanges," is always also to measure oneself against the one with whom one sets up the exchange. See the second essay, ¶ 8.

24. Goethe, *Wilhelm Meister*, Part 4, Book 9 and *Poetry and Truth*, Part 3, Book 14.

25. On this problematic, see my *Don Juan ou le refus de la dette* (with Jean-Yves Masson) (Paris: Galilée, 1991). And in Nietzsche, see *The Gay Science*, trans. Walter Kaufmann (New York: Vintage Books, 1974), ¶ 141: "*Too Oriental.*—What? A god who loves men, provided only that they believe in him, and who casts an evil eye and threats upon anyone who does not believe in this love? What? A love encapsuled in if-clauses attributed to an almighty god? A love that has not even mastered the feelings of honor and vindictiveness? How Oriental this is! 'If I love you, is that your concern?' is a sufficient critique of the whole of Christianity." In *The Case of Wagner*, § 2, Nietzsche writes: "They (men) believe one becomes selfless in love because one desires the advantage of another human being, often against one's own advantage. But in return for that they want to *possess* the other person.—Even God does not constitute an exception at this point. He is far from thinking, 'What is it to you if I love you?'—he becomes terrible when one does not love him in return. *L'amour*—this saying remains true among gods and men—est de tous les sentiments le plus égoïste et par conséquent, lorsqu'il est blessé, le moins généreux (B. Constant)" (Love is the most egoistic of all sentiments, and thus, when it is wounded, the least generous).

Emmanuel Lévinas seems to respond to Nietzsche in establishing an absolute dissymmetry between myself and another, whose correlate is the absence of all demand for reciprocity in the gift of one's self. According to Nietzsche, if this is indeed the true "love," then it is an illusion, since, though more or less dissimulated, the will to power is everywhere operative.

Benjamin Constant showed himself a much keener psychologist than Wagner when, behind all the declarations of "disinterested" love, he was able to read the fiercest egoism, which is exposed in the most blatant way when love is wounded and loses its outward display of generosity.

Far from being a "moral" sentiment, love is, for both sexes, a means of attaining its ends and triumphing over the other. Thus, in woman, the love of man is simply a means of having a child, her only hope for healing and salvation. On this point, once again, Wagner committed the crudest of errors, one which spells his decadence and that of the characters he created: he who, in his operas, always invents "savior" figures, and in whose work the theme of "Redemption" is one of the most recurrent leitmotivs, in *Parsifal* believed that he could "save" a woman (Kundry) by means of a chaste love (that of Parsifal, the innocent and naive knight), whereas, according to Nietzsche, it is obvious that this supposed means of redemption could only spell her downfall. Preaching chastity is a veritable crime against life, and impedes (at the same time as the salvation of women) its eternal return. Because they are impure, sexual life and sensuality are despised and ridiculed by this "virtue" preached by the ascetic ideal and the morality which stems from it. In *Parsifal*, in which the aging Wagner converts to the ascetic ideal, there is a veritable eulogy of chastity, "tragically" cut off from sensuality, whereas it should be understood that the former belongs to a strategy of life, of which it is a necessary ingredient. When the morbidity of man prevents him from being excited by that carnal animal, woman, the stratagem of chastity—the "morbidezza" of woman— furnishes her with a supplementary attraction.[26] Sexual life is not criminal, but chastity, envisaged in its ascetic and tragic opposition to sensuality, certainly is. To the Christians' sin against the Holy Spirit, Nietzsche opposes a far more serious sin, the one committed against life, whose name is Baubô (to deride Demeter, in mourning for Proserpine, Baubô lifted up her skirts and showed her her belly),[27] the sin committed against women and their salvation.

---

26. See *The Genealogy of Morals*, third essay §1–§5, and on all that concerns Wagner's ascetic ideal and *Parsifal*, the false opposition chastity/sensuality, see my "Nietzsche and Wagner." For a thesis which is the opposite of Nietzsche's see Tolstoy's *Kreutzer Sonata*, which one cannot read today without thinking that its virulence and misogyny were designed to provoke a complete rejection of Christianity understood in this way.

27. See my "Baubô, fétichisme et perversion théologique" in *Nietzsche et la scène philosophique* (English translation in *Nietzsche's New Seas*, ed. Tracy Strong and Michael Allen Gillespie [Chicago: University of Chicago Press, 1988]).

When women themselves, or the "emancipated," "refuse" to give birth because they are incapable of it, and hold up a "higher" ideal, they are merely colluding with the ascetic ideal and, like it, they tend toward the negation of life, taking revenge on life and on those women who desire and ensure its return. By fighting for the right to vote and to an education, for equality with the other sex, whose wearing of trousers becomes emblematic, they actually seek to render women inferior to men, to make them lose, in the war of the sexes, the supremacy of which they had assured themselves. These failed women are women's worst enemies, and it would be better if, on the subject of women, they were to remain silent. In *Beyond Good and Evil,* in which, parodying Napoleon, Nietzsche utters the famous *"mulier taceat de muliere"* (woman should be silent about woman), Nietzsche invites women to be suspicious of these famous women, the very height of absurdity, who portray themselves as their spokeswomen; by heeding them, they display the worst taste and betray the perversity of their instincts:

> It betrays a corruption of the instincts—quite apart from the fact that it betrays bad taste—when a woman adduces Madame Roland or Madame de Staël or Monsieur George Sand, of all people, as if they proved anything in *favor* of "woman as such." Among them these three are the three *comical* women as such—nothing more!—and precisely the best involuntary *counterarguments* against emancipation and feminine vainglory. [233]

The "type" of woman—the old maid full of resentment—who, under the cover of idealism, is pernicious to the female sex as a whole, can also be found among those who, anatomically speaking, are men, and who, as idealists, infect all that is natural and innocent in sexual love with their moralism. The typical "old maid," the old maid par excellence, is not a woman, but the dramatist, Henrik Ibsen.[28] In a posthumous fragment, Nietzsche exposes the real motivations of his apparent "idealism," which stem from the will of the weak to establish their supremacy over the strong:

> Your Henrik Ibsen has become very clear to me. For all his robust idealism and "will to truth" he did not dare to liberate himself from the illusionism of morality that speaks of "freedom" without wishing to admit to itself what freedom is: the second stage in the metamorphosis of the "will to power"—for those who lack freedom. On the first stage one demands justice from those who are in power. On the second, one

28. Nietzsche is perhaps thinking particularly of *The Doll's House,* whose heroine is an emancipated woman.

speaks of "freedom"—that is, one wants to get away from those in power. On the third, one speaks of "equal rights"—that is, as long as one has not yet gained superiority one wants to prevent one's competitors from growing in power.[29]

Whether it is a "man" or a "woman" who appropriates this unnatural idealism for his or her own use, the Nietzschean moral code can only condemn this "person" as an idealist, vicious, perverse, and criminal, because a negator of life and of its "sanctity."

A first version of this paragraph ends the text by unmasking the most criminal of "all the idealists," the Wagner of *Parsifal* who, for his crimes, should suffer no lesser punishment than to be put in jail:

> After committing this crime, *Parsifal*, Wagner should not have died in Venice, but in jail. (I recommend this for the inscription on the façade of the theater in Bayreuth—it wouldn't lack wit.) One can imagine what I felt on seeing *Parsifal* during the summer of 1882 when I was pregnant with *Zarathustra*.

In this first version he also cited Article 4 of his "Law against Christianity" which constitutes the end of the *Antichrist:*

> Promulgated on the day of salvation, first day of the Year I
> (30 September 1888 of the false calendar)
> All-out war against the vice:
> The vice is Christianity

Article 4: "Preaching chastity is an open incitement to anti-nature. Disdain for sexual life and sullying it with the notion of 'impurity,' such is the true sin against the Holy Spirit of life." All of the articles of this code promulgated and signed by the Antichrist should be read. In their stead, I cite Article 6, which, more than any other, underscores the transvaluation of values operated by Nietzsche in this, to say the least, revolutionary code:

> One should give "holy" history the name it deserves—"accursed history"; one should use the words "God," "Messiah," "Redemption," "Saint" as insults and to designate criminals.

If some of Nietzsche's theses on women still seem shocking to the "feminists" of today, one must nevertheless recognize that they are inscribed in a general strategy which Nietzsche directs against Christian idealism and its dire consequences for sexuality, and notably femi-

29. *The Will to Power*, trans. and ed. Walter Kaufmann and Roger Hollingdale (New York: Random House, 1967) § 86.

nine sexuality: in this sense, Nietzsche perhaps does indeed, as he claims, "love" women, for he knows, as he states in the third essay of the *Genealogy of Morals* (§ 6), that they could not possibly want a disinterested and "oblative" love, one that appears to be cut off from all pulsional interest.

Moreover, to consider Nietzsche a misogynist[30] is to forget what he always emphasizes: (1) there is no woman "as such," woman as such is herself a historical creation; (2) there are only types of women, for which he tries to establish a differential table (these types themselves being not essences but historical "creations"): perfect women [*wohlgeraten*], and abortive women [*missgeraten*] who are transformed into women; (3) furthermore, he knows that he does not state "the truth" about "woman," but expresses only "his" truths about them, recognizing that these are closely bound up with the image of the mother which he bears within him:

> Whenever a cardinal problem is at stake, there speaks an unchangeable "this is I"; about man and woman, for example, a thinker cannot re-learn but only finish learning—only discover ultimately how this is "settled in him". . . .
>
> After this abundant civility that I have just evidenced in relation to myself I shall perhaps be permitted more readily to state a few truths about "woman as such"—assuming that it is now known from the outset how very much these are after all—only my truths. [*BGE*, 231]
>
> Everyone carries in himself an image of woman derived from the mother; by this he is determined to revere women generally, or to hold them in low esteem, or to be generally indifferent to them. [*HTH*, 380]

Reviewing paragraph three of "Why I am so Wise" (as I demonstrated in *Explosion I*), one can conclude that this image was at the very least ambivalent, since he states there that he would prefer to give up his most abysmal thought, that of the eternal return, rather than—vision of horror—bear the idea that his mother and sister, that riffraff, that dangerous vermin, should return eternally. But the very violence of his assertions about them is symptomatic of his love for these two women and for all the more or less castrating "good little women," against whom he nevertheless protects himself, by refusing all proximity to them—by keeping them at a respectful distance.

—Translated by Madeleine Dobie

30. Derrida has already made this point in *Éperons* (Paris: Champs-Flammarion, 1973); see also my "Baubô."

CHRISTINE DELPHY

The Invention of French Feminism: An Essential Move[1]

"French Feminism" is a baffling topic for everybody, and it is no less so for feminists from France than for feminists from the United States or Britain. There are many aspects to this topic and first of all, of course: what is "French Feminism"?

"French Feminism" is not feminism in France; that must be said at the outset. Feminists in France don't need to call their feminism a particular name any more than American feminists call theirs "American Feminism."

Most feminists from France find it extraordinary to be presented, when abroad, with a version of their feminism and their country of which they had previously no idea. British and American feminists are either fascinated or irritated, but always intrigued, by what is presented to them in Women's Studies as "French Feminism" or "French Theory."

The very attempt to attribute a specific content to a feminist movement shows that we are dealing with an outsider's view. So, even before we start looking at this content, we know that it cannot be a self-definition. This raises the question of the relationship between the way feminists from France see themselves and the way outsiders see them. This relationship bears a resemblance to that between observers and observed, between subjects and objects, a problem often raised in feminist methodology. It raises the question of who has the power to define whom to start with, who calls the shots. This is an important

1. I would like to thank Françoise Armengaud, Laura Cottingham, Judith Ezekiel, and Ailbhe Smyth for their support, their suggestions, and their help in the writing of this paper.

YFS 87, *Another Look, Another Woman,* ed. Huffer, © 1995 by Yale University.

question, because that is what most irritates feminists in France: that a "French Feminism" has been created unbeknownst to them in English-speaking countries. The content given to the category "French Feminism" is important in that respect: for the fact that feminists from France cannot recognize themselves in the picture they are presented with is a source of deeply-felt irritation. But the sole fact of creating a category "French Feminism" with a specific content—whatever the content—deprives feminists from France of the right to name themselves French Feminists. An ideological content—never mind which at this stage—has been given to a geographical specification.

This in turn raises a related issue: why has it been deemed necessary by Anglo-American feminists to specify, in ideological terms, the actions and the writings of feminists from France? And, reciprocally, to give a *national* label to a particular set of ideas or brand of feminism? How relevant *are* national boundaries to feminism—or indeed to other social and ideological movements—and how relevant *should* they be? That question has never been asked, although I think it is central. And finally, how was what is now known as "French Feminism" constructed? Who decided what it was and what it was not? *What went into the bag and what did not?*

What is taught as "French Feminism" has in fact little to do with what is happening in France on the feminist scene, either from a theoretical or from an activist point of view. This has been pointed out several times over the years by French and American scholars and activists.[2] More and more protests are being heard about the voluntary or involuntary distortions and omissions of the Anglo-American version of "French Feminism." The aim of this paper is not, however, to set the record straight: that work is already under way, and although it will take as many years probably to set the record straight as it has taken to get it wrong, it is already off to a good start with Claire Moses's brilliant analysis.[3]

In constructing "French Feminism," Anglo-American authors favored a certain overtly antifeminist political trend called "Psych et

2. See my "La passion selon Wittig," *Nouvelles Questions Féministes* 11–12 (Winter, 1985): 151–56. See also, Claire Moses, "French Feminism's Fortune," *The Women's Review of Books* 5/1 (October, 1987): 44.

3. See Moses, "'French Feminism' in U.S. Academic Discourse," a paper presented at the Berkshire Conference on Women's History, 12 June 1992 (hereafter referred to as Moses 1992a).

po," to the detriment of what is considered, by Anglo-American as well as French feminist historians,[4] to be the core of the feminist movement; and their bias has contributed to weakening the French movement (see Moses 1992a).

Anglo-American proponents of "French Feminism" have also consistently conflated "women writers" with "women's movement" (see Moses 1992a), thus eliminating the activist dimension of that movement. They promoted as "major French feminist theorists"[5] a "Holy Trinity" made up of three women who have become household names in the Anglo-American world of Women's Studies, which itself is increasingly divorced from the social movement: Cixous, Kristeva, Irigaray. This was in spite of the fact, which was never revealed to the non-French public, that the first two are completely outside feminist debate in France—and, not being considered feminist theorists, can hardly be considered "*major* feminist theorists"; and in spite of the fact, which is well-known and has been dealt with diversely by Anglo-American exporters, that at least the first two not only do not call themselves feminists, but have been known to actually denounce feminism.

Although the facts are well-known, they are not seen as a problem. Why? "Never would Americans proclaim nonfeminists to be the figureheads of their own movement."[6] What do you call doing to somebody else what you would not have done unto you? The term "imperialism" springs to the lips. And that is indeed the conclusion reached by both Moses and Ezekiel. They see imperialism at work in the Anglo-American construction of "French Feminism," and, moreover, they see that imperialism as related to domestic agendas: "Opponents have taken as their targets, not its American agents, but the French themselves" (Ezekiel); and "the French . . . are blamed for aspects of ourselves that we do not like but do not take responsibility for (like our racism and our classism)" (Moses 1992a). It is impossible to deny the charge of imperialism: imperialism indeed made the construction of "French Feminism" possible. It is equally impossible to deny that the wish to evade responsibility for one's theories is at work here. I think that the "agents," as Ezekiel calls them, of "French Feminism" wanted

4. See Françoise Picq, *Libération des femmes. Les Années-Mouvement* (Paris: Seuil, 1993).

5. Toril Moi, "Introduction" to *French Feminist Thought* (Oxford: Blackwell, 1987), 5.

6. Judith Ezekiel, Comments on Claire Moses's paper, Berkshire History of Women Conference, 12 June 1992.

to present certain theories as "French" in order that the prestige accruing to what is foreign in intellectual circles, and especially to what is "French," would accrue to that position; and in order to be able to distance themselves from, and not take full responsibility for, the ideas they were defending, as they could always take the stand that they were merely introducing Anglo-Americans to foreign ideas. An added benefit they could expect was that their pretension that these ideas are "feminist" would not be questioned.

But although imperialism, and the motivations behind the imperialist stance, figure prominently in the construction of "French Feminism," they are not the whole story. They are important, even essential, but as a means rather than the ultimate ends. The ultimate ends are domestic, but I contend that the domestic agenda is more ambitious than just hiding behind the "French." Or, to put it differently, the real question is: why is it necessary to hide behind the "French"? I think one has to answer that question first, and to answer it, one has to define the ideological features that are being proposed and promoted under the guise of "French Feminism." What does it say about feminism, and about the central questions of oppression and liberation that feminism poses?

My contention is that the manner in which "French Feminism" addresses these questions—often in an obscure and pedantic style which would require an essay in its own right—is regressive and detrimental to feminism in general, and not only to feminism in France, as noted by Eléni Varikas:

> To reduce "French" feminism to a few particular theoretical positions is not only to obscure the fact that the majority of feminist struggles were fought without knowledge of and sometimes against these positions; it is not only to obscure the most influential theoretical positions of feminist thought in France; even more than that, it is to prevent further thought on the conditions in which these many positions emerged, on what makes them socially and academically acceptable, and on their subversive dynamic.[7]

But before I come to that, I submit that "French Feminism" is not so much a "construction"—a biased and imperfect version of the reality of feminism in France—as an invention: a theoretical statement or

7. Eléni Varikas, "Féminisme, modernité, post-modernisme. Pour un dialogue des deux côtés de l'océan," in Féminismes au présent, special issue of Futur Antérieur (Paris: L'Harmattan, 1993), 63.

series of statements that have only a spurious relation to any other "reality"; that these statements are highly contentious; and that this is the reason why they had to try and be passed off as French.

First I want to establish that the theses of "French Freminism," and therefore "French Feminism" itself, cannot be found in the body of works that its agents refer to, but in their own writings. In other words, I mean that "French Feminism" is not an Anglo-American construction solely, or even mainly, insofar as it selects, distorts, and decontextualizes French writings. That would imply that to find what "it" is, we would have to engage in more comments, distortions, and selections; in brief, we would have to play the game by their rules and chase our tails until doomsday. No, I mean that it is an Anglo-American invention quite literally: Anglo-American writings that are "about" it *are* it.

I will briefly try to characterize "French Feminism" as a political strand, from the point of view of its content, and expose why, on an analytical level, it is not compatible with feminist analysis. My contention is that the problems most apparent in that approach, such as the reclaiming of the "feminine" or a definition of sexuality that leaves no room for lesbianism, are not the *source* of its inadequacy. I propose instead that these claims, which are problematic for a feminist politics, are a consequence of adopting an outdated epistemological framework.

However, these problematic positions come back to the fore when one tries to understand why feminists—or anyone—would want to adopt such a framework. I contend that anxieties about one's sexual and personal identity, threatened by the development of feminism and the blurring of gender lines that it promises, explain the liking exhibited by some women for conceptual frameworks that renege on the approach in terms of gender. That leads me to examine how social constructionism—in particular in the United States—is today often equated with "social conditioning" or "discourse theory," and does not, therefore, present a real alternative to essentialism.

I move on to consider an alternative explanation of the popularity of "French Feminism," in which it is not seen as a response to a contemporary threat, but as a continuation of a "difference" school which has existed within feminism since the turn of the century.

In what may look at first like a conclusion (and indeed was for a time), I then suggest that the reason proponents of that position offered it as "French," and the reason therefore for the invention of "French

Feminism," was to try and deflect the criticism its creators thought they would get—and that they got—from feminists, for offering an essentialist theory. And lastly, in my concluding remarks, I submit that the imperialism exhibited in the invention of "French Feminism" was necessary both to produce a particular brand of essentialism, and in order to pass off as feminist a "theory" in which feminism and feminists need not figure any longer.

FRENCH FEMINISM AS AN ANGLO-AMERICAN FABRICATION

To understand exactly what this "French Feminism" is in relation to feminism is the best way to understand why it was necessary to present it as "foreign." Once that is understood, the particular selection of authors and writings makes sense. And in turn, the distortions brought to the account of the feminist scene in France make sense, once we understand that the particular selection of authors and writings was dictated by ideological choice.

If, on the other hand, we start with the distortions—that is, if we start by comparing the account given by "French Feminism" with the actual French scene—we are left with the realization that there is a huge gap between the two. But how are we to understand how that happened, if we take the proponents of "French Feminism" at their word, that their aim was indeed to give an account of the French feminist scene? We would have to assume that, over a period of fifteen years, scholar after scholar has "misunderstood" the French political or intellectual scene. Inasmuch as we can assume ignorance or misinformation on the part of one or several persons, we cannot assume that all have been blind, and indeed afflicted with the same selective blindness; we cannot assume moreover that no one tried at any time to correct the picture, or to question the dominant account. There were questions and corrections from Anglo-American scholars;[8] and there were protests from feminists from France.[9]

In the hypothesis that the misrepresentation of the French feminist scene was a bona fide mistake, these questions, protests, and correc-

8. See Dorothy Kauffman McCall, "Politics of Difference," Signs 9/21 (1983): 283–93.

9. See Delphy 1985, Moses 1987, and Eliane Viennot, "Review Article," Etudes Féministes 1 (1987): 40–47.

tions were treated with arrogance when mentioned at all.[10] So the hypothesis that the main protagonists of "French Feminism" wanted to give an account and that they were only "mistaken" is untenable. Only the hypothesis that these protagonists had an ideological and political agenda can explain the discrepancies between "French Feminism" and feminism in France, the fact that these discrepancies persisted over a period of years, and, finally, that these discrepancies are not random.

"French Feminism," a fabrication of American, and more widely, English-speaking scholars, was created by a series of distortions and voluntary or involuntary errors about what was happening in France from the mid-seventies on. These distortions have a pattern. We do not have several competing views or definitions which show that the distortions are not random. On the other hand, if we did have competing views, then we would not have "French Feminism." "French Feminism" is thus a highly consensual object in the sense that the only debates about it focus on its relevance to Anglo-American concerns. There are *no* debates about what it *is*. Everybody seems to know what "French Feminism" is. At the same time, it is never really defined and remains elusive. It is therefore impossible to give, in any objective way, an ideological definition to what is an ideological current, and is perceived as such, in feminism.

The only objective way to define it is to say that it is a body of comments by Anglo-American writers on a selection of French and non-French writers: Lacan, Freud, Kristeva, Cixous, Derrida, and Irigaray are the core group. But there are others.

This presents us with two main questions: as I mentioned earlier, the question of the gap between this body of comments and feminism in France will not be addressed here, and I will concentrate instead on the theoretical and ideological pattern it presents. What are the substantive views these Anglo-American authors are promoting or attacking? What are they bringing to the debate on feminism in their respective countries?

But before tackling this, I want to look at its formal definition, that is, its definition as a body of Anglo-American writings. If we accept that "French Feminism" is an ideological and political trend in the countries where it exists as an object of debate, it follows that it has to

10. See, for example, Rosemary Tong's remarks about Viennot in her *Feminist Thought: A Comprehensive Introduction* (Boulder: Westview Press, 1989), 223, or Ezekiel.

be studied as such—and from then on, without quotation marks. It also follows that its message is contained in the sum of articles and books that purport to comment or build on French or other material. It *cannot* be said to consist of what its proponents claim: the complete works of the authors that they comment on, the authors listed above. These are the *referents* of "French Feminism," but they are not *it*. First, Anglo-American authors do not agree on the list of their referents—so that even if we accepted, as they would have us do, that the complete works of their referents is "French Feminism," as that list is infinite, we still would not have a finite and clearly delineated body of writings. Secondly, the supposedly original text of "French Feminism" is a series of bits and fragments taken from a heterogeneous universe. They do not make up an ensemble independent of the comments in which they are incorporated. That justifies seeing this body of comments as a separate entity from its referents, just as the Talmud is rightly seen as distinct from the Torah. We do not possess another text—an original homogeneous text, as in the case of the Torah.

But more importantly, a body of comments is really nothing more nor less than a theoretical statement or statements in the end. Or, put differently, there is no substantive difference between a theoretical work which is about something and a theoretical work which is about somebody. Whatever the detours, you end up saying something about the world, so that there is no legitimate difference of status between the text that presents itself as a "mere" comment, and the text it purports to comment on. These comments—including of course the bits and fragments, the quotes—therefore make up the only text we have of "French Feminism," and it is this body of work which constitutes "French Feminism."

For all these reasons, "French Feminism" is an Anglo-American strand of intellectual production within an Anglo-American context. From now on, when I speak of French Feminism and French Feminists without quotation marks, I am referring exclusively to this Anglo-American body of writings and its Anglo-American authors.

FRENCH FEMINISM AS AN IDEOLOGY OF DIFFERENCE: HOLISTIC VERSUS ADDITIVE EPISTEMOLOGIES

To study and to place this strand within each "national" feminism and feminism at large would require a study well outside the scope of this essay. However, if I tried, from my necessarily partial and impression-istic perspective, to give a description of it, I would say that the features that strike me most—apart from its pretension to be French—are the following:

—the conflation of "women" and "the feminine" and conversely, of "men" and "the masculine";

—the focus on the "feminine" and the "masculine," the belief that such things exist—or should exist—and that they provide or should provide a model for what actual women and men do and "are";

—the belief that "the feminine" and "the masculine" are a universal division of traits; that this division is found in all cultures because it is a trait of the universal psyche;

—the belief that the psyche is separate from and anterior to society and culture;

—the belief that the content of the psyche is both universal—not related to culture—and based on a common condition shared by all humans;

—the positing of a "sexual difference" between women and men which includes morphological differences, functional differences in reproduction, and psychological differences;

—the belief that sexual attraction between people is the desire for "difference";

—the belief that the only significant difference between people is "sex-ual difference";

—the belief that sexual difference is and should be the basis of psychic, emotional, cultural, and social organization, although the word "so-cial" only gets through the pens of French Feminists with some difficulty.[11]

11. See Carolyn Burke, "Report from Paris: Women's Writing and the Women's Movement," *Signs* 3/4 (1978): 843–55 and "Irigaray through the Looking Glass," *Feminist Studies* 7/2 (1981): 287–306; Claire Duchen, *Feminism in France* (London: Routledge & Kegan Paul, 1986); Diana Fuss, *Essentially Speaking* (London: Routledge & Kegan Paul, 1989) and " 'Essentially Speaking'/Luce Irigaray's Language of Essence," in Nancy Fraser and Sandra Lee Bartky, *Revaluing French Feminism* (Bloomington: Indiana University Press, 1992), 94–112; Jane Gallop, *The Daughter's Seduction* (Ithaca: Cornell University Press, 1982); Elizabeth Gross, "Philosophy, Subjectivity and the Body: Kristeva and Irigaray," in *Feminist Challenges*, ed. Carol Pateman and Elizabeth Gross,

One need not go on to stress the point that this approach to the problems raised by feminism is very problematic on analytical and political levels. On an analytical level, it turns its back on the main developments in feminist thinking; on a political level, it has implications that are unpalatable for many feminists.

Whereas some haggle over points of detail, or interpretation, I think it has to be recognized that *any* dealing with "human nature"— whatever form it takes, be it the "aggressiveness" of males, the "constraints of the symbolic order," or the "maternal-semiotic"—is bound to wield very disappointing results for any movement bent on changing the world or even simply on understanding it.

Now, the question is understanding why so many Anglo-American commentators have chosen the human nature approach. And in asking that question, we cannot simply talk about French Feminism anymore: we must include not only the people who write about it, but the people who listen to it, not only the Anglo-American participants, but the people—and in particular feminists—who all over the Western world find that kind of approach so enticing. I and others have tackled

---

(Boston: Northeastern University Press, 1986), 125–43. Alice Jardine, "Pre-Texts for the Transatlantic Feminist," *Yale French Studies* 62 (1981): 220–36, "Introduction to Julia Kirsteva's 'Women's Time,'" *Signs* 7/1 (1981): 7–35, *Gynesis* (Ithaca: Cornell University Press, 1985), and "Men in Feminism: Odor di Uomo or Compagnons de Route?" in *Men in Feminism*, a special issue of *Critical Exchange* 18 (1985): 23–31; Ann Rosalind Jones, "Assimilation with a Difference: Renaissance Women Poets and Literary Influence," *Yale French Studies* 62 (1981): 135–153, and "Writing the Body: Toward an Understanding of l'écriture féminine," *Feminist Studies* 7/2(1981): 246–63; Peggy Kamuf, "Replacing Feminist Criticism," in *Conflicts in Feminism*, ed. Marianne Hirsch and Evelyn Fox Keller (London: Routledge & Kegan Paul, 1990), 104–11; Kamuf and Nancy K. Miller, "Parisian Letters: Between Feminism and Deconstruction," in Hirsch and Fox Keller, 120–33; Dorothy Leland, "Lacanian Psychoanalysis and French Feminism: Toward an Adequate Political Psychology," in Fraser and Bartky, 113–35; Miller, "The Text's Heroine: A Feminist Critic and Her Fictions," in Hirsch and Fox Keller, 11–120; Moi 1987 and Moi, *Sexual/Textual Politics* (London: Methuen, 1985), and *The Kristeva Reader* (Oxford: Blackwell, 1986); Ariel Salleh, "Contribution to the Critique of Political Epistemology," *Thesis Eleven* 8 (1984): 23–44; Naomi Schor, "This Essentialism Which Is Not One," *Differences* 1/2 (1989): 38–58; Paul Smith, *Discerning the Subject* (Minneapolis: University of Minnesota Press, 1988); Gayatri Chakravorty Spivak, "French Feminism in an International Frame," *Yale French Studies* 62 (1981): 154–84, and "French Feminism Revisited: Ethics and Politics," in *Feminists Theorize the Political*, ed. Judith Butler and Joan Scott (London: Routledge & Kegan Paul, 1992), 54–85; Domna Stanton, "The Fiction of *Préciosité* and the Fear of Women," *Yale French Studies* 61 (1981): 107–34, and "Language and Revolution: The Franco-American Dis-Connection," in *The Future of Difference*, ed. Hester Eisenstein and Alice Jardine (New Brunswick: Rutgers University Press), 52–87.

that issue many times over the years.[12] The appeal remains, and it is that of "difference" and, more precisely, of "*sexual* difference." The reasons for the theoretical and political flaws of this approach are also the reasons for its appeal.

The "sexual difference" approach is theoretically flawed on a basic level by the very premises it incorporates, and which are a throwback to epistemological postures that cannot be taken seriously today. I have listed some of them above, but there is a deeper level which makes that approach incompatible with the modern humanities and social sciences, including the so-called postmodern.

Briefly, one can trace back to the nineteenth century the development of a paradigm for understanding the world that I will call, for the time being, structural. This approach, to be found in the natural sciences as well as in the human sciences, considers the whole before it considers the parts. It is the whole, the configuration, that gives meaning to each of the parts. Indeed, it is the whole that gives rise to the parts. In other words, the whole precedes the parts.

This approach, in use in the natural sciences and in mathematics for more than a century, can be found in many models of the human sciences. For example, it is the still uncontested basis of Saussurian linguistics; even though later models have been developed, the basic Saussurian model remains: sounds do not pre-exist the total language, it is the total language which determines how the sound continuum will be cut up into discrete sounds. This model informs contemporary anthropology (not only that which calls itself structural, like the work of Lévi-Strauss), contemporary psychology, and sociology. This understanding of the world is already present in the work of Marx: the total society pre-exists each class, and it is the way it functions as a whole which creates the division principle; the division principle itself creates each class. Classes cannot be viewed independently of one another, as tribes having led their own lives and coming into contact almost by accident, no more than the "a" sound in a given language can be seen as existing independently of the next sound.

12. See my "Rethinking Sex and Gender," *Women's Studies International Forum* 16/1 (1993): 1–9 (hereafter referred to as Delphy 1993a) and "Proto-feminism and Anti-feminism," in my *Close to Home*, trans. Diana Leonard (London: Hutchinson Press, 1984), 182–211; see also Colette Guillaumin, *Sexe, race et pratique du pouvoir* (Paris: côté-femmes, 1992); Nicole-Claude Mathieu, *L'Anatomie politique* (Paris: côté-femmes, 1991); and Monique Wittig, *The Straight Mind* (Boston: Beacon Press, 1992).

For all these reasons, I think *holistic*[13] is the best adjective to characterize the structural approach. Needless to say, all modern and contemporary developments build on that approach. The structural or *holistic* approach is the matrix of all twentieth-century schools of thought, whether they call themselves materialist, social constructionist, or structuralist. The so-called "post" (as in "poststructuralist") trends are not contradictions but further developments of this more general approach.

The contemporary development of research on gender is part of that paradigm: it considers that gender, the dividing principle, is the constituting force behind the creation of genders. To put it simply, this means taking as a starting point that you cannot envision "men" and "women" separately, any more than "the feminine" and "the masculine"; that the two are created one by the other and at the same time. Now this stance has revolutionary implications; it implies that the one does not (indeed) move without the other; that the status of the category "women" cannot change without the status of the category "men" changing at the same time; it implies, moreover, that their respective status and their content are one and the same thing: that it is impossible to change the status of a category without changing its content and vice-versa (see Delphy 1993).

In contrast, French Feminism and the theories, such as psychoanalysis, on which it draws have remained immune to these developments. They go on considering the parts as independent of one another and pre-existing their coming into relation. It uses, from the point of view of the relationship of the parts to the whole, an *additive* approach.

Now such a view implies that the parts, which exist before the whole, have a meaning, and indeed a nature—an *essence*—of their own. It implies furthermore that the parts that make up any reality—the physical, social, or psychic world—are always the same, in number and in content, and are there to stay; therefore, that which we perceive is what *reality* is made up of: if we perceive two sexes for instance, it is because there *are* two sexes; that society or its instances—language for one instance—intervene only to rank these pre-existing realities; that these constituent parts can be shifted around without changing the

---

13. I do not use the term "holistic" in the sense it was given by Quine, although the two are by no means contradictory.

whole; and, conversely, that the only thing that can be done with them is to shift them around; that inasmuch as one wants to shift them around, one has to find their "real" meaning, their "real" essence. The *additive* approach is thus necessarily essentialist.

Only on that basis is it possible to imagine, as French Feminism does, that the only way to "up" the status of women is to up that of "the feminine"; and that, conversely, one of these statuses—that of the "feminine"—can be "revalued" without altering the status of "the masculine." More importantly, that alteration takes place without altering the whole and creating a new whole, and, therefore, new divisions of which "the feminine" and "the masculine" might not be a part (see Delphy 1984 and Delphy 1993).

This is where features of French Feminism which I earlier considered as secondary play a central role, especially the insistence on *not* defining the "sexual difference" it talks about, and leaving it as a mystical object whose mysteries must remain obscure. In order to do that, French feminists must ignore the now considerable work— empirical as well as theoretical—that has gone into cracking open that nut, and on studying the different things to which sexual difference refers. To speak today, without further ado, of undefined "sexual difference" amounts to eliding sex (anatomical), sexuation (gender identity and psychological sex-related differences), sex roles, sexual activity, and sexual preference. All these things are supposed, both in common-sense thinking and in French Feminism, to derive from one another or to be one and the same thing. This confusion is the basis of gender ideology. Psychoanalysis provided the "scientific" version of this common sense ideology, putting sexual difference under one form or another—the penis, "castration," or the mother-child bond—in the place of the ultimate principle.

Feminism started—a long time ago—deconstructing all these links; extricating sex from sex role and sex identity; it has even forged whole new concepts, such as *gender,* to account for this deconstruction. From the early distinction between sex and sex roles, it has proceeded through the second half of the twentieth century to break down "sexual difference" into more and more component parts, only arbitrarily and socially related to one another, to the point where even sexual desires have been dissociated from the anatomical difference between females and males, and heterosexuality has lost its aura of naturalness and necessity.

GENDER THEORY AS A THREAT TO IDENTITY

This is all very threatening, not only to men, but to women as well, and the realm of sexuality—sexual practice and sexual preference—is particularly sensitive, invested as it is in contemporary society with the capacity to fill subjectivity: to provide a personal identity. Sexual activity both defines people as male or as female and defines them as *people*, in a society where you are *nobody* if you are not one or the other. At the same time, sexual activity is imbued with a strong sense of guilt and shame. People do not relish having to think that it is up to them—they don't readily let go of the idea that it has all been decided for them in some part of their hormone-influenced cortex. They do not like being, as they see it, "free-floating," with no sound "natural" basis for their tastes, which they experience, rightly, as irresistible impulses.

What has to be taken into account, too, or maybe first, is that gendered societies such as Western societies create their own subjectivities and in particular, as mentioned above, the inability to have an individual identity that is not a gendered identity. Our very languages preclude that possibility: how long can you talk about someone without saying "she" or "he"? (It's even worse in French, but only marginally.) What the language imposes has been confirmed by psychosocial studies: the notion of "human being" does not exist in our societies, or rather, there are two ideas of "human being." There is a "male human being" and a "female human being."[14]

This is our psychological make-up, what we've inherited not only from our childhood, but from every minute we've spent on this earth. This is being shattered by the findings of feminism about the social construction of gender. But how are we to integrate this newly acquired knowledge, which remains highly intellectual, with our "immediate" perceptions?

The two clash, and there's nothing we can do about it. We may know—or, rather, try to imagine—that gender is socially constructed, that is, arbitrary in its form and its very existence. But how are we to reconcile that with the evidence of our eyes which shows a very sturdy, all-pervasive, immovable gender on which all reality seems to be founded?

14. See Marie-Claude Hurtig and Marie-France Pichevin, "Masculine-Feminine: A New-Look Essentialism," a paper presented to the fifth Conference of the International Society for Theoretical Psychology, Bierville, France, April 1993.

IS SOCIAL CONSTRUCTION THE SAME THING AS "SOCIAL CONDITIONING"?

One of the many shortcomings of contemporary theory, maybe particularly in the United States, is the false perception that what is socially constructed is somehow shallow, or superimposed, or easily overthrown.

This perception shows a naive contempt for the workings of society and is grounded in an implicit belief that somehow underlying social and cultural structures, there exists a "human nature" that could surface if given the chance. But there is no human nature, and we have no other perception or possibility of action than those given by society. There is no "beyond" (or indeed "before") social construction.

Only this kind of belief in an individual—or universal—nature, one that somehow pre-exists "social conditioning," can explain the belief that if we feel "male" or "female" it cannot be "all social," or the opposite but symmetrical belief that we can opt out of gender on an individual basis.[15] If there is something that is the most particularly American in French Feminism, it must be the belief that presumes, even when it does not say so, the existence of a primal individual, and reduces social construction to "social conditioning" or "socialization."

But social construction is not something that happens when you're not looking—it is what happens all the time, in all societies, and it started happening long before we were born. It is coterminous with being human, because this is the world that we find and there is no other: there is nothing else "underneath," contrary to what so many American writings, especially postmodern, seem to imply.

However, maintaining a belief in a "beyond" or "before" social and cultural organization together with an intellectual adherence to social constructionism, is not an American trait: it is a general inability to come to terms with the implications of social constructionism, an inability that is both an intellectual shortcoming and an emotional reluctance. Actually, it is remarkable that, gendered as we are in our psychological make-up, we (at least some of us) can even *envision* the non-necessity of gender.

The inability to correctly understand subjectivity as socially constructed, but *not* amenable to voluntaristic behavior, puts feminism

15. See Judith Butler, *Gender Trouble: Feminism and the Subversion of Identity* (London: Routledge & Kegan Paul, 1990).

between a rock and a hard place, and this is particularly visible in the American intellectual scene today. On the one hand, those who remain convinced that the category "women" exists feel that the only foundation for it must be essentialist—grounded in "Nature"—whereas those who supposedly take a social constructionist view argue that the implication is therefore that the category "women" does not really exist: "If gender is simply a social construct . . . what can we demand in the name of women if women do not exist?"[16]

I want to linger on this "simply social." This understanding of "social" amounts to equating social construction with what is called in everyday language "social conventions": something that you can take or leave—and if you leave it, at the worst you will be seen as impolite. Alcoff and Butler have different positions, the first wanting to stay with the category "women," the second not. But they share a philosophical "idealism" in their perception of human life and subjectivity. Either it is "real" and must be based in "Nature" (not "simply" social), or it is "social" and therefore "unreal" and can be undone by individual volition. Even though they differ in the outcome they favor, neither of them assumes a truly social constructionist view. Both Alcoff and Butler can envision the nonexistence or disappearance of the category "women" without at any time considering the implications of that for the category "men"—a category which therefore must be presumed to stay, and to be able to stay all by itself. In a social constructionist view, which is necessarily holistic, either the two categories exist, or neither. The fact that Alcoff and Butler can imagine one of them subsisting without the other reveals that they adhere to an *additive* world view, where the parts exist independently and can change or move independently of one another. What is still lacking is a notion that human arrangements are both social—arbitrary—and material: external to the action of any given individual.

It is difficult not to link this defect in social constructionist thinking in the United States to the way in which the only contesting of essentialism comes from women who are steeped in "French Theory." French Feminists and French Feminism are being "reprocessed" as "postmodern," and even though some, such as Linda Nicholson,[17] point out the incompatibility between the essentialism of classic

16. Linda Alcoff, "Cultural Feminism versus Post-Structuralism," *Signs* 13/31 (1988): 405–36.

17. Linda Nicholson, ed., *Feminism/Postmodernism* (London: Routledge & Kegan Paul, 1990).

French Feminism and the structuralism of "poststructuralism," the two are inextricably connected in the dozens of titles and mind-blowing new appellations that seem to crop up every day.

Inasmuch as one can make sense of the frenzy of incessant renaming that has seized Anglo-American academe, it appears that the heady mixture of Foucault and Derrida has given rise to something called "theory of discourse" or "deconstructionism." In this theory everything is a text, and the old contest between "reality" and discourse has been done away with: better, it has been won by discourse, of which "the text" is the best incarnation. All other things—such as social practices, institutions, belief systems, and subjectivities—are only bad approximations of the text.

Thus what seems to have happened is that as soon as it was rediscovered and used against essentialism,[18] social constructionism was watered down: it was conceptualized as constructionism without the power of society behind it; or, the power of society was reduced to that of an always interpretable and, moreover, multiple "discourse." Social constructionism is equated with male authors and with a nominalist version of itself which deprives it of any real content. Commenting on these developments as exemplified by Joan Scott's *Gender and the Politics of History,*[19] Joanna Russ writes:

> To say that language influences reality . . . is one thing. To say that nothing else exists . . . is another thing entirely. . . . One of the advantages of aging is that the second time you see the same damn nonsense coming around again you can spot it in one-tenth of the time it took you to recognize it the first time. The nineteen fifties' literary emphasis on the autonomy of texts was an escape into a realm divorced from the nasty world in which professors were being kicked out for being "subversive," and witch hunts against homosexuals were a regular feature of public life. Current reality is also mighty unpleasant; how nice it would be if it *were* only language and we could control it by controlling language, or if attempts to do anything else were impossible or useless. And look how important that would make us.[20]

18. See Alcoff; Butler; Fraser; Nicholson; Jane Flax, "Post-modernism and Gender Relations in Feminist Theory," *Signs* 12/4 (1987): 621–43; Joan W. Scott, "Deconstructing Equality Versus Difference," *Feminist Studies* 14/1 (1988): 33–50.

19. Joan Scott, *Gender and the Politics of History* (New York: Columbia, 1988).

20. Joanna Russ, Letter to the Editors of *The Women's Review of Books* 6/4 (1989): 4. This letter is about Claudia Koonz's review of Joan Wallach Scott's *Gender and the Politics of History.*

So the explanatory power of social constructionism, along with the fact that it was developed in feminism by feminists, and particularly by French, British, and Italian materialist feminists[21] is being ignored.[22]

Maybe some feminists do not want to accept the political implications of unadulterated social constructionism: that things can change, but that it will be long and arduous, and that we do not have an infinite power over our own individual lives, nor, to start with, over our own brains. Maybe they do not want to accept that even though things—including our own thoughts—present themselves to us qua individuals as external constraints, they are not imposed on us by God or Nature and that we, qua members of society, share in the responsibility for changing or not changing them.

DIFFERENCE AS A PERMANENT FEATURE OF TWENTIETH-CENTURY FEMINISM

In this attempt to explain the appeal of conceptual frameworks based on naturalistic premises, I have taken for granted that French Feminism is a contemporary reaction to a contemporary problem: that the progress of social constructionist views is, on a personal level, threatening to many people, because they let us envision a future where we might not have gender to rely on as a basis for our personal identity.

However, this emphasis on "difference" is not new. We find it throughout the history of feminism, which it has split since its very beginnings. The debate between these two currents of feminism is still alive and well, and its terms—"Difference" versus "Equality"—are still amazingly similar after a century and a half. There is a tendency to

21. See Delphy 1984 and 1993a; Delphy and Diana Leonard, *Familiar Exploitation: A New Analysis of Marriage* in *Contemporary Western Societies* (Cambridge: Polity Press, 1992); Guillaumin 1992; Guillaumin, "The Practice of Power and Belief in Nature," *Feminist Issues* 25 (1981): 25–31; Hurtig and Pichevin, "Masculine-Feminine"; Hurtig and Pichevin, "The Body as Support and Mediator of Sex Relations," in Lisa Adkins and Leonard, *The Other French Feminism*, forthcoming; Hurtig and Pichevin, "Salience of the Sex Category System in Personal Perception: Contextual Variations," *Sex Roles* 22/5–6 (1990): 369–95; Celia Kitzinger, *The Social Construction of Lesbianism* (London: Sage, 1987); Mathieu; Monique Plaza, "'Phallomorphic Power' and the Psychology of 'Woman,'" in Adkins and Leonard; Paola Tabet, "Les mains, les outils, les armes," *L'Homme* 19/3–4: 5–61, "Fertilité naturelle, reproduction forcée," in *L'arraisonnement des femmes*, ed. Mathieu (Paris: Editions E.H.E.S.S.), 61–146, "Du don au tarif: les relations sexuelles impliquant compensation," *Les Temps Modernes* 490 (1987): 1–53, and "Imposed Reproduction: Maimed Sexuality," in Adkins and Leonard.

22. See Stevi Jackson, "The Amazing Deconstructing Woman," *Trouble and Strife* 25 (Winter 1992): 25–31, and Adkins and Leonard.

pretend that it is over or that one can go "beyond" it. But despite their promising titles,[23] articles that purport to "transcend" the debate always end up on one side or the other, and I see several reasons why this is so and, in fact, cannot be otherwise.

These two positions cannot be reconciled at an analytical level. One relies either on the conceptual framework I have tentatively described as holistic/social constructionist, or on an additive/essentialist framework. But positions are ultimately expressed by people, and although we often assume that people are coherent, they are not. They therefore come up with theoretical positions that mix elements resting on different and contradictory premises. So the fact that essentialism and social constructionism are combined in some, or even most positions, does not make them logically compatible. Furthermore, people's incoherence can extend to their endorsing positions which at the outset might seem at odds with what they think. This has led activists such as Carol Anne Douglas to wonder whether theory really mattered for feminism.[24]

In spite of all this, there *is* a logic to conceptual frameworks that makes eclecticism impossible to pursue beyond a certain point that is reached all too soon. Although social constructionism and essentialism are seldom presented in a pure form, for the reasons just outlined, they still are irreconcilable. Indeed, it is *because* they are seldom presented in a pure form that they can be seen as not completely antagonistic. However, that pure form exists and it consists of their intrinsic possibilities and limits—whether they are used or not at any given time. Some things are conceivable in social constructionism but not in essentialism and vice-versa. And the fact that we do not have to think them now does not mean that we will not need to think them tomorrow; on the analytical level as well, there are moments of reckoning. We have not yet thought through social constructionism, because it is emerging precisely *against* common sense, essentialist thinking, and because it is resisted in the area of gender by those men who use it in every other area.

The impression that using one conceptual framework or the other does not make much difference is probably misleading. Dorothy Stet-

23. See Scott. Also, see Louise Toupin, "Une histoire du féminisme est-elle possible?" *Recherches féministes* 6/1 (1993): 25–53.
24. Carol Anne Douglas, Review of "Is the Future Female?" by Lynne Segal, *Off Our Backs* (January 1989): 16.

son has convincingly shown[25] that it was difference feminists in the Women's Bureau who defeated the passage of the E.R.A. Molly Ladd-Taylor makes the same point: "Maternalism and feminism coexisted and at times overlapped until the 1920s, when the bitter debate over the Equal Rights Amendment drove them apart."[26] In other words, there *are* different political agendas and times of reckoning when these differences can no longer be smoothed over.

Even though these different political agendas are not necessarily linked in a one-to-one way with different analyses, just as one cannot assume such coherence on the part of individuals, it is equally clear that there are correspondences between analytical frameworks and political agendas in general, whether in respect to feminism or in respect to other political questions.

The tendency to gloss over divergences is due to an unrealistic belief that basically we all want the same thing. It is, or should be, apparent by now that we do not all want the same thing, no more than "we" wanted the same thing during first-wave feminism or at any time between the two waves. We have to accept that not all women conceive of their interests in the same way, and that their different ways can be conflictual, as was strikingly demonstrated in the debate over the E.R.A.

I have for a long time (see Delphy 1984 and 1993a), like others, believed that only a faulty analysis, which could be sorted out by debate, led some Western women to argue that the way out of oppression lay in specific rights for women and the buttressing of gender identity, when so many women in other countries, especially in fundamentalist Muslim countries, are trying desperately to get rid of "codes of personal status" and other specific "rights" that are in reality a curtailing of citizenship for women.[27] But I believe now that we don't have the same vision of "liberation." Evidence of this is presented by the highly emotional rejection, by feminists I call "radical"—that is, looking for and wanting to eradicate the roots of patriarchy—of the group-identity sought by proponents of "difference"; and by the

25. Dorothy Stetson, *Women's Rights in the U.S.A.* (Belmont: Brooks/Cole, 1991).

26. Molly Ladd-Taylor, "Toward Defining Maternalism in U.S. History," *Journal of Women's History* 5/2 (1993): 110–14.

27. See A.E.L.F.H., "Les luttes de femmes en Algérie," and Marie-Aimée Hélie-Lucas, "Les stratégies des femmes à l'égard des fondamentalismes dans le monde musulman," *Nouvelles Questions Féministes* 16–18 (1991): 17–29 and 29–63.

equally highly emotional disgust expressed by them at our vision of a world that would make room for all individual differences, and also consider all differences as individual.[28]

To continue interpreting divergences within feminism as mere misunderstandings, or as different strategies, is to bury one's head in the sand: some divergences are not about different ways of achieving the same goals, *they are about different goals.* The most striking illustration of this proposition is found, I think, in the very terms of the debate about "Difference" versus "Equality." Among the oppressed groups of humankind, only women oppose "difference" to "equality," and that formulation alone is reflected in titles such as *Beyond Equality and Difference.* In the introduction to this paradigmatic book, "Contextualizing Equality and Difference," the only "contextualization" which would indeed make it possible to go "beyond" the question of "Difference" versus "Equality" is never once mentioned.[29] Such a contextualization would be the preliminary admission that "the opposite of 'equality' is 'inequality.'"[30]

DESTABILIZING FEMINISM

The main reason that its inventors invented their brand of feminism as "French" was that they did not want to take responsibility for what they were saying and, in particular, for their attempt to rescue psychoanalysis from the discredit it had incurred both in feminism and throughout the social sciences. They pretended that *another* feminist movement thought it was great—that in fact it was all the other, admittedly strange, movement was interested in.

That took some doing, a process which is excellently described and

---

28. For the sake of being understood, I use the term "differences," although I think it is a loaded term in the context of the discussion of sex and gender, especially since "differences" are never referred explicitly to their implicit referent, be it the dominant category, or the realm of human action where they acquire, or do not acquire, relevance, and furthermore in that "differences" are, at the most, opposed to "sameness" (see Scott). But levels of sameness—for example, belonging to the human species—are the unsaid but necessary context of finding differences within that level, in the same way as levels of differences—for example those between humans and other animals—are the unspoken basis for finding sameness.

29. "Contextualizing Equality and Difference," in *Beyond Equality and Difference,* ed. Gisela Bock and Susan James (London: Routledge & Kegan Paul, 1992), 1–13.

30. Christine Planté, in her "Questions de différences" in *Féminismes au présent,* wonders why Joan Scott, who makes this clear in her 1988 article, does not apply this insight to her analysis of the Sears Case.

analyzed by Claire Moses (1992a). Moses points out that at the time of the famous 1978 *Signs* issue, "the Prefaces always identified Cixous, Kristeva, and Irigaray as French 'writers' or 'intellectuals,' never as 'feminists.'" She goes on to note that the French movement was consistently presented by Elaine Marks and Isabelle de Courtivron as "in discontinuity with historical feminism"; that Domna Stanton (in the 1978 *Signs* issue) identifies language as the site of feminist struggle in France. Moses gives many examples of the way the French movement was misrepresented. The fact that it was a movement that shared many traits with other movements—in terms of preoccupations, analyses, campaigns, demands, activism—was not only ignored, but denied. It was said that there was a movement, but a movement of writers who "problematized the words 'feminist' and 'feminism'" (Marks and de Courtivron, cited in Moses 1992a).

One could go on, taking up factual errors in Anglo-American writings to this day and showing the distortions that the French movement suffered, and still suffers, at the hands of these writers. I want to focus here on one point in particular, and that is the personal and ideological closeness to psychoanalysis of the women selected by French Feminists, and their equal distance from feminism.

It has been noted by Moses that French Feminism was equated with "women writers," that two of the three writers in question are antifeminist and that only one—who has only recently started calling herself a feminist—has been read and commented upon by feminists from France. But if it has been mentioned that they are Lacanian, nowhere does it ever appear that two of them are practicing psychoanalysts: Irigaray and Kristeva. In the way that Cixous's and Kristeva's antifeminist declarations are, variously, treated as nonrelevant, the fact that they are not part of the feminist debate in France is considered as so irrelevant as to be not even worth mentioning. It is implied that actual feminists from France look up to these writers, which is necessary in order to make them look significant to the domestic reader. Their real importance in France is never evaluated—for instance, by the number of times they are quoted or appear in feminist discussions.

What is implied by portraying these women as important in feminism is that whether one calls oneself a feminist or not is not relevant; what is further implied by asserting that they are important for feminists in France is that feminists in France do not consider that relevant either. The message is that in order to speak in or of feminism, one does not need to be a self-defined feminist. The impact this had on domestic feminism was to blur the frontiers between feminists and nonfeminists.

However, this is not a consistent policy. At other times, Kristeva and Cixous are, on the contrary, reclaimed as feminists, in spite of themselves. This is a spectacular manifestation of imperialism. Kristeva's or Cixous's outspoken antifeminism can be dismissed in a way that no Anglo-American's opinion could be dismissed: "Despite their disclaimers, it is difficult not to classify Kristeva and Cixous as feminists" (Tong, 223).

It is suggested that they do not know their own minds. There is a level of contempt here that is truly unbearable. But if one manages to forget and forgive the condescension, what is the message to the Anglo-American reader? Again, it seems to be that writings meant as anti-feminist are just as important to feminism as feminist writings. Again, the line is blurred, and the feminist debate opens up to welcome anti-feminist opinions, which are to be treated *on a par* with feminist opinions.

That was opening the way for things yet to come: the introduction into feminism of Freud and Lacan, first as "French Feminists," then as feminists *tout court*, and finally as "Founding Fathers." The redeeming of psychoanalysis has now been achieved; and not only thanks to French Feminism, since Juliet Mitchell, Nancy Chodorow, and Carol Gilligan have paved the way for this development, albeit with a *soft* version of psychoanalytic essentialism. Proponents of French Feminism were able to use this opening to offer the real hard stuff: unreconstructed continental psychoanalysis. And the Anglo-American scene has been transformed to the extent that a book on psychoanalysis is seen as intrinsically part of feminist theory, in spite of the total absence of any discussion of feminism (see Gallop). That is something that could not have happened before the invention of French Feminism, and which could still not happen in France, whoever the author. (Marcelle Marini did write a book on Lacan, but that was not seen as part of her feminist writing; in fact it was actually seen as slightly odd.)

But the most interesting feature of French Feminism is the way it deals with essentialism. Most French Feminists do not hold up essentialism as a "Good Thing." But they often promote it by saying that it is not essentialism. A good deal of their time is taken up "defending" Irigaray against accusations of essentialism (see Schor 1989 and Fuss 1989, especially 55–83). But why exactly? Is it because they are convinced that Irigaray is not essentialist? They cannot be, as Irigaray makes no bones about it, and never tries to defend herself against something she does not see as an indictment. Anglo-American essentialists are in a more delicate position: they want the thing without the sting. And since of course this is not possible, what they are accomplishing on their domestic scene is a regression. Everybody talks about essentialism, but nobody knows what it is anymore, as essentialist theories are presented as nonessentialist. Even Freud and Lacan, whose essentialism was established a long time ago in *all* quarters, not only in feminist circles, are now being "revalued" and absolved.

Moreover, in an apparently contradictory, but really coherent movement, essentialism is increasingly presented as something which, although it cannot be endorsed outright, might not be "the damning criticism it is supposed to be" (Smith, 144). Paul Smith and Diana Fuss credit Irigaray with such sophistication that, it is implied, she can only "seem" essentialist; on the other hand, if she were found to be (and not just seem to be) essentialist, then, it is implied, might she not have a good reason? Although they cannot decide on the matter—Fuss even writes that "Irigaray both *is* and *is not* an essentialist" (Fuss 1989, 70)—they agree that if she is, it is a strategy, even "a key strategy . . . not an oversight" (Fuss 1989, 72). Thus, under the guise of trying to understand complex European thinking, Anglo-American authors are working their way towards a rehabilitation of essentialism.

CONCLUDING REMARKS: IMPERIALISM AS A TACTIC FOR ELIMINATING WITH ONE FELL SWOOP FEMINISM . . . AND WOMEN

The invention of French Feminism is contemporary with the invention of "French Theory." The two follow the same lines and indeed are, to some extent, the same thing. What is striking to the French reader, in the writings of the seventies as well as in more recent writings, is the manner in which all feminists from France are lumped together, regardless of their theoretical, esthetic, or political orientation. Wittig, for instance, is cited early on in the same breath as Cixous, and sometimes she is defined as belonging to the same strand, "écriture féminine." There is more than ignorance at work here. Even when it is recognized that Wittig cannot be in the same strand since she is very vocal about repudiating "écriture féminine" and all that it stands for, she is still always quoted in conjunction with the "Holy Three," very seldom by herself or in conjunction with Anglo-American feminists who are theoretically and politically close to her. The same of course holds true for Cixous: her plight is exactly symmetrical, although for reasons that should be clear by now, I feel for Wittig. Michèle Le Dœuff, who is not particularly bashful about her theoretical stand, is also lumped together with the essentialists, "despite her disclaimers," as Tong would put it (Tong, 223).

Do the stars of "French Theory"—who are also the masterminds behind the women, according to French Feminists (see infra)—fare better? No. Lacan, Derrida, Foucault, and Barthes are all one in the Anglo-American compulsion to unify and homogenize the "French," thus denying them any individuality. How is it possible to lump together in the same article, never mind in the same sentence, writers such as Foucault and Lacan, who come from totally opposite traditions, and who furthermore are very open about their disagreements?

Anglo-Americans have created whole new schools of thought—or at least academic trends—by comparing French writers who cannot be compared, by "putting in dialogue" people who have nothing to say to each other, and by giving this ready mix names like "poststructuralism" and "postmodernism." How will that improbable mixture withstand the test of time? Not very well: Foucault's social constructionism will *not*, even with the help of the Marines, ever blend with Lacan's essentialism.

And why are French authors—male or female, feminist or not—almost never compared to their Anglo-American counterparts, however similar, but only to other French writers, however different? Because that would show that there are differences among them, on the one hand, and similarities between them and their commentators or translators in the Anglo-American world, on the other. Internal homogenization and external differentiation: this is how groups—national, ethnic, sexual—are constituted. In exactly the same way, French authors are seen as a group which is defined by, and only by, its difference to the group which has the power to name; thus they are constituted as an Other.

If one has to admit that the work of writers can be interpreted, and that the word of the author on his or her own work need not be the last, or the only one, it is an entirely different kettle of fish to pretend that these works can be totally abstracted from their objective, historical contexts. And this is precisely what is being done, to female and male writers who were born in France. Moreover, if Anglo-Americans have the right to "take their good where they find it," as the French say, and to use quotations from France—or any other part of the world—to create their own theories, the line must be drawn at calling that creative endeavor "French Theory." Nobody owns their own writing; but everybody deserves a fair hearing, and that is what the French often do not get. They are entitled to be understood and appreciated, or dismissed, for what they did or said, not hailed or damned for what some other French person did or said: "It all happens as if the word French erased or diminished the serious tension between the works of Cixous and Irigaray (or those of Lyotard and Derrida)" (Varikas, 64). Interestingly, Anglo-American commentators who do try to put, say, Foucault or de Beauvoir in perspective, and to understand why they said what they said when they did, do *not* call that "French Theory."[31]

Claire Moses writes eloquently about this:

> We . . . in the role of imperial have expropriated some one aspect of French culture, used it for our purposes, with little regard for the French or the French context . . . with little interest for the people themselves. . . . The aspect that interests us is the least characteristic but the most different from our feminism; the more characteristic aspects bore us. We have exoticized French Feminism, decontextualized it, used it for our purposes, with little interest in French activists. In so doing, we have abused our power—involving ourselves, unwittingly, in a power struggle among French women and conferring prestige and status on one side—the psych et po group—which proved destructive to the interests of French women. [Moses 1992a]

When I read Claire Moses's paper, I had a flash of recognition—and, yes, gratitude—at seeing what I have been thinking for years so clearly and beautifully expressed. Then I had to write another paper, this time for *Nouvelles Questions Féministes,* on the Hill-Thomas hearings and its meaning for France and for feminism. I read Claire's paper again, and was struck this time by a sentence on the same page: "The French (and more generally 'Europeans') are blamed for aspects of ourselves that we do not like but do not take responsibility for (like our racism and classism); Europe or France is tainted; we are pure."

And I remembered having written exactly the same words just a few days before, but about the French caricature of the United States and Americans. The Hill-Thomas controversy was presented in France as a

---

31. See Sonia Kruks, "Gender and Subjectivity: Simone de Beauvoir and Contemporary Feminism," *Signs* 18/1 (1992): 89–111.

proof of American racism—to make their point, the media simply *overlooked* the fact that Hill, like Thomas, is African-American. There were headlines on "The New McCarthyism," on "sexual fundamentalism" and "the feminist lobby"; weeklies warned: "Puritanism, feminism and attacks on private life. . . . Is the American model threatening France?" (cited in Ezekiel 1992). The media use knee-jerk anti-Americanism, but fill it with a new content: it is everything that is progressive in the United States that they condemn. Kristeva's husband, Philippe Sollers, who has written a best-seller about his womanizing (*Femmes*), is in the forefront of the battle. There was, too, a domestic agenda: a year later when, forced by Europe, France had to legislate on sexual harassment, all the officials warned against "Americanization"; as a result we got the most restrictive law on the books to this day, a law that makes a mockery of sexual harassment.[32]

I have argued above that French Feminism was invented in order to legitimate the introduction on the Anglo-American feminist scene of a brand of essentialism, and in particular a rehabilitation of psychoanalysis, which goes further than the native kind expressed by Sara Ruddick, Chodorow, or Gilligan. The other feature of this intellectual current, which is definitely not exhibited by Ruddick, Chodorow, or Gilligan, is that it questions the very bases of what defines a feminist theoretical approach. In the usual definition, a feminist theoretical approach is tied to a political movement, a movement aimed at effecting actual change in actual society and in actual women's—and men's—lives; the main feature of this tie resides in the *questions* that are asked of the objects under study. That necessary tie does not mean that some abstract activist instance dictates the topics to be studied, but that any feminist—scholar or not—should be able to argue the relevance of the questions she raises to the feminist movement as a whole. In order to demonstrate that hypothesis, I will turn to a case study of one of the key moments of the whole operation: Alice Jardine's *Gynesis*.

In this work, "French Theory" is constituted as a "whole" by a series of rhetorical manoeuvres that use distortion and generalization, imperialism and exoticism. First, the feminist movement in France is cast as D.O.A. in the "socialist" era, after a series of murderous struggles, from which it is supposed not to have recovered. So, *exit*

---

32. See Delphy, "The Hill-Thomas Controversy and French National Identity," *Nouvelles Questions Féministes* 14/4 (1993): 3–13.

French Feminism in the usual sense of "feminist." Feminists are still there, however. How is Jardine going to dispose of them? We have already been told that feminism, "that word," "poses some serious problems." It does, indeed, if, like Jardine, one can think of only one place to look for it: the dictionaries! She then dismisses the feminists "who qualify themselves as feminists in their life and work" (Jardine 1985, 20), because that would be too simple.

But here plain factual distortion gives way to imperialism: what counts is only what *I* say counts. It is not only because it would be too simple that actual feminists from France will not be discussed, but because: "When in the United States, one refers to . . . French feminisms, it is not those women one has in mind" (Jardine 1985, 20). There is something circular or tautological in the argument: "I will not interest myself in those women because they are not of interest to me." But circularity and tautology, as exemplary expressions of self-centeredness, are essential components of imperialist thinking.

In the next sentence, American interest is what constitutes feminists from France as important or not important in an objective, real way: these women are said to "have a major impact on theories of writing and reading" (Jardine 1985, 20). The place where that "major impact" is supposed to have happened is not specified: it may be the United States, it may be the whole world—isn't it the same thing? And Jardine lists: Cixous, Kofman, Kristeva, Lemoine-Luccioni, Montrelay.[33] Then she moves on to say that "the major new directions in

---

33. At the time Jardine's piece was published, and at the time it was written, Women's Studies and Feminist Studies were undergoing the only period of expansion they have ever known in France. A research program had been launched in the National Center for Scientific Research in 1983 which lasted until 1989. At the time Jardine was in France writing about the "Parisian scene," it was under way. It was extremely varied in its ideological and theoretical orientations, as it regrouped on its board the Who's Who of Women's Studies in France. Over a period of six years, it examined more than three hundred research projects and funded eighty, in all disciplines and on all topics, including, of course, literary criticism. Why is it that most of the names Jardine lists never appear in the bibliographies of any of these projects, even of the few that were psychoanalytically-oriented, if they made such a "major impact"? And why is it that Jardine does not mention this program, which was the talk of the—admittedly provincial—town of Paris and which she could not have helped hearing about?

Similar tactics are used by Moi: "The publishing history of French feminism in English-speaking countries confirms the overwhelming impact of the three names of Cixous, Irigaray and Kristeva" (Moi 1987, 5). A somewhat disingenuous and even perverse statement on two accounts: first, the publishing history of these three writers in English is supposed to prove their popularity *in France!* And secondly, that publishing history is not so external to Moi as she, pretending to "discover" it, would have us think.

French theory over the past two decades . . . have . . . posited themselves as profoundly . . . anti- and/or post-feminist" (Jardine 1985, 20). This is a strategic move which overturns all previous understandings about what kind of thinking is useful for feminism.

But the best is yet to come: this said, she proceeds to explain that she will deal with the *men*, because "the women theorists in France whose names have been mentioned here are . . . in the best French tradition . . . direct disciples of those men." And although she does "not mean this as a criticism," she comments that these women's work consists of "rewritings of the men . . . repetitions and dissidences from those men" (Jardine 1985, 21).

We are given to understand that these women, who are antifeminist, are, however, the producers of the most important work for feminist thinking; that their thinking comes from men, to the extent that they need not be considered themselves. The reader may be surprised. But this is where the exoticism comes in to confuse and guilt-trip us: that is the French brand of feminism, and even though it may seem strange, what if feminists from France like it? As in all imperialist discourses, there's a mixture of fake respect for the culture and condescension. Enough respect to warrant the attention of the American reader: "French Feminism" is important, we must listen to what it has to say. But that respect is really condescension: for what sort of feminists can feminists from France be if they take as their major theorists women who not only are antifeminists but who merely parrot men? On what sort of clichés in the reader's mind is Jardine counting? What sort of stereotypes are necessary to believe that of French feminists, indeed of any *feminists*?

But she insists it is "in the best French tradition." So subservience to the men is seen as both unique to the French[34] and not so damnable as it might seem: from the moment it has been deemed "French," and since the French are an interesting culture, it cannot be condemned as easily as all that. Jardine extends the cultural relativist wing to protect

---

By all accounts, her *Sexual/Textual Politics* was decisive in starting that trend. And what was the thrust of that book? To pit "Anglo-American feminist criticism," which she finds disappointing, against what she calls—coining the phrase—"French feminist theory," and whose first chapter is entitled "From Simone de Beauvoir to Jacques Lacan," thus establishing Lacan as a "feminist theorist," a paradox not even the most psychoanalytically-oriented feminists in France would have dreamed of defending.

34. Again, Moi uses the same tactics: "French feminists on the whole have been eager to appropriate dominant intellectual trends for feminist purposes, as for instance in the case of the theories of Jacques Derrida and Jacques Lacan" (Moi 1987, 1).

it. Could she have sent the same message using an American example? Could she have decided that So-and-so is an important writer for feminist issues even though that person does not address the topic, or worse, is against feminism? Could she say that today the most important American writers for feminism are Katie Roife or Camille Paglia? And if she did, where would it place her? But why could she not do so? After all, opponents are important. They do need to be discussed. But is it the same thing to say that Patrick Moynihan's theses must be discussed and to say that he is the main theorist of and for feminism?

There are three points that need to be made here. It is true that, since there exists a continuum of feminists and antifeminists, it creates particular problems, which have been noted by Judith Stacey,[35] for "drawing the line," especially when writers with clearly antifeminist views, such as Jean Elshtain or Paglia, call themselves feminist, as they increasingly do in the United States today. As mentioned earlier, the point has been raised regarding Irigaray by Maryse Guerlais and Eléni Varikas[36] in France, and it is a difficult one. Although Irigaray's work is not used in Women's Studies in France, her theses are very popular with important parts of the women's movement in Italy, and smaller but still significant audiences in France and Holland. However, inasmuch as there are, in feminism as elsewhere, definitional problems for borderline cases, these problems are always situated, precisely for this reason, at the margins; they do not touch on the core.

Writers who situate themselves vis-à-vis feminist questions are part of the feminist debate—including those who *oppose* feminism; but even though the latter are discussed, they are not treated in the same category as writers who define themselves as feminist. Feminists have always discussed antifeminists: one could even say that this constitutes a major part of feminist writing. Exposing and analyzing patriarchal ideology has been on the feminist agenda from the very beginnings of feminism. But antifeminists and feminists have distinct places in feminist analysis. Patriarchy and its intellectual productions are an *object* of study, they are not and cannot be a *means* or a *tool* of feminist analysis.

35. Judith Stacey, "Are Feminists Afraid to Leave Home? The Challenge of Conservative Pro-Family Feminism," in *What is Feminism?*, ed. Juliet Mitchell and Ann Oakley, (Oxford: Blackwell, 1986), 219–49.

36. Maryse Guerlais, "Vers une nouvelle idéologie du droit statuaire: *Le temps de la différence* de Luce Irigaray," *Nouvelles Questions Féministes* 16–18 (1991): 63–93; and Varikas 1993.

The case is quite different with writers who are not necessarily hostile to feminism but who *do not* address feminist issues. The question is not: "Friend or foe?" It is: "What do they bring to the discussion?" This is the case in France for Kristeva, who does not address the questions raised by feminism because she does not know what they are. Her only information about feminism is the kind of caricatures circulated by the media. This is the case also for women like Montrelay or Lemoine-Luccioni, who are traditional psychoanalysts and cannot even be described as "antifeminist," since that implies engaging with feminist ideas, which they do not. Their position is best described as a traditional "male-supremacist" or "prefeminist" view; and it is so widely held in France by psychoanalysts that feminists have never felt the need to discuss those three in particular.[37] So here the point is rather: could Jardine, or any other supposedly feminist writer, decide that an English or American author, whose work is not considered relevant and is not discussed by English and American feminists because *she or he does not discuss feminist questions,* represents what is most interesting in the feminist scene of those countries?

This is, in fact, exactly what Jardine, and with her, most other French Feminists are saying: that there is no difference between feminist thinking and patriarchal thinking from the point of view of their use for feminist analysis. Further, they imply that addressing questions which are relevant for feminism is irrelevant for participating in the feminist debate. That makes feminism itself an irrelevant position.

This could not be argued from a domestic position, using domestic examples: straw women had to be invented who, supposedly from *within* feminism, were questioning and invalidating a feminist approach; but it had to be a feminism so strange, so foreign, that this would be as credible as it was improbable. It had to be "French Feminism." The second part of the message is: if the "French" can do it, why can't we? And they did.

Feminism could not be invalidated from within the French Feminists' own culture, i.e. Anglo-American culture; men could not be reinstated as the main interlocutors, as the arbiters of all knowledge, including feminist knowledge, from a domestic position. Introducing

37. This is why Cixous and Irigaray, who know what feminism is, must be distinguished one from the other, the first being antifeminist, and the second being feminist by her own definition. Furthermore, both must be sharply distinguished from the second group—Kristeva, Montrelay, and Lemoine-Luccioni—who do not know what feminism is and who are neither feminist nor antifeminist, but *pre*-feminist.

"French women" was the way to introduce the idea that to be antifeminist and to be part of the feminist debate was acceptable; the next step was to do away with the women and to reveal the men behind them, according to the purported native women's wishes, so that men could be, once more, center stage, in feminism as well as everywhere else.

Promoting essentialism was the main motive behind the creation of French Feminism; but there was a further, and when one thinks about it, not vastly different, reason for that invention; and that was putting Women's Studies scholars "in dialogue" again with male authors.

EPILOGUE *IN THE FORM OF AN (IMAGINARY) TRANSATLANTIC DIALOGUE*

My undergraduate students assure me that feminism is no longer necessary because we've solved all that, and various female colleagues and graduate students derive it from two white gentlemen, ignoring twenty years of extra-academic feminist work and writing. I would say that we've been betrayed, were not such a remark one of the banalities of history. And so heartbreaking. [Russ, 4]

I want to add: and academic.

The price paid by resistant women is literally incalculable (that is, I know of no currency in which its cost can be counted). It is thus not at all surprising that the temptation to "dilute" the challenge is not always resistible, or resisted.[38]

---

38. Ailbhe Smyth, "Haystacks in My Mind or How to Stay SAFE (Sane, Angry and Feminist) in the 1990s," a paper presented at the WISE Conference, October 1993, Paris.

Contributors

ANDREW BENSON studied at Oxford University and the University of Athens. He has been a translator of Portugese and French for European Communities, Brussels; Council of Europe, Strasbourg; and Carrefour des littératures (1991–1993).

KARL ASHOKA BRITTO, a Ph.D. candidate in the department of French at Yale University, is currently writing a dissertation on interculturality and identity in the novels of Pham Van Ky, V. Y. Mudimbe, and Maryse Condé.

NICOLE BROSSARD, a native of Montreal, is the author of many works, including novels (*French Kiss, Picture Theory, Mauve Desert*), poems (*Daydream Mechanics, Lovhers*), and essays (*The Aerial Letter*). She has also co-edited an *Anthologie de la poésie des femmes au Québec* (1991).

MARYSE CONDÉ is Professor of Francophone Literature at the University of Maryland and the University of Virginia. Her works include *Segu and the Children of Segu* (Ballantine), *I, Tituba, Black Witch of Salem* (University of Virginia Press), and *Tree of Life* (Ballantine). Her next novel in translation, *Crossing the Mangrove*, will be published by Anchor-Doubleday.

DAVID DEAN is a Ph.D. candidate in the department of French at Yale University.

CHRISTINE DELPHY is a researcher with the Centre National de la Recherche Scientifique. She is also the cofounder (with Simone de Beauvoir) of *Questions Féministes* and of *Nouvelles Questions Féministes*, which at this time is the only women's studies journal

YFS 87, *Another Look, Another Woman*, ed. Huffer, © 1995 by Yale University.

published in France. Her latest work is *Familiar Exploitation (etc.)* (Polity Press, 1992).

ASSIA DJEBAR, born in the Algerian town of Cherchell in 1936, was originally trained as a historian. She has had a multiple career as novelist, playwright, poet, stage director, and film director. Djebar is now simultaneously finishing her eighth novel and starting on her third film. Two of her recent novels have been translated into English: *Fantasia: An Algerian Cavalcade* (Quartet, 1988) and *Women of Algiers in their Apartment* (University of Virginia Press, 1992). A translation of *Loin de Médine* is forthcoming.

MADELEINE DOBIE is an Assistant Professor of French at Tulane University. She recently completed a Ph.D. in French at Yale University. Her dissertation is entitled *Foreign Bodies: The Figure of Oriental Women in Eighteenth- and Nineteenth-Century French and British Literature.*

BARBARA GODARD is Associate Professor of English, Women's Studies, and Social and Political Thought at York University. Her recent translations include Nicole Brossard's *Theseourmothers* (1983), *Lovhers* (1986), and *Picture Theory* (1991), and France Théoret's *The Tangible Word* (1991). She is the author of *Talking about Ourselves: The Cultural Productions of Canadian Native Women* (1985) and *Audrey Thomas: Her Life and Work* (1990), and has edited *Gynocritics/Gynocritiques: Feminist Approaches to the Writing of Canadian and Quebec Women* (1987).

NOAH GUYNN, a Ph.D. candidate in the department of French at Yale University and an editorial assistant at *Yale French Studies*, is currently writing a dissertation on gender and sexuality in the Middle Ages.

LYNNE HUFFER is Assistant Professor of French at Yale University. She is the author of *Another Colette: The Question of Gendered Writing* (University of Michigan Press, 1992), and is completing a book entitled *Beyond the Mother: Gendered Fictions of Literary Authority.* She is currently working on performativity in contemporary theory and fiction.

LUCE IRIGARAY is a philosopher, psychoanalyst, and teacher, and has held positions at the Centre National de la Recherche Scientifique, the University of Paris, Erasmus University, and the Collège International de Philosophie, among other places. She is the author of over fifteen books, including *Speculum de l'autre femme* (1974), *Ce sexe qui n'en est pas un* (1977), *Ethique de la différence sexuelle*

(1984), and *Je, tu, nous: pour une culture sexuée* (1990). Most of her works have been translated into English.

SERENE JONES is Assistant Professor of Theology at Yale Divinity School where she teaches in the areas of Reformation, Feminist, and Contemporary Systematic Theology. She is the author of *Rhetoric and Doctrine in John Calvin's Institutes* and is presently at work on *Feminist Theory and Theology*.

PEGGY KAMUF teaches French and Comparative Literature at the University of Southern California. She is the author of *Fictions of Feminine Desire* and *Signature Pieces*. She has also translated numerous texts by Jacques Derrida and is the editor of *A Derrida Reader*.

SARAH KOFMAN was Professor of Philosophy at the Université de Paris I. She has written twenty-seven books about women, art, and literature, seven of which are about Nietzsche and six about Freud. Several of her works have been translated into English, including *Nietzsche and Metaphor* (Stanford, 1993) and *The Enigma of Woman* (Cornell, 1985).

MARY LYDON is Professor of French at the University of Wisconsin, Madison. Her book *Skirting the Issue: Essays in Literary Theory* (University of Wisconsin Press) is forthcoming.

CLARISSE ZIMRA teaches world literatures and comparative literary theory at Southern Illinois University, Carbondale. She has published articles on writers of North Africa and the Carribean, as well as collaborated on the American publication of Djebar's *Femmes d'Alger* (University Press of Virginia, 1992).

The following issues are available through **Yale University Press,** Customer Service Department, P.O. Box 209040, New Haven, CT 06520-9040.

69 The Lesson of Paul de Man (1985) $17.00

73 Everyday Life (1987) $17.00

75 The Politics of Tradition: Placing Women in French Literature (1988) $17.00

Special Issue: After the Age of Suspicion: The French Novel Today (1989) $17.00

76 Autour de Racine: Studies in Intertextuality (1989) $17.00

77 Reading the Archive: On Texts and Institutions (1990) $17.00

78 On Bataille (1990) $17.00

79 Literature and the Ethical Question (1991) $17.00

Special Issue: Contexts: Style and Value in Medieval Art and Literature (1991) $17.00

80 Baroque Topographies: Literature/History/Philosophy (1992) $17.00

81 On Leiris (1992) $17.00

82 Post/Colonial Conditions Vol. 1 (1993) $17.00

83 Post/Colonial Conditions Vol. 2 (1993) $17.00

84 Boundaries: Writing and Drawing (1993) $17.00

85 Discourses of Jewish Identity in 20th-Century France (1994) $17.00

86 Corps Mystique, Corps Sacré (1994) $17.00

Special subscription rates are available on a calendar year basis (2 issues per year):
Individual subscriptions $24.00
Institutional subscriptions $28.00

ORDER FORM   **Yale University Press,** P.O. Box 209040, New Haven, CT 06520-9040
I would like to purchase the following individual issues:

_____

_____

For individual issue, please add postage and handling:
Single issue, United States $2.75   Each additional issue $.50
Single issue, foreign countries $5.00   Each additional issue $1.00
Connecticut residents please add sales tax of 6%

Payment of $_____ is enclosed (including sales tax if applicable).

Mastercard no. _____

4-digit bank no. _____ Expiration date _____

VISA no. _____ Expiration date _____

Signature _____

SHIP TO _____

_____

_____

See the next page for ordering other back issues. Yale French Studies is also available through Xerox University Microfilms, 300 North Zeeb Road, Ann Arbor, MI 48106.

The following issues are still available through the **Yale French Studies Office**, P.O. Box 208251, New Haven, CT 06520-8251.

19/20 Contemporary Art $3.50
33 Shakespeare $3.50
35 Sade $3.50
38 The Classical Line $3.50
39 Literature and Revolution $3.50
41 Game, Play, Literature $5.00
42 Zola $5.00

43 The Child's Part $5.00
44 Paul Valéry $5.00
45 Language as Action $5.00
46 From Stage to Street $3.50
47 Image & Symbol in the Renaissance $3.50
52 Graphesis $5.00
53 African Literature $3.50
54 Mallarmé $5.00
57 Locus in Modern French

Fiction: Space, Landscape, Decor $6.00
58 In Memory of Jacques Ehrmann $6.00
59 Rethinking History $6.00
61 Toward a Theory of Description $6.00
62 Feminist Readings: French Texts/American Contexts $6.00

Add for postage & handling

Single issue, United States $3.00 (Priority Mail)   Each additional issue $1.25
Single issue, United States $1.80 (Third Class)   Each additional issue $ .50
Single issue, foreign countries $2.50 (Book Rate)   Each additional issue $1.50

YALE FRENCH STUDIES, P.O. Box 208251, New Haven, Connecticut 06520-8251
A check made payable to YFS is enclosed. Please send me the following issue(s):

Issue no.   Title   Price

_____

_____

Postage & handling _____

Total _____

Name _____

Number/Street _____

City _____ State _____ Zip _____

The following issues are now available through Kraus Reprint Company, Route 100, Millwood, N. Y. 10546.

1 Critical Bibliography of Existentialism
2 Modern Poets
3 Criticism & Creation
4 Literature & Ideas
5 The Modern Theatre
6 France and World Literature
7 André Gide
8 What's Novel in the Novel
9 Symbolism
10 French-American Literature Relationships
11 Eros, Variations...
12 God & the Writer
13 Romanticism Revisited
14 Motley: Today's French Theater
15 Social & Political France
16 Foray through Existentialism

17 The Art of the Cinema
18 Passion & the Intellect, or Malraux
21 Poetry Since the Liberation
22 French Education
24 Midnight Novelists
25 Albert Camus
26 The Myth of Napoleon
27 Women Writers
28 Rousseau
29 The New Dramatists
30 Sartre
31 Surrealism
32 Paris in Literature
34 Proust
48 French Freud
51 Approaches to Medieval Romance

36/37 Structuralism has been reprinted by Doubleday as an Anchor Book.
55/56 Literature and Psychoanalysis has been reprinted by Johns Hopkins University Press, and can be ordered through Customer Service, Johns Hopkins University Press, Baltimore, MD 21218.